Her Prayer for Peace

Her Prayer for Peace

A Collection of Stories from the
Lifelong Journey of Motherhood

MONICA B. STALEY

With Contributions from 33 Christian Mamas-
New, Seasoned, and In-Between

Copyright © 2024 by Monica B. Staley

All rights reserved. No part of this book may be reproduced or transmitted in any form or by any means, electronic or mechanical, including photocopying, recording, any information storage, and retrieval system, without written permission of the author except in the case of brief quotations embodied in critical articles and reviews.

For information on distribution rights, royalties, derivative works, or licensing opportunities on behalf of this content or work, please contact the publisher at the address below:

Farmhouse Publishings, LLC
P.O. Box 333
Spearfish, SD 57783

Scripture quotations marked (ESV) are taken from THE HOLY BIBLE, ENGLISH STANDARD VERSION®, Copyright© 2001 by Crossway, a publishing ministry of Good News Publishers. Used by permission. Scripture quotations from The Authorized (King James) Version. Rights in the Authorized Version in the United Kingdom are vested in the Crown. Reproduced by permission of the Crown's patentee, Cambridge University Press. Scripture quotations marked (NIV) are taken from THE HOLY BIBLE, NEW INTERNATIONAL VERSION®. Copyright© 1973, 1978, 1984, 2011 by Biblica, Inc.™. Used by permission of Zondervan. Taken from the Holy Bible: Easy-to-Read Version (ERV), International Edition © 2013, 2016 by Bible League International and used by permission.

Although the author and publisher have tried to ensure that the information and advice in this book were correct and accurate at press time, the author and publisher do not assume and disclaim any liability to any party for any loss, damage, or disruption caused by acting upon the information in this book or by errors or omissions, whether such errors or omissions result from negligence, accident, or any other cause.

ISBN (Hardcover): 979-8-9881344-6-6
ISBN (Softcover): 979-8-9881344-8-0
ISBN (Ebook): 979-8-9881344-7-3

Design by Heidi Caperton
Editing by Kendra Paulton

Printed in the United States of America

wellnessbymonicabstaley@gmail.com
www.wellnessbymonicabstaley.com/
linktr.ee/wellnessbymonicabstaley

To my husband, Ryan. Your support and faith in me helped make this devotional possible. Thank you for always supporting and encouraging me (in motherhood). When I'm doubtful, when I'm fearful, when I'm straight-up losing it, you are steadfast for us. I love you. *Thank You, Lord, for Ryan. You made him so wonderfully!*

To my kids, Hope Juliette and John Ryan. You little stinkers (along with your dada) are the biggest blessings in my life! You make me laugh; you make me cry… Both tears of joy and tears of exhaustion. Without you, gosh… I can't even put into words (or remember!) life without you in it. I love you so much and thank you for loving me and forgiving me every day. I pray you both come to rely on God as much as I'm learning to. I pray you love Him and others richly. I pray you do hard things, especially when it benefits others and glorifies God. If you become parents, and I pray you do, I hope you'll read this and be reminded of how much God loves you. Lastly, the journey to motherhood and motherhood itself has brought me closer to God. Thank you, Hopey and Johnny, for being the (best!) reasons why I now try to rely on Him more than myself. (Some days and moments, I'm better at this than others; it's a constant prayer of mine.)

To my own mama, thank you! Thank you for your strength and commitment to raising my sisters and me in faith. Thank you for authentically modeling motherhood love and Christian living for us! I love you.

To my mother-in-law. Thank you for prayerfully raising my earthly best friend to have Christian values, incredible patience, and a heart of gold! I love you.

Table of Contents

Introduction . . . . *xv*

The Mamas Who Made this Devotional Possible . . . . *xviii*

The Structure of this Devotional . . . . *xix*

Week One: Losing Yourself in Motherhood 1

Week Two: Raising Kids for Jesus 6

Week Three: Losing a Baby/Child – Miscarriage, Stillbirth,
and the Loss of a Child 11

Week Four: When We Faithfully Obey God, He Can Work
against Sin and Evil in Our Families 16

Week Five: Christian Mom Friends: Be One, Have Many 21

Week Six: Postpartum/The Fourth Trimester 26

Week Seven: When Our Kids Leave Our Nest, They're Still
in the Arms of Jesus 31

Week Eight: Mothering with Childhood Trauma 36

Week Nine: Balance in Motherhood 40

Week Ten: Reflection; Miracles in Motherhood (Vol. I) 45

Week Eleven: Growing in Motherhood through Faith in God . . . 48

Week Twelve: Growing Your Prayer Life because You're a Mother . . 52

Week Thirteen: Modeling Faith to Our Children by
Mothering (and Living) with God 56

Week Fourteen: Personal and Worldly Expectations
in Motherhood 61

Week Fifteen: Comparison: The Thief of Joy
(Plus Judgment and Envy) 67

Week Sixteen: God's Grace for Us Mothers 72

Week Seventeen: God's Grace Instead of a Mother's "Perfection" . . . 77

Week Eighteen: Showing Our Humility and God's Grace
to Our Kids. 82

Week Nineteen: Motherhood after Infertility;
Secondary Infertility 87

Week Twenty: Reflection; Miracles in Motherhood (Vol. II) 93

Week Twenty-One: God Leads Mamas of Children
with Medical Needs. 97

Week Twenty-Two: Worry in Pregnancy. 103

Week Twenty-Three: A Mother's Hope in Christ when
Little Lives are at Stake. 109

Week Twenty-Four: Our Children are God's Children First;
He Loves Them More than We Do. 114

Week Twenty-Five: When Our Kids Hurt, We Hurt,
but God's Provision is True 119

Week Twenty-Six: Mothering within God's Will and
Perfect Long-Term Plan for Our Kids 124

Week Twenty-Seven: Mothering and Marriage 129

Week Twenty-Eight: Mothering after Divorce and
in Stepmotherhood. 135

Week Twenty-Nine: The Influence of Society/Peers and
Their Sin on Our Children 140

Week Thirty: Reflection; Miracles in Motherhood (Vol. III) 146

Week Thirty-One: Does Motherhood Ever Get Easier?. 149

Week Thirty-Two: Extreme Anxiety in Motherhood 153

Week Thirty-Three: What Might You Share with a
New Mom Who's a Believer in Jesus? (Vol. I) 158

Week Thirty-Four: What Might You Share with a
New Mom Who's a Believer in Jesus? (Vol. II) 164

Week Thirty-Five: What Might You Share with a
   New Mom Who's a Believer in Jesus? (Vol. III) 170
Week Thirty-Six: Gratitude in Motherhood 177
Week Thirty-Seven: Motherhood and Our Children: Idols? 182
Week Thirty-Eight: Overwhelm in Motherhood 187
Week Thirty-Nine: Avoiding Mom Guilt as a Working Mom . . . 192
Week Forty: Reflection; Miracles in Motherhood (Vol. IV) 198
Week Forty-One: Jesus is a Mama's (and a Kiddo's) Best Friend . . 201
Week Forty-Two: Trials and Struggles in Motherhood Can
   Grow Our Faith 205
Week Forty-Three: Helping Our Children in Their Faith
   and Prayer Life 210
Week Forty-Four: Disciplining Our Children with the
   Love of Jesus 216
Week Forty-Five: How to "Know" when Your Family is
   Complete – Biologically or through Adoption 222
Week Forty-Six: When a "Helper" Needs Help 228
Week Forty-Seven: Christ's Peace in Our Mama Hearts 234
Week Forty-Eight: Sin and Spiritual Health in Motherhood 240
Week Forty-Nine: Caring for Yourself when You Become
   a Mother 247
Week Fifty: Reflection; Miracles in Motherhood (Vol. V) 253
Week Fifty-One: Worry, Worry, and More Worry
   in Motherhood 257
Week Fifty-Two: Trust, Trust, and Even More Trust
   in the Lord 263
Next Steps 268
Things to Say or Not to Say when it Comes to Infertility 269

Acknowledgments *271*
Notes (Resources for Mamas) *273*
About the Author. *277*

Introduction

Hi! I'm Monica, and I've wanted to be a mother my whole life! I waited years to find my husband, and together, we waited years to conceive due to unexplained infertility. While it's harder than anything I've ever done, being a mother is more than worth the challenges. It has also been well worth the wait.

Early on in my motherhood journey, I asked my two older sisters, who each have two children, "Why didn't you tell me how hard motherhood is?" But now, I understand. Yes, it's really hard. But it's also really lovely! Motherhood is love in action. Such love is the greatest thing in this world!

This is the first work I've written, aside from a few blog posts on my personal wellness website. While I enjoy writing, I've never really considered myself to be a writer. But whatever we do or don't consider about ourselves is not of much consideration to God. God put this devotional on my heart after the hardest 18 months of my life: My first 18 months of motherhood. I could not ignore His call.

I'll share more about my early motherhood journey throughout the course of this devotional. (To cut to the chase, see the last paragraph of **WEEK FORTY-SEVEN: Christ's Peace in Our Mama Hearts**.) Still, my current biggest struggles in motherhood include: 1) relying on God more than myself; 2) having patience and self-control with my children; and 3) dealing with the various extremes of "mom guilt." **(See: WEEK THIRTY-NINE: Avoiding Mom Guilt as a Working Mom.)**

Her Prayer for Peace

On December 30, 2020, I learned I was pregnant with not one but two babies! *You are such a generous God, Lord!* I stayed home with my twins, Hope ("Hopey") and John (I call him "Johnny," and my husband calls him "JR") until they were just shy of 18 months old. At that time, per the referral of one of our contributing mamas, we sent them to "school" a few days per week at one of the churches we attend. Hope and John still love it there! This gave me great peace of mind and also gave me some time to participate in a very special Bible study.

Just before Hope and John started school and just before I started that Bible study, I had hit rock bottom with worry and fear in motherhood. Thankfully, I also (finally!) hit my knees in personal prayer and prayer with other Christian mamas. That's when motherhood changed for me… more to come!

The author of that very special Bible study is another one of the amazing contributors to this devotional (more on these mamas soon). Megan Nielsen wrote a book of her own called, *A Beautiful Exchange – Responding to God's Invitation for More*.[1] Along with the book, she created a study journal, a video teaching, and a worship playlist, plus the other participants and I met virtually once a week. While the content was rich and vast, the actual point of the study was to simply spend more time with the Lord. During this time, we were to sit and ask God what He wanted us to know, hear, be, and do. I had just gotten some free time in my schedule, and while I was excited about the study, honestly, I was eager to be more present in my wellness business. But I knew spending time with the Lord was never a waste of time. I pressed on; I'm so glad I did! Throughout the course of the study, God called me to write a devotional for mothers. Here is a glimpse into the dialogue I had with the Lord:

> *Are you sure, God? Motherhood is still really hard, God. Who wants to hear from a mother who's not even sure she can offer words of encouragement to other mamas when I'm still so discouraged myself sometimes? But oh, You're right, Lord… I don't live in constant worry and fear like I once did. I've grown to trust You more and more, Lord. To pray to You more and more. Thank You for hearing my prayer for peace*

in my mama heart, Lord. I've also leaned on the many other Christian mamas You've put in my life. Thank You for each of them, Lord. Include them? You want me to write a devotional for moms and include how You've worked in the lives of other mamas, too? Okay, Lord. I trust You to make time in my schedule for this. I do think it will benefit other Christian mamas. Lord, thank You for the opportunity to share how You love and care for mothers; how You answer her prayer for peace. I love You. Amen.

And so, this devotional came to be! My hope and prayer is that it blesses you, encourages you, and, most of all, I hope it reminds you how much God loves you, mama. He's always with you and loves to give you His peace, especially when motherhood is hard, which is really very often. We're in this together, mama. You, me, and every other mother, along with the greatest supporter around, the God of the universe.

The Mamas Who Made this Devotional Possible

Thirty-three Christian mamas, myself included, contributed to the content of this devotional! I am so grateful for each of them. While I, myself, am currently a 39-year-old mama of twin toddlers from the Midwest, the content of this devotional comes from mamas in their 30s to their 70s, with one to six kids of all ages, mamas from several ethnic backgrounds, different Christian denominations, and addresses from all over the United States. I prayerfully came up with three questions to ask them:

1. Please share a time/season in your life when your Christian faith was tested as a result of motherhood. How did Jesus care for you and draw you back during this time?

2. Has there been a time in your life when you truly felt the peace, wisdom, and guidance of Jesus in terms of parenting your child/children? How did Christ's peace, wisdom, and guidance show up for you during this time?

3. What might you share with a new mom who believes in Jesus?

From their answers, I highlighted specific topics that became the weekly chapters of this devotional book. To my contributors, *thank you!* Thank you for taking time out of your crazy-busy lives to share how God has loved and cared for you, and how He gave you His peace, in the hardest and best moments of motherhood. My prayer is that your time was well spent in this kingdom work, and as a result, this devotional blesses many, many mothers around the world!

This is a devotional for moms, by moms, ideally to be experienced with other moms!

 Bible Study/Small Group Study Guide

Introduction

The Structure of this Devotional

There are 52 topics, one for each week of the year, that make up the content of this devotional. Every ten weeks, we will pause, reflect, and hear about a mother and child who experienced a miracle of God's grace. We will cover a wide range of topics. I tried to rely on God's direction regarding the order in which each topic appears. You may go in chronological order (my personal preference) or jump around. I encourage you to study one topic every week for a year. Some weeks, you may feel like a topic was written just for you. In other weeks, you may struggle to personally relate. Either way, there's a message of God's love, support, and peace in every story and testimonial! If you can't relate to a particular topic at the present moment, there may come a time when you can. Or, you may know another mama who can relate. In that case, my hope is you feel better equipped to support and pray for that mama.

Try to read the start of each topic/week on Sunday or Monday. Answer the reflective questions in your own personal prayer journal and dig deeper into the Bible verse(s) when you can, ideally within the first couple of days of the week. Be in prayer. Ask God what He wants you to receive from Him in each of the weekly teachings. I then encourage you to re-read the weekly topic and the reflective questions in the middle of the week to see if anything new stands out after the second reading.

If you haven't already, pray for or connect with another mom by the end of the week. We are not alone in motherhood! God is always with us, and He is a relational God Who has put other amazing moms in our lives to help support us on the journey. As you round out your week, thank God for any revelations He's given you and be in prayer with Him. On the following page, is a sample weekly schedule.

Sunday &/or Monday	Prayerfully read the weekly topic through.
Tuesday & Wednesday	Answer the reflective questions, dig deeper into the Bible verse(s), and pray.
Thursday & Friday	Re-read the weekly topic, reconsider the reflective questions, and pray.
Saturday &/or Sunday	Pray for/connect with another mom, pray, and give thanks to God.

I know you're busy, mama. While this is a weekly devotional (as you'll hear throughout), spending time with the Lord every day will never be a waste of your precious time. I promise!

I am so excited for you, mama!

Week One

Losing Yourself in Motherhood

This feels like a good place to start. Whether you're a stay-at-home mom seven days per week, or you're home in the mornings, evenings, and on the weekends, or maybe your kids are grown, and now your grandchildren are your focus; there's just no doubt about it… Raising and serving our kids is a full-time (Divine) vocation!

This feeling of 'losing ourselves' in motherhood is normal. Suddenly, we have transitioned from answering mostly to our (and our spouses') needs and plans to our children's physical, mental, and emotional demands and needs. These needs most often come before attending to our own preferences and can quickly spiral into such a hopeless feeling! Oh, but mama, it doesn't have to be that way! Let's hear some wisdom from other mamas and glean from their experiences.

Gina is in her 30s, with four young to school-age children. She shares these beautiful words on losing ourselves in motherhood: *I recall the beginning of my motherhood journey being filled with many extremes. I was overwhelmed with joy, love, and fulfillment, along with anxiety, fear, and even anger. I was constantly serving. I remember hearing many of my mom friends say things like, "I feel like I'm losing myself." I reflected often on this feeling and found myself explaining that it felt like I was "shedding." I shed my sense of control, pride, vanity, perfection, selfish tendencies, and even some of my dreams. Shedding is a painful process. I would always run to the Lord in prayer and begrudgingly tell Him about how much this hurt and that it was all too much. I remember counting how many years I'd have until I could have my life back: my body, my sleep, my brain. I would tell Him, "Surely this isn't how we are supposed to love."*

I remember one day in particular; I was having a breakdown in front of the crucifix and asking the Lord how He could expect me to do this motherhood thing. As I gazed at our Lord's outstretched arms on the cross with His head slightly bent downward as if looking at me so lovingly and yet also uncomfortably, He gently reassured me, "You can do it because I have done it first. This is My body, given up for you. I will do it with you. It's not your job. Let go and surrender to Me so I can lead you, your marriage, and your children. I love them more than you do." Now, when I hear moms worry that they are losing themselves, I encourage them to lean in because shedding the old is how He makes way for the new (Ephesians 4:22-24).

I just have to pray after that. *Lord, thank You for amazing mamas like this. Thank You for her courage to go to the Cross. Thank You for speaking to her and for her sharing with me so I can share with many other mamas struggling with feeling like they're losing themselves in motherhood. Amen.*

We'll hear more from this wise mama in the weeks to come. **(See: WEEK NINE: Balance in Motherhood and WEEK THIRTY-ONE: Does Motherhood Ever Get Easier?)** Her peace, wisdom, and guidance come from the Lord!

Kary is in her 30s, with two young to school-age children. She shares: *It is a big change as a woman to go from a person to a home. You are forever your baby's home, and they'll want to be close to you.*

I can't help but see the parallel of how our kids want to be at home with us and how God wants us to be at home with Him! God wants us to lose ourselves in *Him* rather than feel like we are losing ourselves in motherhood. When we trust God and allow Him to lead us in motherhood, we can more abundantly be a home for our children.

> GOD WANTS US TO LOSE OURSELVES IN *Him* RATHER THAN FEEL LIKE WE ARE LOSING OURSELVES IN MOTHERHOOD.

Alyssa is in her 30s, with four young to school-age children. She shares: *Laundry has truly been an area of my life that has grown with me as my spirituality and my family have grown. It's the folding that kills me. I had to find a way to cope with it and lose that feeling of dread, procrastination, and the mountain I couldn't climb. It was just my lane. After I discovered podcasts and Christian audiobooks, I brought Jesus with me to do laundry. Now, when I fold laundry, I am listening, laughing, meditating, and contemplating. Nap time became 'my time' while I did laundry on our bed (so it had to get done). I flipped the script from dread to giving myself a reward for doing this detestable household chore. Today, I'm proud to say I've grown, and I neither dread it nor mind it. The 8-11 loads a week can still be overwhelming if we feel lost in it, but it's the mindset that matters! (Pro-tip: We've switched to a commercial machine now!)*

Have you ever felt like you've lost yourself in socks, washcloths, and lovies? I included this contribution in this week's topic of losing yourself in motherhood because I think it's important to note that we can feel like we've lost ourselves in all aspects of motherhood, including the piles and piles and piles of laundry. Even with two kids and a husband, sometimes it feels like all I do is gather, carry, load, hang dry or load, carry, stare at, and also dig through clean baskets of laundry for several days, eventually fold, and eventually put away about a million articles of clothing and towels every week.

How interesting that the solution from our first and last mamas' experiences this week was to bring Him into motherhood with us! We, too, can benefit from the Lord's servant's heart as we serve our children. Whether praying on our knees in front of a crucifix or folding jammies with the Word in our earbuds, He reminds us how precious we are to Him and how He longs to guide and support us so that when we trust in Him, we feel His peace and never feel lost. We are not meant to mother alone, mama. God wants to mother with us, and He also wants us to be in community with other Christian mamas. I'm so glad you're here, mama! **(For more support — See WEEK THIRTY-SIX: Gratitude in Motherhood and WEEK FORTY-NINE: Caring for Yourself when You Become a Mother.)**

Bible Verse

"…just as the Son of Man did not come to be served, but to serve, and to give his life as a ransom for many" (Matthew 20:28 NIV).

Prayer

Lord, we love our children so much. Thank You for the gift of their lives in our life. Thank You for reminding us to lean on You, and to share the responsibilities of serving and raising our kids with You. We trust You to guide us, Lord. We trust we are not doing this alone but that You are here with us. Help us to view motherhood as a blessing of service as we grow. Thank You for honoring us with a responsibility that parallels Your own, Jesus. Give us the strength and peace to serve our kids with Your guidance. Help us not to experience a loss of who we were but rather a gain of growth with the blessing of our children. Help us to serve our kids as we become who they need us to be through You. We love You. Amen.

Reflective Questions

1. Have you ever felt like you're losing yourself in motherhood? How would you describe who you were before you were a mother? How would you describe yourself since you became a mother? What are the similarities and differences? How has the Lord grown you in motherhood?

2. What did you most relate to in this week's topic? What did you learn? Consider what the Lord would like you to focus on and pray about right now.

3. Do you know a mama who could use the encouraging truth of this week's topic? In bold fellowship, reach out to her in the next few days. Remind her how much God loves her and how He longs for her to rely on Him and His peace as she mothers her children.

Week Two

Raising Kids for Jesus

As I write this, my kids are a little over two years old. We've been praying to and singing about Jesus with them for a while now. Their language skills are developing more every day, and it is just the sweetest sound to hear them say His name, "Jesus!" It's even sweeter to hear them sing the truth, "Jesus loves me." Oh, my heart! In this section, we'll hear from mamas who have prioritized raising their kids to love Jesus.

Angela is in her 40s, with two school-age children. She shares about some of the challenges of raising kids for Jesus: *Raising children (mine are currently ten and six years old) in a society where Christianity–faith in general–feels nearly obsolete is a tricky and constant test. Teaching children to love and obey the Ten Commandments and the timeless messages that are repeated over and over in the Bible, like, "Love one another as I have loved you" (John 15:12), and "As you wish others would do to you, do so to them" (Luke 6:31); is so much tougher to live by when it is so very apparent that I am one of the few mothers still teaching her babies that these are words to live by.* (We'll hear more from this strong mama in **WEEK TWENTY-NINE: The Influence of Society/Peers and Their Sin on Our Children.**)

Lord, please reward this mama's efforts. I pray You bless her with peace and encouragement as she trusts You to guide her in raising her (Your) children for You. Please also send her some Christian mom friends with whom to raise their kids for Jesus together!

I'm so grateful this mama's done some of the work for us! These verses and concepts are messages we can share with our young kids as we teach them the English language. In between saying, "gentle hands" and "teeth are for eating," we can also pour God's truth, goodness, and teachings into them as well.

'J' is for 'John,' it's also for *Jesus*!

"Mama loves you so much. Jesus loves us even more! Can you show Mama what loving and treating each other with love looks like?"

Our young kids are like sponges. They understand much more than they can communicate. With the help and guidance of Jesus, we can raise our littles to know and love Him from an early age. That foundation will serve them as they age and encounter times when they need to rely on it. While we always have Jesus, a community of Christian mamas is such a blessing, too. Let us all seek them, love them, pray for them, and be them. It makes a difference! **(See: WEEK FIVE: Christian Mom Friends: Be One, Have Many.)**

Janette is in her 30s, with three young to school-age children. She shares: *I started answering this question with so many practical parenting tips. When you boil it all down, there is one main mission of motherhood if you follow Jesus: To make lifelong Jesus followers. All of the other advice and hard seasons of parenting fade away in comparison to our calling to teach our children about Jesus and how to walk with Him. In each hard season of parenting, focus on extending grace and love to your child to show them a glimpse of their Heavenly Father. As they grow, use every hard moment with your children as an opportunity to turn their hearts and attention to the Lord. Use naughty moments to teach them about God's grace and point them to the work of Jesus on the cross instead of instructing behavior. Make sure they understand that we as parents aren't God but that we serve Someone much higher because we, too, sin and need a Savior! Make your home a place where they can learn about Jesus, ask questions about Jesus, and, God willing, choose to follow Jesus themselves.*

Amen. But I'm reading this and thinking, *Gosh, I didn't do this very well at breakfast this morning.* I'll repeat her words: *We are not God.* But I know I can rely on Him more, bringing His teachings and His character into tough moments with my kids. I know every Christian mama can relate to having this prayer and intention. We are not perfect, but He is, and every time we remember to rely on Him, every time we practice this, He rewards us. So much of raising kids for Jesus is about allowing God to raise us as the mothers He wants us to be! **(See: WEEK ELEVEN: Growing in Motherhood through Faith in God and WEEK SEVENTEEN: God's Grace Instead of a Mother's "Perfection.")**

> SO MUCH OF RAISING KIDS FOR JESUS IS ABOUT *allowing* GOD TO RAISE US AS THE MOTHERS HE WANTS US TO BE!

Pam is in her 50s, with five school-age to adult children. She shares victory in Jesus, even within tragedy: *I lost my husband suddenly about six months ago. All five of my kids, ages 18 to 28, have shown grace, resilience, and faith in how they have coped with this tragic loss. In their moments of grief, they are finding ways to continue to honor their dad. Very proud mama right here. You feel like all the things we as parents have done along the way have come together, so they get to evolve into people helping and connecting with others. I've spent many years praying on this, so I'm so joyful to see this happen in a season of sadness for them.*

My heart is filled with joy that this mother and her children are prayerful people. *Thank You, Lord, for being near to this family, especially now.*

A great book and website about teaching children to pray is *Raising Prayerful Kids: Fun & Easy Activities for Building Lifelong Habits of Prayer* by Stephanie Thurling & Sarah Holmstrom.[2] But don't forget to pray for and create your own prayer life, too! It sounds a little obvious, but we can so easily get focused on praying for our kids and their prayer lives. However, our own prayer life is vital, as well. **(See: WEEK TWELVE: Growing Your Prayer Life because You're a Mother.)**

We can teach them the lessons of the Bible, and we can do our best to model the life of a faithful servant in front of our children. Still, the power of prayer and expecting God to hear and deliver on our prayers (in His perfect way) is a crucial piece of the equation in raising prayerful kids for Jesus. Mama, pray for the expectation that the Lord will help You raise your kids for Him. **(See: WEEK FORTY-THREE: Helping Our Children in Their Faith and Prayer Life.)**

Bible Verse

"Train up a child in the way he should go; even when he is old, he will not depart from it" (Proverbs 22:6 ESV).

Prayer

Lord, our relationship with You is the greatest gift in this life. We love our children so much! We want them to have a close relationship with You, too. Use us, Lord. Use us to show Your love to our family. Guide us, Lord. Please guide us in responding to the challenges of motherhood in a Godly way. Grow our faith, trust, and reliance on You, Lord. Live and breathe in us so we can more easily breathe faith, trust, and reliance on You into our children. Help us to pray to You for our children every day. Lord, we pray You also bring other Christian mamas into our lives. We want to raise our children for You in a community of other believers. We love You. Amen.

Reflective Questions

1. Were you taught any Bible verses or specific Biblical teachings as a child? If so, how have they impacted you? Have you shared these or other verses or teachings with your children? If not, set aside some time or put a date in your calendar when you'll share concrete truths about Jesus with them.

2. How's your personal faith and prayer life right now? Are you confident in your ability to model and share the love of Jesus with your children? Whether your answer is yes or no, or somewhere in between, spend some time in prayer. Ask God to guide you.

3. Do you pray for your children? How often? Spend some time journaling on what you want for your children. How do you want God to bless them? Share your thoughts and journal with your husband or a friend. Pray for your children. Pray also for God to help you remember to rely on Him and His peace, especially in the tough moments of motherhood.

Losing a Baby/Child – Miscarriage, Stillbirth, and the Loss of a Child

*L**ord, this is a hard week to write and read. Please hold the mama who has experienced the loss of a child extra closely this week. Please help the mama who hasn't experienced the loss of a child to glean something this week that allows her to better support and pray for a mama who has.*

Emma is in her 30s, and has two young (earthside) children. She shares about the loss of her middle son at 17 weeks gestation: *We were absolutely crushed. I immediately started questioning why God would take him away from us when we so badly hoped to raise good and virtuous Christian children. Although suffering is a mystery, it is when we are at our weakest that we are more likely to run to God and cling to Him. Through suffering, He gives us an opportunity to grow closer to Him. My husband and I felt God's presence (what we call "pearls of His goodness") more clearly than we ever have in our lives. We immediately experienced this during the birth of our son, which was an extremely peaceful and holy experience. There was no doubt that God was wrapping us in His arms and showering us with His mercy and love. We had no doubt that Johnny was in paradise. Our meeting had only been delayed, not stolen.*

Several of the nurses, doctors, and other health care professionals who helped care for us at the clinic the day we learned he no longer had a heartbeat, and again at the hospital, when I gave birth, have since mentioned what a "spiritual" experience it was for them, despite many of them not being Christian. I believe they felt God's presence. God not only allowed us to grow closer to Him through Johnny's death, but He also made His presence known to others.

God has showered us with those "pearls of His goodness" since that time, including the gift of our new son Frederick, who would not be here if Johnny was not in Heaven. Our oldest son has a beautiful relationship with his brother in Heaven that we hope will continue as he gets older. He even asked to show Johnny his new undies he got in preparation for potty training… Oh, the precious two-year-old mind!

For all those who have lost a child know that there is beauty that is initially hidden amidst the devastation. God is good. Your child in Heaven is happier than you could ever imagine, and they are in a paradise more incredible than our brains can fathom. They will only ever know joy and happiness since they are in the presence of God for eternity. You, your spouse, and any other children you might have now have their very own guardian angel to watch over you and pray for your family. You will see many "pearls of God's goodness" throughout the experience and for years to come.

This mama's faith and perspective inspire me. I remember getting the initial text from her that they'd lost their Johnny. Her pain, joy, and how she saw God use their experience to show His goodness to others moved me to sorrowful and joyful tears. (I do want to note that this is not the only way to grieve/experience a loss. God loves us and wants to give us His peace no matter how we respond.)

Amara is in her 30s, with two young (earthside) children. She shares: *Losing Mia tested my faith, but it also opened my eyes wider to Jesus. I saw so many "God moments" because I was open to seeing Him through my journey of grief. I leaned on Him more than anything. He taught me how to love a child that wasn't even on earth. One moment that really sticks out to me is when I* was at Mia's funeral. I was so mad at God because I couldn't hold Mia at the hospital because she was too fragile, but then I was able to hold her casket at the funeral, and I didn't even know she was in there. I thought they had already buried her. They gave her to me and said, "Here you go, you can hold her." I just knew that was God's way of saying, "Hey, she's here, she's close to you, and now she's close to Me." Jesus cared for me through it all.

Thank You for that blessing-filled moment for my friend, God. One of many things that I love about this mama is that she speaks about her earthside children just as much as she speaks about sweet Mia in Heaven. She has been open about their loss of Mia for as long as I've known her. It reminds me of how being open about my infertility was and has been cathartic and healing for me. Again, it's not necessary, but if it feels right to open up about a loss, I pray that the Holy Spirit empowers mamas and gives them the healing peace to do so.

Bri is in her 30s, with two young to school-age (earthside) children. She shares about her multiple miscarriages: *When we miscarried each time, it was something that just kind of derailed my faith. I had never questioned God's "intentions" before, and it made me reconsider everything that I had known growing up. The community of believers we spent time with really picked me up and helped me to remember God's sovereignty and goodness even in life's hard circumstances. His character and goodness are not impacted by the weight of loss or the hurt of our hearts.*

> HIS CHARACTER AND *goodness* ARE NOT IMPACTED BY THE WEIGHT OF LOSS OR THE HURT OF OUR HEARTS.

The truth in that last sentence is golden. There is hurt here on earth, but our God in Heaven is full of goodness. That can be a hard truth to believe when we're in pain. Surrounding ourselves with people who love us and love God is an absolute gift, especially when our hearts are broken.

In closing this hard week, two of our three mamas shared about a type of special communication God had with them in their time of grief: "pearls of His/God's goodness" and "God moments." We can feel God's presence at any time and in many ways. But when our hearts are suffering and breaking, God meets us in His special way while (hopefully, eventually) also growing our faith in Him. **(See: WEEK FORTY-TWO: Trials and Struggles in Motherhood Can Grow Our Faith.)** His tender heart and love for us can be felt in a particular way during difficult times in life. Perhaps giving this a name allowed these mamas to feel especially cared for while their hearts tried to heal.

Bible Verse

"When the righteous cry for help, the LORD hears and delivers them out of all their troubles. The LORD is near to the brokenhearted and saves the crushed in spirit" (Psalm 34:17-18 ESV).

Prayer

Lord, I pray for the mother who has lost a child. I pray she seeks You, over and over, for comfort and for Your healing peace. May she know You are with her child forever. Please help us to be there, in community, for a mother who's lost a child. Help us to show them Your love. We trust You. We love You. Amen.

Reflective Questions

1. Did anything surprise you in this week's shares?

2. If you have lost someone in your life, how were God and other Christians there to support and pray for you? Consider how you might do the same for someone who's experienced the loss of a loved one, especially a child.

3. What does it mean to you to trust God, especially when hard things happen in your family?

Week Four

When We Faithfully Obey God, He Can Work against Sin and Evil in Our Families

Last week was a hard week. This week, I'll share a couple of stories of how God rewards us as we faithfully obey Him, even/especially when it's hard. There is sin and evil in this world. God has indeed overcome the world! I pray these stories are an encouragement and a reminder to you that in the thick of hard times, God is working all things for good.

Beth is in her 60s, with three adult children. She shares: *I grew up in a home where both of my parents chose to walk away from the church. Our home was flamboyant, theatrical, and run by my own mother's emotions. High or low, we all reacted to match her in order to keep the peace. I loved my parents, and we grew up supported and loved, just with NO exposure to or knowledge of Jesus. When I found Jesus as a newly married young woman of 21, I knew He was what I had been seeking all my life. I was so excited to share Jesus with my parents, but they rejected it all profoundly and emphatically.*

When I had our first daughter, their first grandchild, everyone was so excited and loving. At that time, my mother had been experimenting with writing, having always wanted to write books. She wrote a book about a little girl who was a witch! She gave the witch in her book my daughter's name and dedicated the book to her. My mother presented me with the draft excitedly, asking me to read it and give her feedback. It was scorching to read, terrifying, satanic, and a complete crushing blow to my spirit. The Lord literally commanded me to rise up and rebuke not only the book but my own mother. I was clearly told to "Choose you this day whom you will follow" (Joshua 24:15)! I heard the Lord's voice clearly and audibly. It was a crossroads I was standing at that required me to lay down my personal life and choose to pick up the cross of Jesus and boldly claim His name, His grace, His mercy, His love, and trust in His provision. Laying this out to my mother, whom I loved and saw as so lost and yet so confrontational regarding my faith, was one of the hardest things I've ever had to do. I then let her know that this was unacceptable and that if she chose to move forward in publishing the book, using my daughter in any way attached to it, we would need to step back from our relationship with her in order to honor the Lord.

For weeks, I wandered my house feeling empty and alone, so ripped away from my mom. Jesus would draw me into the Psalms and Proverbs for comfort daily. I could not stay away from His Word, needing it like I needed water. I heard Him whisper love from every corner of my home. It was a long, hard season of waiting on Him in trust and lifting up my mother to Him, trusting in His deliverance for all of us from this situation. He did! Not only did Mom decide that her relationship with us was more important, but she never published that book. In fact, once she humbly told me this and asked for forgiveness, the book literally disappeared! To this day, she cannot find that draft, doesn't know where she put it, and cannot remember the plot at all.

This example of God rewarding us for our obedient faith in Him, even when it hurts, amazes me! *Lord, You disappeared something tangible from hands and disappeared intangible thoughts from the mind. You are so powerful. May we never forget the supernatural power You hold! You are good and greater than all evil!*

Her Prayer for Peace

Billie is in her 60s, with four adult children. She shares: *One of my daughters and her husband became addicted to drugs a few years ago. Through this time, my grandchildren were removed by Child Protective Services from their home and brought to my home. There were many attempts by me and others to help them get clean and get back on track. Things escalated several times. For nine months, I prayed and prayed for sobriety for them. I prayed for my grandchildren. It wasn't until I heard that I needed to turn everything over to God that things changed. I knew I needed to back away and let Him do the work only He can do. This was guidance I had not expected, so with everything in me, I laid everything down. I stopped contact and stopped any further attempts to help. Once I did this, I felt a sense of peace. It was crazy how peaceful I felt. How could this be? With all the trauma, turmoil, and potential disaster that could happen, how could I feel peaceful? Once again, God told me to be still and let Him work. I took that step back, even with many others coming at me, questioning why I wasn't helping. The peace that I had was so hard to describe.*

> GOD TOLD ME TO BE *still* AND LET HIM WORK.

Then, my daughter and her husband lost their home. They were living in their truck. They were losing everything, including their children. I loved them from afar and prayed all day, every day, but I knew I needed to stay strong. Then came a sudden turn of events. Within two weeks, my daughter and son-in-law were suddenly in rehab; they had housing lined up for them and their children; they had a caseworker who was assigned to personally help them get their lives back; they were both in therapy; my son-in-law got a job; and much more. I knew only God could have pulled this off!

When I finally spoke with my daughter, she told me that one cold night, as they were trying to stay warm in their truck, God spoke to her. He told her to get on her knees and give it all to Him. They both did it together and prayed for forgiveness and help to get clean and get their lives back. From that moment on, things began to turn around. To this day, I know that had I not listened and stepped away to let God do His work, things probably would not have turned out for good. This season also brought my daughter so much closer to God and helped to build her faith.

Wow, another amazing example of God rewarding us for our faithful obedience to Him, even when it hurts! His ways are better than our ways; when we listen to Him, our families are rewarded! From helpless to full of help, resources, and hope, our God is greater than all sin! **(See: WEEK FORTY-EIGHT: Sin and Spiritual Health in Motherhood.)**

Bible Verse

"He replied, 'Blessed rather are those who hear the Word of God and obey it'" (Luke 11:28 NIV).

Prayer

Lord, help us to hear Your voice. Help us to know Your desires and heed them. Help us to trust that You love us, You want to care for us, and that You are always working everything out for good. Thank You, Lord, for showing up for these mamas. Thank You for guiding them to do, and not to do, what You wanted of them so Your will could be done. Sometimes, it feels hard to obey, but please constantly remind us that You only want to bless us and our families! We love You. Amen.

Reflective Questions

1. Have you ever heard a directive from the Lord? Was it hard to obey? Was it eventually worth it? If not, ask the Lord to share with you. Take time and expectantly wait for the Lord to speak to you.

2. What were your biggest takeaways from the first story that was shared, where the Lord gave a directive to do something specific?

3. What were your biggest takeaways from the second story that was shared, where the Lord gave a directive to NOT do something?

Christian Mom Friends: Be One, Have Many

I just returned from Mom's Life, a small group at a local church where every other week, we study the Word and then a topic of interest for Christian mothers.³ As such, I'm especially pumped for this week's topic! I truly cannot emphasize how important my Christian mom friends have been to me, my marriage, and my children since I became a mom. Mom's Life is similar to MOPS (Moms of Preschoolers), now known as The MomCo, which is a global organization for Christian mamas of kids five and under.⁴ My local MomCo group meets ten times during the school year. Various speakers come in, sharing topics of interest to Christian mamas, and we have small group discussions and prayer time. It's fellowship at its finest! Whether a small group at church, an in-home Bible study, or a virtual prayer group (the possibilities are endless!), authentic and vulnerable connections with other Christian mamas are an absolute blessing from God.

Over the last three years (my pregnancy included), I have sought after Christian mamas with whom to do life and motherhood. Please use the resources I've listed here and in the Resources for Mamas section at the back of the book as a starting point to finding the support of like-minded mom friends. If making friends doesn't come naturally to you, or there are logistical barriers, please pray about it! Ask God for Christian mom friends, and expect Him to direct you and/or bring them into your life. Keep praying! I'm trying to imagine having too many Christian mom friends; I can't! Neither can our first contributing mama in this week's topic.

Megan is in her 50s, with four young adult children. She shares: *When my first child was born, I felt alone and frustrated. Jesus provided an amazing community of moms through the ministry of The MomCo. The MomCo was a place where I could be myself and connect with other women who were experiencing similar things. Eventually, the incessant sadness subsided, but thankfully, the friendships did not. Some of those women are still my best friends today! We aren't crying over physical exhaustion anymore; now, we share laughs and tears as we navigate the emotional roller coaster of teens and young adults!*

I'm from the Midwest, and this contributor lives in the western part of the United States. Our kids are over a decade apart, yet we both benefited from The MomCo. I'm about to start my third year in The MomCo, and I'm just so grateful God put it on my heart to sign up! There is always Jesus, fellowship, lots to learn, support to give and receive, plus there are always treats! It's a blessing now, and I know I will have forever Christian mom friends because of it.

Jill S. is in her 60s, with three adult children. She shares: *I definitely had times where my faith in myself as a mother was tested. I knew that motherhood would be a part of life, and I knew there would be challenges that went along with it. What kept me sane was surrounding myself with other women who were in the throes or had experienced motherhood. This included playgroups, Bible studies, and things that nurtured my soul and kept me from being unrealistic in my expectations*

> WHAT KEPT ME SANE WAS SURROUNDING MYSELF WITH OTHER *women* WHO WERE IN THE THROES OR HAD EXPERIENCED MOTHERHOOD.

of motherhood. *I sought counsel in prayer, meditation, Scripture, and trusted friends.*

I love how this contributor mentioned how her Christian mom friends helped her with *unrealistic expectations of motherhood.* **(See: WEEK FOURTEEN: Personal and Worldly Expectations in Motherhood.)** I also love how she noted how she connected with both God and *trusted friends.*

Alyssa is in her 30s, with four young to school-age children. She shares: *God showed me the gift of family and community. None of us are independent. Since then, I have truly appreciated the truths of a "village." I have been a part of the village for others. They have been the village for me. Our family continues to be interdependent. Think about how many people there are to help you deliver that little peanut. It is a lie of the enemy that tells us that we can't trust the good people in our world. There's something about having three under three in your home that takes away all of your independence. I couldn't go to any public place other than the tiny local grocery store on the corner without extra hands.*

This mama makes such a cool point in the middle of her share! Between my 30 hours of labor, eventual C-section, and then the subsequent four days in the hospital, I bet there were over 25 complete strangers helping us with our newborn twins. It should be natural to continue to receive (and give) love and support from/to others, preferably other Christians.

Kary is in her 30s, with two young to school-age children. She shares: *I would say people are serious when they say, "It takes a village." Utilize your village!* I'll reiterate here that if you don't have a village yet, pray for one. God will provide!

Pam is in her 50s, with five school-age to adult children. She shares: *It's ok to reach out to other folks who have walked the parenting journey. The truth is more people have been in the same shoes, on the same road, and they mostly give you solid answers and direction.*

Most people really do want to be helpful! Especially if you're going through a specific challenge, seeking Christian families who've gone through something similar can be especially valuable. For example, connecting with other mamas who've experienced infertility is an opportunity for me to share how God supported and loved me during that time in my life.

(See: WEEK NINETEEN: Motherhood after Infertility; Secondary Infertility.)

Christine is in her 30s, with three young to school-age children. She shares: *As much as getting advice can be abundantly helpful, you should always pray to God for which advice applies to you and your child and what doesn't.*

As this last contributor noted, and I'm so glad she did, it's important to always seek God's support first and to also pray about any advice you receive from other Christian mom friends. I recently heard it said, to go vertical before going horizontal. (There's more on praying for our families, growing our faith as mothers, and mothering with God in later weeks.)

I could have added several more contributions, but hopefully, you now understand how important Christian mom friends are! When things in life are hard, we seek resources to help. Motherhood should be no exception! **(See: WEEK FORTY-SIX: When a "Helper" Needs Help.)**

Bible Verse

"For lack of guidance a nation falls, but victory is won through many advisers" (Proverbs 11:14 NIV).

Prayer

Lord, I praise You again for all the Christian mom friends with whom You've blessed me. Especially those who took time away from their families to contribute to this devotional! Those mothers have helped create a community of moms who are strangers, except in Christ. Please bless them and their families for their contributions. I pray that you bless these readers. I pray this reader actively pursues Christian mom friends who love You and seek to raise their children with Biblical principles and

God's love. Lastly and most importantly, may we seek You first, Lord. Help us to pray to You before we phone a friend or ask Google. Help us to also pray for Your discernment when we receive advice from other Christian mamas. You have all the answers, Lord. May we take the time to seek You and be blessed by You. We love You. Amen.

Reflective Questions

1. Take a moment to jot down the names of your best friends in your village. Are they followers of Christ?

2. After praying, wait for His direction in taking one step closer to connect with (more) Christian mamas. Where has the Lord led you?

3. When was the last time you prayed for another Christian mother? Make an effort to at least pray for, and at most connect with, a Christian mom you know at least one to three times this week.

Week Six

Postpartum/The Fourth Trimester

If you're reading this as a pregnant, first-time mama, you've probably deduced that "the fourth trimester" (often lasting much longer than three months) will be both challenging and wonderful. Even if your kids are grown, you'll hopefully find this week's shares valuable. I wish I had focused on these words and truths while I was still pregnant and in the throes of new mamahood. But I do find them helpful, even now! A pregnant mama will likely find herself soon saying things like, "I can't do this," in the near future. The truth is *you* may not be able to. But God can! There are a million joyous moments when we become mothers. This week's contributors will share about the hard moments and how they relied on God, the Father of us all, to get through.

Megan is in her 50s, with four young adult children. She shares: *The first season that came to mind when my faith was tested was the new, itty-bitty infant phase. While pregnancy wasn't horrible for me, life with a newborn was NOT easy. I didn't tip into postpartum depression, but the baby blues were in full swing. I was exhausted (for obvious reasons!) and cried at the drop of a hat.*

This volatile emotional state was difficult because I couldn't seem to get a handle on my emotions. Until then, I prided myself on my ability to stay calm, cool, and collected in most situations. I wasn't able to "hold it together." I felt alone and frustrated. I wanted to enjoy my newborn, but the tears wouldn't abate. I no longer had time to linger in the mornings with Jesus, but He met me in new and tender ways through moments with Him in breath prayers and providing an amazing community of moms through TheMomCo. **(See: WEEK FIVE: Christian Mom Friends: Be One, Have Many.)**

Have I mentioned how much of a blessing this devotional has been for me, too? I had never heard of "breath prayers" before! We all have many motherhood moments, postpartum and beyond, when we are about to lose our cool! Since I had never heard of these specific types of prayers, I did a little more research.[5] What I found is that breath prayers should be no more than eight syllables so they easily fit into one exhale. Take a deep breath and then exhale your prayer. Examples given include: "Help me rest; give me peace." "Make clear my way, Oh Holy One." "Out of the darkness, into the light." And, "Fill me Spirit, with Your love." I really like how, in the thick of the craziness, I can quickly say, "God, give me [patience(!), kindness, goodness, faithfulness, gentleness, self-control, love, joy, and peace]."

Thank You, the fruit of the Spirit (Galatians 5:22), for having all the prayerful buzzwords we mamas need every day! When hormones are raging, mental capacity is stretched, and we are likely running low on sleep, these breath prayers could be the simple game-changer we need with the ultimate goal of *more of He, less of me*! Our next mama goes a little more into when and how she uses breath prayers in early motherhood and beyond.

Chelsea is in her 30s, with four young children (including twin infants). She shares: *My faith is being tested right now. Motherhood takes a lot of mental capacity, and I am often stretched for time for myself. I need to be purposeful and make time for God so I can be better guided in my parenting and hopefully feel like I have more mental capacity. I recently received a devotional of one-minute prayers to say over my children. The devotional is* One-Minute Prayers to Pray for Your Kids *by Hope Lydia and Michelle Lind.*[6] *I'm trying to make time each day to read this devotional. As a new mother of four, I can still find one minute to pray! Because the truth is, I couldn't parent without God. He gives me patience and wisdom. When I am about to lose my patience, I say a breath prayer. Most recently, my two-year-old has tested my patience. I constantly am asking God to give me the strength and patience to parent such an independent and strong-willed toddler! Breath prayers are so helpful. They are quick, few-word prayers that are spoken with an exhale. I often say, "God, give me patience." These have helped me get through the toughest moments when I am about to lose my cool!*

Regarding sleep deprivation, Janette is in her 30s, with three young to school-age children. She shares: *Sleep has been a hard-won battle at our house. We have not (until recently!) slept consistently through the night for six years, thanks to our three children. Two separate sleep consultants and a pediatric sleep doctor helped to get us to where we are today. I can't even count the number of nights I spent with a child in a dark room, pleading with God for sleep. One night, on the floor of the kids' room, I felt the Lord telling me this wasn't about my kids sleeping but about me growing. I needed to change my perspective from, "Give me what I want" to, "Make me who You want me to be." I have found when I am able to take this attitude, my circumstances may not change, but I do, and that makes all the difference.*

> I NEEDED TO CHANGE MY PERSPECTIVE FROM, "GIVE ME WHAT I WANT" TO, "*Make* ME WHO YOU WANT ME TO BE."

That gave me goosebumps! Thank You, Jesus! While older kids may continue to have trouble sleeping, I included this mama's share this week because I think sleep deprivation is generally most pertinent in the infant stage. However, the lesson *"Make me who You want me to be, Lord"* is woven throughout every age and every stage of motherhood!

Kary is in her 30s, with two young to school-age children. She shares: *The season that has been most difficult for me is the postpartum trimester. I struggled, thinking it was way harder than I had expected. God continued to care for me by placing supportive people in my life. My husband, family, and in-laws helped out in incredible ways to welcome our new baby.*

Postpartum/The Fourth Trimester

Community, community, community! In desperate moments, sleep-deprived, and all things postpartum, our loving God hears our desperate cries. Even if all we have the strength for is a single breath prayer, God hears, sees, and knows our every need. You may indeed find your postpartum self saying; I can't do this! Just remember that HE can! God doesn't always call the equipped, but He always equips the called! We were called to be mothers, and our Lord can't wait to hear us call out to Him for guidance, support, and peace as we walk out our calling of motherhood. **(See: WEEK ELEVEN: Growing in Motherhood through Faith in God.)**

Bible Verse

"Trust in the LORD with all your heart and lean not on your own understanding; in all your ways submit to him, and he will make your paths straight" (Proverbs 3:5-6 NIV).

Prayer

Lord, in between breath prayers, I pray the postpartum (and every) mama finds her knees and asks You how a particularly hard circumstance in motherhood may be an opportunity for growth, for You to mold her into who You want her to be. Lord. I pray that each reader (especially new moms) gets in the habit of saying, "More of He, less of me!" Thank You for the gift of motherhood. Our babies are gifts from You. We need You to help us, Lord! Give us patience, Lord. Give us the strength to trust and rely on You the most. And please, Lord, give us rest! We love You. Amen.

Reflective Questions

1. If you're currently pregnant, meditate on what you've just read. Find an accountability partner who promises to lovingly remind you to trust and rely on God several times a day after your baby is born.

2. Whether your baby is seven days, seven months, or seven years old, consider how you trusted and relied on God in the early days of motherhood and also in the last week. How do the seasons compare for you? How might you allow Him to equip you more in your calling of motherhood this week?

3. Consider several hectic scenarios with your children. Then, prayerfully write down at least three breath prayers that will support you during these times. Practice praying these prayers now and throughout the week. Pray and ask God to remind you to seek Him amongst the craziness!

4. Because postpartum and motherhood can be lonely, let's circle back to last week's topic again. After praying to God, wait for His direction to take one more step toward connecting with (more) Christian mamas.

Week Seven

When Our Kids Leave Our Nest, They're Still in the Arms of Jesus

Last week, we read about diapers. This week, we'll read about dorm rooms. As a mama of toddlers, I'm thinking more about closed or open-toed jammies than sending my kids off to young adulthood, but as I've heard many, many times (and I'm sure you have too), it "apparently" goes by fast. (Am I the only one who feels like my two-year-olds have been here way longer than two years?!) The wisdom and peace God has given the mamas we'll hear from this week is vast. Their faith and trust amaze me.

Jill J. is in her 50s, with two adult children. She shares: *When my kids entered high school and became independent, I had to trust and pray they were making the right decisions as I wasn't by their sides all the time. It was during this time that I truly dug deeper into my faith and relationship with Jesus. I started attending daily Mass occasionally to have my time with the Lord and to pray for my family. This was my time to trust and see that Jesus cared for me. In motherhood, we must trust, trust, and trust some more. Sometimes, it's hard to trust and keep the faith when life is so busy, and there is barely time for yourself. Step back and allow yourself just 10-15 minutes to be thankful and grateful for everything that is going on around you, as crazy as it may be at times. Trust me, before you know it, the "crazy" is gone, and your time to parent, teach, and mold your children is, too. That is when you really do have to TRUST and have FAITH that you did your job as a mom! As parents, we need to be reminded that our children are not ours; they are GOD's, and He trusted us to love, teach, and care for them while they are young so that when they do go off on their own, they do so with the faith, knowledge, and confidence we instilled in them.*

I just have to ask: If you have littles at home, are you struggling to relate to there being no more "crazy?" Are you freaking out a little bit that there will come a time when we will just send our children off into the world (all alone)? Mama, if I'm honest, this terrifies me. I mean, I send Hope and John to "school," but I still get alerted to how much they ate, if they peed or pooped on the potty, how long they napped, and also any and all circumstances around every little bump, bruise, or scratch they may get while they're away from home. Plus, I get photos capturing their experiences, happiness, and safety.

So, I think this is the point: First, our children are never all alone, ever. Jesus is always with them! As this mama said above (and I find myself getting weirdly protective just writing this), our children are not ours; they are His! God is always with them. This is most reassuring when we firmly believe this and have also taught our kids this truth. *I want this level of trust and belief, Lord, I pray!* **(See: WEEK TWENTY-FOUR: Our Children are God's Children First; He Loves Them More than We Do.)**

I also love how this mama started by sharing how when her kids became more independent, she spent more time with the Lord, becoming more dependent on Him. I love that, and so does He. I imagine Him sitting with this mama, holding her while she prayed for her children–His children–that He loves more than we ever could.

Next, I love how she suggests stepping back in gratitude. When we're truly grateful, we're unable to experience negative emotions at the same time. The lack of patience, the worry, and the "hanger" I can experience in the crazy moments simply disappear when I look at and pray about my kids with thankfulness. **(See: WEEK THIRTY-SIX: Gratitude in Motherhood.)**

At 39 years old, I still learn from my mom (and she never misses an opportunity to teach me!). However, most of the "molding" of our children, especially when it comes to their faith in Jesus, is done within the very first formative years of their lives. That feels like a lot of pressure to make sure I did my job as a mom! But as parents, we need to be reminded again and again that our children are not ours alone. When we lean on Jesus, He equips us with His wisdom *to love, teach, and care for our children while they are young. So then, when they go off on their own, they do so with the faith, knowledge, and confidence we instilled in them* through Jesus Christ.

Cassandra is in her 50s, with six school-age to adult children. She shares: *I thought things would be easier as my oldest child grew older and that once he became an adult, I would have fewer worries and responsibilities. However, as he grew and began to interact with the world, I realized that I had less and less control over his environment and who had access to him. Daily, I have to let go and let God have His way, and trust God to send angels to be a hedge of protection* (Psalm 91) *around my oldest child, even now that he's an adult.*

> DAILY, I HAVE TO LET GO AND LET *God* HAVE HIS WAY.

Releasing control, letting go, and letting God is something I'm praying hard about right now. And it's a good thing, because while I may try to be in control now, it's definitely not possible when my kids are no longer under my roof! But thank God, that when our kids leave our nest, they're still in the arms of Jesus! I can imagine this mama praying every morning for the protection of her son. It gives me peace just thinking about it. I think I'll join her, and by the time Hope and John leave our home, I pray I have the peace of knowing Jesus is always by their sides and in their hearts.

I want to conclude this week with some prayers one mama personalized for her kids. Tamara is in her 50s, with two young adult and adult children:

Father, I thank You that my sons' steps are ordered by You and that they are surrounded by Your hedge of protection according to Psalm 91.

Father, I thank You that no weapon formed against them will prosper. (Isaiah 54:17, personalized)

Father, I thank You for Your favor that surrounds them like a shield. (Psalm 5:12, personalized)

Lord, You are amazing, and Your goodness and mercy follow them all the days of their lives. (Psalm 23:6, personalized)

Lord, You keep them from hurt, harm, or danger of every kind. (Psalm 91, personalized)

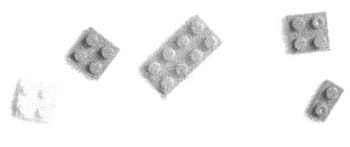

Bible Verse

I invite you to write out your own personalized versions of the above verses.

Prayer

Lord, I pray for the mama whose child is leaving their home. I pray she seeks You and feels Your presence and protection over her and her child. Give her the peace only You can provide, Lord. For those of us with littles at home, help us practice giving up control and trusting You with our children right now. Equip us, Lord, to show them Your ways as they're written in the Bible and also through our actions. As our children become more independent from us, may we (and they) become more dependent on You. Thank You for the gift of raising and loving Your children, Lord. We love You. Amen.

Reflective Questions

1. Reflect on your current stage of motherhood. How can you more fully rely on God now so you're more reliant on God in your future motherhood?

2. Reflect on a time in your life when you didn't know the outcome of something important to you. Did you pray to God? Did you trust in Him? Did you receive His peace? Whether you answered yes or no, spend some time relating that experience to motherhood.

3. Pray about one area of motherhood wherein you can release (at least some) control to God right now.

Week Eight

Mothering with Childhood Trauma

The Oxford Dictionary defines trauma as "a deeply distressing or disturbing experience; emotional shock following a stressful event or a physical injury, which may be associated with physical shock and sometimes long-term neurosis; physical injury (in medicine)." After reading this, I wanted more context around "neurosis" which is defined as "a mental condition that is not caused by organic disease, involving symptoms of stress (depression, anxiety, obsessive behavior, or hypochondria), but not a radical loss of touch with reality; excessive and irrational anxiety or obsession."[7] Oof. It's some heavy and serious stuff, but I love how our first mama shares how God has worked to heal her of her childhood trauma.

Jonnie is in her 40s, with two young adult children. She shares: *God has used motherhood to sanctify me and heal so much of my childhood trauma with my own mother. What I will say is that motherhood brought up a TON of fear for me as a trauma and abuse survivor. That fear has the power to either control you and your decisions or drive you straight to the One Who has conquered fear and death itself. As a child of a narcissist, I never felt like I had any control, and*

I think that is why my default was to go to God for help since I knew I could not do it alone. Fear and anxiety have been commonplace for me in parenthood, and I have to say, that experience has kept me super close to Jesus. His wisdom and guidance have shown up over and over, but always when I felt the weight of facing the fear of letting go.

> FEAR HAS THE POWER TO EITHER CONTROL YOU AND YOUR DECISIONS OR DRIVE YOU STRAIGHT TO THE ONE WHO HAS *conquered* FEAR.

In a follow-up conversation with this mama, who is so wise and whose faith is so steadfastly woven into every area of her life, motherhood included, she further noted: *We as humans cannot manage fear. When we try in our own strength to manage fear, we are always left fearful because only God can manage fear. He has given us the gift to manage love, not fear, so we must go to Him with our fears (Philippians chapter 4).*

I'm so grateful for this mama's humble heart and for her love for God. Notice how she didn't say her childhood trauma just went away but that her continued fear and anxiety has given her an opportunity to continue to rely on God. That's what He wants! As she noted in her first sentence, it's likely in this process of her continuously going to God in times of fear and anxiety in motherhood that God continuously sanctified and healed her of her childhood trauma every time she clung to and relied on Him.

Bri is in her 30s, with two young to school-age (earthside) children. She shares: *Parenting kids has really made me look internally and sit with the heartache of my own childhood and how ignored I felt. I was held to high standards and reprimanded when those expectations weren't met. I sat with my frustration one night after an evening of tears and tantrums by my four-year-old. Why couldn't she just speak kindly and be reasonable? It was then that God gently reminded me of the times I had felt unseen and unheard. The times I felt like my needs were pushed aside and how I needed a love that was unconditional… That could only come from the Father. I went back to my daughter and sat with her in bed, frustrated and hurt. I reminded her of how I try to love her the best I can, but we also need the love of Jesus to satisfy our hearts' cries.*

God's love for us is greater than we can even imagine. We love our children as much as possible, but the love that's possible for us is finite, unlike God's infinite, unconditional love. **(See: WEEK TWENTY-FOUR: Our Children are God's Children First; He Loves Them More than We Do.)** That's hard for me to write and hear, but it's the truth. Mama, we must rely on God's love for us and our children to help us mother them, especially if that wasn't our experience in our own childhood.

Christine is in her 30s, with three young to school-age children. She shares: *With one of my daughters, Jesus' peace and wisdom come to me when her anxiety flares, and I know that I can help her walk through it. God has given me so many different periods of anxiety/depression, and what I have learned I will share with her to help ease her experiences.*

Sometimes, our adult anxiety and depression can stem from things that happened in our own childhood. Even if these or other traumas aren't happening to our children, they can still experience "emotional shock following a stressful event." It's a gift to be able to support our children in ways similar to how we've been (or how we wish we would have been) supported. For us and for our children, God is the number one healer of trauma of any kind. But many resources are available to help families navigate healing from trauma, restoring mental health, and building a strong foundation in Christ. (See: *Mental Health Sermon Series* in the Resources for Mamas section.[8])

Bible Verse

"There is no fear in love, but perfect love casts out fear. For fear has to do with punishment, and whoever fears has not been perfected in love" (1 John 4:18 ESV).

Prayer

No matter what we've experienced, Lord, I pray we parent from faith, not fear. Mature us and our faith in You, so when we become anxious or fearful, we draw closer to You, casting our cares, anxieties, and fears at your feet (1 Peter 5:7 and Psalm 55:22). I pray for *more of He, less of me*. Help us relinquish control of our worries in motherhood and instead lean more on You, no matter what we experienced in our childhood. Thank You for being a God that never gives up on us. Thank You for saving us. Lastly, Lord, I pray our love for our children comes closer and closer to Your infinite, unconditional love for us. Help us to experience Your love so we can better show it to our children. Your perfect love casts out our fears. Help us to draw closer to You, Lord. We love You. Amen.

Reflective Questions

1. Prayerfully reflect on your own childhood. What childhood traumas might you be carrying with you into adulthood? Do you have someone to forgive? Have you thanked God for being your Savior recently?

2. How might you take this week's topic into mothering your own children? How might we show up differently in motherhood when we've cast our cares on the Lord and received His perfect, no-fear love?

3. Read, meditate on, journal, and pray about Philippians chapter four.

Week Nine

Balance in Motherhood

Some people say "balance," others say "harmony." I try to remember to say, *Jesus, Jesus, and more Jesus.*

Gina is in her 30s, with four young to school-age children. She shares: *When I give myself to Him totally, He helps me find balance in motherhood by setting healthy boundaries and sometimes by setting aside my needs for others. It's all done in prayer because I trust Him to lead me.*

There's a lot to unpack from this short but significant share! I'm asking myself this question right now: Have I given myself to Him totally? Have I ever, even for a few minutes, given my total self… my past, present, future, my family, my everything to God? When we give ourselves back to Him (as He's from where we came), we receive in return a harmonious balance in our lives and in motherhood. You'd think it would be an easy choice to make then, every moment of every day, with that kind of reward! Well, maybe it's easier for you than it is for me!

Oh, I need this week of reminders and encouragement, mama! I'm over here clutching my life and my motherhood so tightly, oftentimes hardly leaving any room for God to empower and enlighten me. *Jesus, help us trust You more. You are our source of balance and peace in motherhood. We trust You, we trust You, we pray. Help us get out of Your perfect and balanced way, Lord, so that You can do Your great work in us!* **(See: WEEK TWENTY-SIX: Mothering within God's Will and Perfect Long-Term Plan for Our Kids.)**

This mama also mentioned having healthy boundaries. For me, this means guarding my eyes and my ears. That is, for example, not watching or listening to the filth and evil that, often unknowingly, creates space between my heart and God's, leaving me feeling unbalanced. Sometimes, I cave and watch filthy shows on Netflix, but they never make my heart feel good. So, then, I pray. Sometimes, I find myself playing the comparison game on social media.

But actually, as a side note, I usually really enjoy social media. I try to post positive content, so I see a lot of positive content. You have the choice of whether or not to follow someone. If someone's content makes you feel bad about yourself, you can pray for them and then unfollow them. When comparison comes up for me, I try to stop it as soon as it starts, and I pray for the other person in the confidence of God. This is how I guard my heart! **(See WEEK FIFTEEN: Comparison: The Thief of Joy (Plus Judgement and Envy).)**

Lastly, setting aside our own needs for another's needs is exactly what Jesus did for us. To do this for our children is part of motherhood. And while it's an honor to mirror Jesus' selflessness, it can be hard sometimes. We're not paid to be mothers! It's often a thankless job, but it is the most important job there is! By praying and trusting in Jesus, He gives us the strength to do what our imperfect, unbalanced humanness cannot.

Alyssa is in her 30s, with four young to school-age children. She shares: *Schedule Jesus at least once a day. Your schedule isn't always yours, so find it when you can or in the midst. Find your thing. Ask Jesus to help you figure out that time and to spend your time doing whatever Jesus wills you to do. Remember that being married is a vocation. Being a mom is part of that vocation. He will give us sufficient graces to accomplish His will. We will find an oasis in Christ so that we can pour out from an overflowing spirit.*

We won't last long white-knuckle surviving. I have truly found some balance once I started practicing the Sabbath. That doesn't mean a day without doing... Sabbath is active! Yes, laundry is included in that as time for listening to God. It's time to go out in our community, serve the poor, serve our church, host or attend Bible study, do something with our hands instead of just sitting at a desk, play a sport with our kids, and go out to eat. My time is from noon on Saturday to noon on Sunday. Trust that God can do more in six days than we can do in seven. We'll never feel like we're giving enough to our children, spouse, self, and in the way we serve others. Isn't one of the best things about God that He tells us that we're not supposed to be enough? He will give to us faithfully and abundantly, and we are to share it. The gifts of others around us and the omnipotent, omnipresent, and everlasting God are more than enough. Pray, Jesus, I trust in You. Jesus, help me to do Your will today. Lord, keep me from the things in my day that do not glorify You. Please help me. Strengthen my relationships. Whatever those other things are on my mind, those things must be worldly. Even if they are "good," if they aren't glorifying You today, help me to avoid them so that they will not diminish the way I live to be sanctified by You. The world lies. Keep your eyes and confidence up, sister!

> *Trust* THAT GOD CAN DO MORE IN SIX DAYS THAN WE CAN DO IN SEVEN.

There is so much goodness here! First, if you work outside the home (or work from home, as I do), it's important to remember that we have a vocation that is more important than the one for which we're paid. Again, this often-thankless job of motherhood is the most important job, and yet we find ourselves, for instance, seeking balance in who we were and what we cared about before we were mothers, compared to who we are now and what we care about now. **(See: WEEK FORTY-NINE: Caring for Yourself when You Become a Mother.)**

As this mama said, it is through Him that we are able to pour from an overflowing cup… If we trust in Him, pray to Him, and do as He tells us. I love how she also reminds us of the importance of prayerful rest! *Trust that God can do more in six days than we can do in seven.* I'm trying to think of a 24-hour period in a week where I don't work at all. Especially since I started writing this devotional, on top of my wellness business and motherhood, I have stayed quite busy. There are seasons in life, sure, but you can bet I'm praying about trusting God fully with my time.

If this mama of four, who also owns her own business, can set aside time for a Sabbath rest, so can I. And so can you... with Jesus' help! His promises are true for us all. I am a big fan of hiring childcare or swapping care with another Christian mom friend to spend time with my husband or time alone doing something I love. We may not get a regular 24-hour Sabbath from motherhood, but we can prayerfully focus more on honoring God with our children. And I bet He will honor us with a sense of balance and peace in return.

Lastly, I included this mama's words about not being enough this week because we really do put so much effort into our children. This can leave us feeling depleted and longing for more balance. Again, when we lean on Him, He fulfills us as only He can do. I love her series of prayers to God as well. All of these prayers help us accomplish *more of He, less of me*, which will always leave us feeling more balanced with who we were created to be. Our story is to be His glory. When it's not, that's when we feel out of balance and most in need of Him. Remember that He is always there for us... totally.

Bible Verse

"She watches over the affairs of her household and does not eat the bread of idleness. Her children arise and call her blessed; her husband also, and he praises her: 'Many women do noble things, but you surpass them all.' Charm is deceptive, and beauty is fleeting; but a woman who fears the LORD is to be praised. Honor her for all that her hands have done, and let her works bring her praise at the city gate" (Proverbs 31:27-31 NIV).

Prayer

Lord, we need You only. Help us to seek You totally, Jesus. Show us what we need to stop to have more of You in our lives and as part of our motherhood. Open our tight fists, Lord, and give us Your peace and balance in abundance instead! As our Bible verse this week says, I pray we "fear the Lord," that we seek, pray, and trust You, and then we are "praised" and feel balanced and whole in our Creator God. You are all we need. We love You. Amen.

Reflective Questions

1. Have you given yourself totally to God? What healthy boundaries could help you do so? Create a list and hold yourself accountable (maybe by another Christian mama) and also in prayer.

2. Do you take a Sabbath? If not, plan out your perfect, restful, God-honoring Sabbath. Please share it with your husband, and prayerfully make it a reality for you and your family.

3. Do you believe God is more than enough? Pray and meditate on this truth as it relates to trusting Him in finding balance in life, as a mother, and as a child of God.

Reflection; Miracles in Motherhood (Vol. I)

Woohoo! You made it to week ten, mama! Go YOU and go GOD! We've covered a variety of topics in the past nine weeks, and my hope is you've been in prayer, in action, and in rest with the Lord. God is on the move! He's working to connect you with amazing Christian mom friends. He hears your breath prayers for patience. He hears you praying for other Christian mamas who've experienced challenging times in motherhood (that you may not have experienced).

God IS ON THE MOVE!

Take some time to reflect on the last nine weeks:
1. How has God's love and peace for you changed you and impacted your family since you started this devotional?
2. What have been your three biggest takeaways so far?
3. Is there a topic you'd like to re-read this week?

4. Is there a mama you thought of in weeks three, six, or eight, but you forgot to pray for her or reach out to her? Now is your opportunity! Don't let this week go by without praying for her or connecting with her.
5. Do you find yourself seeking, trusting, and relying on God for peace, wisdom, and guidance in motherhood, even 5% more than you did nine weeks ago?

Let's pray. *Lord, thank You for the mama reading these words right now. She has been seeking You, Lord. She has been working on relying on You to help her love and raise her children, children who are Yours first. She loves You, Lord. Show her Your love for her right now, Lord. Surround her with Your abundant love, grace, and peace for her. Continue to be present with us, Lord, as we continue week after week, yearning to be with You as we mother our children. Protect the time we carve out to be with You, to honor You, and to be guided by You in this journey of motherhood. Lord, thank You to each mama whose contributions have made up this devotional. Please bless them and their families, Lord. Help me use their words to bring honor and glory to You. I pray this devotional blesses the mamas reading it. Thank You for blessing us with motherhood. We love You. Amen.*

This week, I'll share a miracle of God – from Julie, a mama in her 60s, with four adult children. She shares: *When you pray for God to protect you and then you see that protection unfold right before your eyes, emotions simply unravel. You may cry because of what could have happened, and then get on your knees and thank God from the depths of your being for sparing your child's life, for protection from disability, or for keeping your child free from the suffering of serious illness. All of that being said, if anything dreadful does happen, it does not mean that God didn't answer prayer. Many wonderful, Godly, prayerful people have gone through devastating accidents and illnesses causing disability and even death, yet the grace of God was still with them. I am sure there have been many times that Christians have been protected, and we were never aware of it, as well.*

I believe I still have the little Aladdin loafer that my young son had on when he ran to his father, who was operating the riding lawn mower. When my husband noticed him out of the corner of his eye, my son was almost there and my husband didn't have time to fully stop the mower or the blade. My husband turned off the deck and thrust out his arm to push my son away. At that moment, my son's foot went under the still-spinning blade, which sliced open the top of his shoe but left his foot unharmed. I saved the shoe as a reminder of God's grace.

I promised the mamas who contributed to this devotional that their shares would remain anonymous except for their first name and approximate age. Still, I'll just say this: If God hadn't extended His grace that day, these words may have never been written. My children, Hope and John, may have never been born. My exact challenges in my first 18 months of life as a new mom may not have brought me to my knees for Jesus in the exact way that they did. He may not have rescued me with His peace in the exact way that He did. As a result, He may not have put it on my heart to write a devotional for moms because, in all this, I've learned how much mothers absolutely need Jesus! *Thank You, Jesus, for Your grace! Thank You for this miracle!*

I hope this reflection week has blessed you. Some of the topics in this devotional are hard. Some we can relate to more than others. A week where we pause to review and reflect can be really helpful. And hearing a story about the gift of God's incredible grace reminds us how great our God truly is! It's also a reminder to ask God to protect our families, to be weak and vulnerable, pleading for God to keep our children healthy and safe. In place of fear for our children's safety, we can ask the Lord to give us His peace. If tragedy happens, we can still pray to the God Who loves us.

This week's Bible verse sums this up well:

"But he said to me, 'My grace is sufficient for you, for my power is made perfect in weakness.' Therefore I will boast all the more gladly of my weaknesses so that the power of Christ may rest upon me. For the sake of Christ, then, I am content with weaknesses, insults, hardships, persecutions, and calamities. For when I am weak, then I am strong" (2 Corinthians 12:9-10 ESV).

Week Eleven

Growing in Motherhood through Faith in God

I felt like God was teaching me things that were really hard for me to do, but I knew He was making me grow in motherhood. Amen! So, that's it for this week… Go pray and reflect, sweet mama. But really, these words from Amara, who is in her 30s, with two young (earthside) children, could have come right from my very own heart. Maybe yours, too? This week we begin a three-week series on faith and prayer life in motherhood.

Janette is in her 30s, with three young to school-age children. She shares: *I felt the Lord telling me this wasn't about my comfort but instead about growing me. I needed to change my perspective from, "Give me what I want" to, "Make me who You want me to be." I have found when I am able to have this attitude, though circumstances may not change, I do, and that makes all the difference.*

Ever since I first read this mama's words, I've heard the Lord tell me the same type of thing in my own recurring, challenging moments in motherhood. And so, I pray: *Grow me and change me, Lord. Please grow me by growing my faith and trust in You. Help me be better in this situation, help me be more compassionate when my son does this, help me be more patient when my daughter does that. I, of course, pray for You to work in and through my children, keeping them healthy and safe, but my most fervent prayer for my children is actually a prayer for myself. Make me who You want me to be, Lord, for the benefit of my children. Grow me in this area of motherhood, Lord. Please make me who You want me to be!*

Cassandra is in her 50s, with six school-age to adult children. She shares: *When I became a mother, internally, I was in turmoil, conflicted, and sometimes even seething with anger and frustration. I remember praying repeatedly, "God, give me patience!" whenever I would encounter these emotions. When my son was born, I felt such joy and thought God made me a mom, so I must have patience now! (I'm sure God chuckled at my logic.) However, eight weeks in, my son was crying inconsolably one night, and I was sobbing because I felt anything BUT patient. I remember saying out loud, "I give up – I surrender! I thought I was in control of the situation and my feelings, but clearly, I am not. God, I need You now more than ever!" At that moment, my son stopped crying, and I was amazed to see him quietly fall asleep. What I realized was that I was expecting God to sprinkle patience over me like some magic fairy dust, and poof – I would be patient! The truth is that, oftentimes, there is a process we must go through to become what and who God desires us to be.*

I could have included this share during week six when we covered the postpartum/fourth trimester phase, but I think this process my friend speaks of is exactly that: an ongoing process that extends well beyond the fourth trimester. While the early days of motherhood have their fill of firsts and harder-than-normal, God-seeking moments, our growth doesn't end there. Motherhood is a lot like pregnancy. You're not sure how your body will do it all, but slowly, you begin to grow and expand until your baby is finally born. Our physical body changes first, then eventually, with the help of God, other changes occur too. We need God in order to grow and expand our faith life and our Godly motherhood. God grows our faith as we grow to rely on and trust in Him.

Emma is in her 30s, with two young (earthside) children. She shares: *It is when we are at our weakest that we are more likely to run to God and*

GOD GROWS OUR FAITH AS WE *grow* TO RELY ON AND TRUST IN HIM.

cling to Him. Through suffering, He gives us an opportunity to grow closer to Him.

We love our kids. Suffering is part of loving. Jesus did this first. As our kids grow (and suffer), we suffer with them as we prayerfully focus on growing our faith in Jesus Christ (and modeling this for them). **(See: WEEK TWENTY-FIVE: When Our Kids Hurt, We Hurt, but God's Provision is True.)** He suffered for us first, and He is the solution to all our suffering! *Thank You for making us grow in motherhood, Lord! The growth, the changing, the process, and our suffering are worth it since it brings us more faithfully to You in motherhood and in life.*

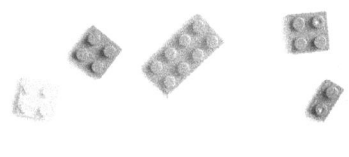

Bible Verse

"Listen to advice and accept instruction, that you may gain wisdom in the future. Many are the plans in the mind of a man, but it is the purpose of the LORD that will stand" (Proverbs 19:20-21 ESV).

Prayer

Lord, we need You. We need to have strong faith in You for motherhood. You blessed us with our kids; help us remember to give You our most challenging moments in motherhood. When suffering in motherhood brings us to our knees, remind us we're in the perfect position to pray and receive You, our Holy Solution. As we grow in our faith and grow in our relationship with You, help us to come to You more quickly and more often so we may be strengthened by Your holy, supernatural power to mother our children how You want us to. Grow us, change us, Lord.

Make us become who You want us to be. Grow us, Lord, for our children. Help us with this process, over and over again, as we grow to rely on and trust in You more. We love You. Amen.

Reflective Questions

1. When the challenges of motherhood bring you to your knees, what typically happens next?

2. How do you think God might be yearning to grow and change you as a mother? Prayerfully ask Him.

3. Outside of motherhood, where in suffering has God met you? Reflect on this, noting how your faith differed before and after suffering. **(See: WEEK FORTY-TWO: Trials and Struggles in Motherhood Can Grow Our Faith.)**

Growing Your Prayer Life because You're a Mother

The most common, recurring answer to the third question I asked the mamas who contributed to this devotional: *What might you share with a new mom who's a believer in Jesus?* was to pray to, study with, and spend quiet time with the Lord daily. (During weeks 33, 34, and 35, we'll learn from all of their answers to this question.) After last week's topic, I hope this week on growing your prayer life guides your heart to want to spend more time with our Heavenly Father, for your own personal benefit and for the benefit of your motherhood. Here's what our contributing mamas share:

Beth is in her 60s, with three adult children. She shares: *As a new mom, I cannot encourage you enough to dig into the Word daily. Start your day early in the morning, before your household wakes, in the Word with Jesus. Wait upon Him, listen to Him. The day will be busy enough, full enough, and exhausting enough on its own to tire you out, so you won't have that time at the* end of the day because a mom's job is never done, no matter how young or old your children are. I encourage you to make a place in your home that is "Mom's prayer corner," where you begin every day alone with Jesus. Don't give that up, not even for a day! Put Jesus first and listen to Him. He wants this time with you to feed you, guide you, and nurture your motherhood journey in His quiet, loving grace and mercy. He stands as a gentleman and waits, knocking at the door of your heart. It is your job to open that door, welcome Him in, and sit at His feet and listen.

Even now, with all three of my own children grown, married to wonderful believers, and growing their own households, I still begin my day early with Jesus, laying all before Him, waiting upon His wisdom and abiding in His grace. My prayers for my children have grown and shifted as they have grown into adulthood. All of them still remember being young children coming out in their jammies, finding Mommy in the Word, and spending time with the Lord before our family day began. I remember the days I let that time go, skipping it in order to meet the needs of a hectic day, I would always feel disconnected somewhat, not centered, and not fully present, nor capable of meeting the demands of the day. These early morning times with Jesus are still like air to my lungs. I encourage young moms to embrace this as well. You'll never regret it!

Carmie is in her 70s, with three adult children. She shares: *I would tell any mom, new or experienced, that it's really important to make time for Jesus in your life in order to deepen your faith. Just try to carve out a few minutes each day of quiet time to either study the Word of God or just pray. Sometimes, I just sit and listen; God speaks to those of us who have quiet time. It's hard to find that quiet time; you have to work really hard at it. Even schedule it like you do other appointments and make it a top priority in your life.*

GOD SPEAKS TO THOSE OF US WHO HAVE *quiet* TIME.

Billie is in her 60s, with four adult children. She shares: *Things will be hard. There is no instruction manual that comes with our beautiful children. We do, however, have words of wisdom and guidance from the One Who can answer all questions. When things are hard, just breathe, pray, and listen! He will guide you – always. As parents, we feel responsible for our children and try to fix everything. We think that's our job. While that is partially true, God may have other plans where we need to take His guidance, not ours. On the flip side, always remember to thank Him for all the blessings with your child. Even for the times in life and in motherhood they test you to your limit, this is when God can shine brightly through you. God is good all the time, and all the time, God is good.*

Heather is in her 40s, with two school-age children. She shares: *Pray every single day that God gives you what you need to be the best mother to your children. It's so much easier to do life with God's guidance versus going at it alone.*

Lastly, Pam is in her 50s, with five school-age to adult children. She shares: *Sometimes, getting back to your faith and praying keeps you sane along with everything else, and it helps give you strength to deal with hard things.*

By praying to, studying with, and spending quiet time with the Lord daily, we inevitably experience more growth, support, and peace in our prayer life and in our motherhood.

Bible Verse

"Call to me and I will answer you, and will tell you great and hidden things that you have not known" (Jeremiah 33:3 ESV).

Prayer

I love that verse in Jeremiah, Lord, because it reminds me that we don't (need to) know everything! We don't have to because You do! But we need to pray and spend time with You in order to glean from You, Lord. Help us spend more time with You, praising You, and praying to You. When our children test us to our limits, let us see You shine brightly through us, Lord. We know when we spend more time with You, our children will experience You more through us. Thank You for that, Lord! We love You. Amen.

Reflective Questions

1. Consider your current prayer life. Are you regularly in awe of God in life and in motherhood? Do you feel encouraged, supported, and inspired by God? If not, I encourage you to spend time with Him until He amazes you and until you feel His strength and peace every day.

2. Do you easily accept help, or do you try to do everything on your own? Pray that God may use your prayer life to show you how helpful He is! **(See: WEEK FORTY-SIX: When a "Helper" Needs Help.)**

3. What objections came up right away when you read this week's topic? Time, space, etc.? Pray about it all. Ask God to meet you where you are, to bless your schedule, and to strengthen your prayer life through and with Him.

Week Thirteen

Modeling Faith to Our Children by Mothering (and Living) with God

There's some overlap between this week's topic and the topics of the last two weeks. I ended up sandwiching "Growing your prayer life because you're a mother" between "Growing in motherhood through faith in God" and now, "Modeling faith to our children by mothering (and living) with God," because all of these topics are, at their core, about being prayerful. As we live each day prayerfully, we are showing our kids firsthand what it looks like to grow and be radically changed in the ways God so desires for us and for them.

Jan is in her 70s, with three adult children. She shares: *My own dear mother set such a strong example. I witnessed her living her life in faith, prayer, and study, showing much strength. It was such a blessing. So, whether it's your own mother or another woman, seek and be that example of shining faith.*

If you had that Godly, prayerful example in a mother growing up, this may come more easily to you. But even if you didn't, remember that, ultimately, we are talking about seeking Jesus! If you're seeking Him, He will show up whether you saw your parents follow after and pray to Him or not! What I'm really learning to do right now is to open my tight fists of loving control over my children's lives so I can receive God's help in mothering and raising them. Then, my prayer is that my kids will see this and know and experience my faith in Him so they can do the same.

I think to do this well, we must know and believe in God's perfect plan for us all. **(See: WEEK TWENTY-SIX: Mothering within God's Will and Perfect Long-Term Plan for Our Kids.)** He will equip us to put His plan for our family and our life into action when we are tuned into Him. Again, God does not necessarily call the equipped, but He always equips the called who seek Him. We were called to be mothers! It's this very act of showing our kids that we yearn for God to equip us that allows them to open themselves up to God's help in their own lives. This takes humility instead of pride, strength to *let go and let God*, and trust and peace instead of worry or fear. **(See: WEEK EIGHTEEN: Showing Our Humility and God's Grace to Our Kids.)**

Jonnie is in her 40s, with two young adult children. She shares: *Don't confuse fear and worry with guiding your children. As parents, we often parent from fear, not faith. We think we shape and affect our children far less than we actually do. We are to shepherd them and encourage them toward the Lord.*

She goes on to talk about our own process of growing and changing to be who the Lord wants us to be, being shepherded by Him, as well: *God created us to experience bliss and peace. That is our role as parents to let their little lives unfold, teaching them faith in God, meditation, and to live according to His Word. Then God helps them to become who He created them to be... blissful and peaceful, too.*

Mothering (and living) with God means accepting His guidance because we need it to do the best job. Doing so provides us with His peace. Exemplifying faith for our children means showing them how we pray for, expect, and utilize God's guidance in day-to-day activities and also while going through challenging times. Our kids can see when we're worried. They can also see the peace we have when we trust in God, inviting Him to mother with us. **(See: WEEK FORTY-SEVEN: Christ's**

Peace in Our Mama Hearts.) I love to be reminded that our faith is not ours to hold on to, but it is ours to give away. Who better to give our faith to than our children?

> OUR FAITH IS NOT OURS TO HOLD ON TO, BUT IT IS OURS TO *give* AWAY. WHO BETTER TO GIVE OUR FAITH TO THAN OUR CHILDREN?

Julie is in her 60s, with four adult children. She shares: *I think motherhood brought me even closer to God and helped me understand the necessity for involving Him and invoking His blessing, wisdom, and, sometimes, even begging for His intervention on behalf of my children. Jesus proved so very worthy of our trust over and over again. At this point in my life, looking back and trying to recall the struggles of parenthood—and there are many, of course—it is easy to see that God has a long-term plan (see Jeremiah 29:11), and I am only a part of His workings in the life of each child.* **(See again: WEEK TWENTY-SIX: Mothering within God's Will and Perfect Long-Term Plan for Our Kids.)**

She goes on to say: *There are some things I knew how to do, to teach, to encourage, and there were some things (indeed, many things) about which I had little knowledge and over which I had no control. So, you pray a lot, encourage, and do your very best to have your kids face everything with their relationship with God and good character as priorities. Watching this play out and seeing God's care and provision draws me ever closer to Jesus.*

There's so much goodness here, but for the sake of this week's topic, I want to focus on this part of her share: *You pray a lot, you encourage, and you do your very best to have your kids face everything with their relationship with God and good character as priorities.* Modeling prayer and being in a relationship with God, (praying, trusting, experiencing His peace within His guidance) is one of the best ways for our children to know how to be in a relationship with God. As we've read the last couple of weeks, when we suffer and lean on God, He grows and changes us in motherhood and in life. The same goes for our kids! We need to mother (and do life) with the One Who gave us life and gave us our kids. And we need to show our kids this process in our own lives so they know how to work through it themselves. By modeling this, our children can learn how to be in relationship with God, too.

These last couple of shares are reminders that God has/wants to equip you to mother the children you've been given and to share Him with them throughout the blessings and challenging moments of motherhood and life.

Kacie is in her 30s, with three young to school-age children. She shares: *You are enough, and you are the perfect person for this job. God made you with your current situation in mind and in His perfect timing. The most important thing you can do is share the love of Jesus with your children… Everything else can follow.*

Cassandra is in her 50s, with six school-age to adult children. She shares: *Your relationship with Christ becomes even more significant as you begin your journey as a mom. Learn how to turn to Him for everything, not just the critical or challenging moments. Jesus is truly your best friend!* **(See: WEEK FORTY-ONE: Jesus is a Mama's (and a Kiddo's) Best Friend.)**

We share the love of Jesus by sharing Jesus with our kids and by loving them as He loves us (which we can do most effectively *with* His help). Don't be afraid to pray in front of your children, mama! Let them hear your quiet breath prayers. Let them see you hit your knees for Him! Let them see you praise Him. When they're hurting, we can talk about how much we love them as their mamas and how much more God our Creator loves them! When they see this in you, they will know it's right and good to have their own relationship with Christ, too. This is modeling our faith in God for our kids!

Bible Verse

"'As a mother comforts her child, so will I comfort you;…'" (Isaiah 66:13 NIV).

Prayer

Lord, thank You for comforting us and guiding us. Thank You for being the best example of how we should comfort and guide our children – with You! Help us remember to treat You like our best friend! You are always present and available to strengthen, guide, grow, and change us in motherhood and within Your will for our life. Let our life be an example of a woman and mama who loves You and who seeks You, Lord. Let our children see us seek You and see us grow with Your guidance. We pray for our children to seek You and seek to love others as You love them. Help us show them Your love and who You are, Lord. We love You. Amen.

Reflective Questions

1. During the last couple of weeks, reflect on how God has met you and changed your heart. How has this change and growth shown up in your prayer life? Have your children seen you pray more? If not, try praying in front of them today!

2. Do you have a faith or prayer mentor? Someone you saw praying and seeking God as you grew up? If so, have you thanked them lately? If not, do you have someone like this now? If not, pray to God for a prayer warrior and mentor in your life. Pray for a Christian mom friend who seeks to do motherhood and her life with God by openly praying to and seeking Him and His guidance.

3. Do you know/see that your children have a personal relationship with God? If not, what have you learned about how you can better exemplify and model faith to them? Be intentional this week to find one specific way you can tangibly model your faith in God to your children.

Personal and Worldly Expectations in Motherhood

We're heading in another direction this week, but we'll revisit mothering with God in the coming weeks. Having Christian mom friends who are open and honest can be the best example of worldly versus Godly expectations in motherhood. Being vulnerable about the reality of motherhood and how challenging it can be, especially if our previous personal expectations have faded away, allows others to be vulnerable, too. I'll quote again what one mama shares about her early days of motherhood.

Jill S. is in her 60s, with three adult children. She shares: *What I did feel was that motherhood would be a part of life, and I knew there would be challenges that went along with it. What kept me sane was surrounding myself with other women who were currently in the throes or had experienced motherhood. This included playgroups, Bible studies, and things that nurtured my soul and kept me from being unrealistic in my expectations of motherhood. I sought counsel in prayer, meditation, Scripture, and trusted friends.*

Personally, I'm not sure what I was thinking, but I had absolutely no idea how hard motherhood would be. I had no idea how much I would learn and how much I would need to learn to rely on God. How much I would need His peace in my heart. I babysat and nannied starting at age 12. I knew how to change a diaper, that babies shouldn't sleep with blankets or bumpers, I understood that kids thrived with routines, and I even thought I knew nearly every baby/toddler song there ever was. But I wasn't prepared for 30 hours of labor. I wasn't prepared for a chronic illness in one of my newborns. **(See: WEEK TWENTY-ONE: God Leads Mamas of Children with Medical Needs.)** And I certainly wasn't prepared to encounter all-new motherhood things with two children at the same time! Add hormones and not a ton of sleep to the mix, and I simply had no idea how much I'd need the Lord and His support and peace as a mother!

I also had no idea how much I could love another human being. In the years before we got pregnant, we were diagnosed with unexplained infertility. **(See: WEEK NINETEEN: Motherhood after Infertility; Secondary Infertility.)** With every negative pregnancy test, I saw my dream of holding a sweet, sleeping newborn with my husband's blue eyes slip further and further away.

While motherhood has a million sweet moments, like holding your sleeping baby, I now know there are many hard moments, too. My world was transformed when having a family went from a prayer and a sweet dream to interrupted sleep and poop literally everywhere. And then came specialist doctor's appointments and infant blood draws, and well, you fill in the blank because literally anything goes in motherhood! While I couldn't prepare myself for the love I'd feel, my expectations of a fairytale life as a mother flew right out the window.

Simply put, mothers need God and other God-loving mamas to help us

> MOTHERS NEED GOD AND OTHER GOD-LOVING MAMAS TO HELP US REORIENT OUR EXPECTATIONS AND WALK IN THE *fullness* OF MOTHERHOOD.

reorient our expectations and walk in the fullness of motherhood... the dreamy, the good, and also the hard!

Alyssa is in her 30s, with four young to school-age children. She shares: *I think that motherhood has taught me that this worldly expectation of being an independent woman is broken. Being an independent mom is overrated. I know now that I was learning prudence and patience. It was good for me.*

Christine is in her 30s, with three young to school-age children. She shares: *I think as I came into motherhood, I had this idea of what a mother should look like. I pictured gentleness, patience, and full devotion. As I became a mother, I often felt that I didn't portray those things and often felt at odds with who I naturally was as a caregiver versus this image in my mind. I think my frustration with myself turned into frustration with God and how He created me. I wondered why He would make me a mother if He didn't build me actually to be a mother in the way I idealized one. I think the fact that Jesus continues to provide for me in such amazing ways and how much His love shows through is what draws me back. It causes me to take a step back and sit in the fact that Jesus made me, He loves me, and He will help me be the mother HE wants me to be. Not the mother that society or even the mother that I personally tend to think is the right ideal.*

Oh, mama, I hear your heart! I'm also reminded of the mama who shared, *I was expecting God to sprinkle patience over me like some magic fairy dust, and poof – I would be patient!* **(See: WEEK ELEVEN: Growing in Motherhood through Faith in God.)** From where do these expectations even come? The world, inauthentic friends, or maybe our unmet expectations from our own mothers? I know many amazing mothers who are sometimes impatient with their children, so why do we tend to think we'll become this perfectly patient mother just by being blessed with children? Mama, that's one of the reasons I wanted to write this devotional. God knew I was in for some serious growth and change in order to be the mother He wants me to be for the children He's given me. Mama, in order to best serve our children, we must rely on our Father. It's in sharing these realities that, together, we can work to dissolve worldly expectations of what it looks like to be a ("perfect") mother. **(See: WEEK SEVENTEEN: God's Grace Instead of a Mother's "Perfection.")**

But–spoiler alert–the "perfect" mother doesn't exist. Unless we think of a perfect mother as someone who makes mistakes, learns and grows, all while consistently leaning on God for help.

The truth is, when we see a mother who we think checks all the boxes, for one, she simply doesn't. But two: she's most likely leaning heavily on the Lord as He works through her! He promises to do that for us, but we need to constantly remind ourselves to rely on Him. Again, may we cultivate relationships with mamas who encourage us and are also vulnerable about the realities of motherhood! As someone who's very active on social media, I suggest only following mamas who tactfully share the hard along with the good and the holiness of motherhood. On social media there's an incredible opportunity to unite and inspire, but often, people don't share their real lives, and so the result can be unmet, unrealistic expectations for the rest of us. (We will cover the slippery slope of comparison more next week.)

A note on social media and motherhood: After reading *M Is for Mama: A Rebellion Against Mediocre Motherhood* by Abbie Halberstadt,[9] I had to check myself on social media. The author explains that motherhood is a profession from God. We can tactfully share (and even laugh over) the real-life moments of motherhood without belittling our need for God or our gratitude for the children He gave us. For instance, I no longer post about needing wine after bedtime. I like to drink wine sometimes, but what I really need is God. Only God can give us the tools we need to mother our children according to His perfect will. Let us work to meet HIS expectations of our motherhood, but only with His help, grace, and peace!

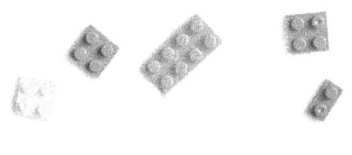

Bible Verse

"Now to him who is able to do immeasurably more than we all ask or imagine, according to his power that is at work within us,…" (Ephesians 3:20 NIV).

Prayer

Lord, work inside us. Give us Your power to meet YOUR expectations for us in motherhood. Help us experience *the Cross before us, the world behind us*. Help us not to compare ourselves to others. Help us to seek Christian mom friends who will be on this journey with us… A journey to seek Your expectations of us with Your help, grace, and peace. Help us to be the mother who encourages other mothers while being authentic and vulnerable. Help us seek the Cross and not things of this world in life and in motherhood. The world gives us false messages. Lord, thank You for overcoming the world! We love You. Amen.

Reflective Questions

1. What expectations of motherhood did you have before you became a mother? Was there a reality check for you?

2. Pray and ask God what He expects of you in motherhood. Ask Him to journey with you and ask Him to bless you with Christian mom friends who want in on this holy journey, too.

3. Do you share unrealistic stories of motherhood with friends, family, or on social media? How can you contribute to erasing worldly expectations of motherhood and replacing them with Godly expectations and tools?

Week Fifteen

Comparison: The Thief of Joy (Plus Judgment and Envy)

It seems only natural to go from expectations to comparison in motherhood, and then potential judgment and envy. First, what a gift God gave us and our children: the miracle of life! In doing so, He blessed us all with special gifts, talents, and passions that He hopes we'll use to glorify Him in the process of helping others. But when we compare ourselves or our children to others, especially when it results in judgment or envy, we may become unappreciative of the way God uniquely created us.

Pam is in her 50s, with five school-age to adult children. She shares: *Sometimes, on the outside, it looks so easy for the mom next door, but we all have our struggles... Sometimes, we hide them well. I have also learned not to compare my children's journeys to each other or to other families.*

We all have our struggles! There's not a person in the world that doesn't. When we're tempted to compare, judge, or envy others, we must remember that this is a temptation of humanity... Eve envied God first. She wanted what He had. And so, the fall of temptation and sin began. But with God's strength, we can pray to compare, judge, and envy less. **(See: WEEK FORTY-EIGHT: Sin and Spiritual Health in Motherhood.)**

Julie is in her 60s, with four adult children. She shares: *Don't compare your children. Don't say, "He's my smart one," or, "She's my (whatever, fill in the blank)." This can take away from the sibling's aspirations and/or confidence in an area.*

This is a great reminder, especially with twins, kids close in age, or those of the same gender. God made our kids with their own unique gifts, talents, and passions, too! We may not see these fully develop until they're older, so when they're younger, we can pray about how to best support our children and God's plan for their lives.

Christine is in her 30s, with three young to school-age children. She shares: *God has created each individual uniquely. That means that your children are unique, and so are you. What motherhood will look and feel like for you differs from that of ANYONE else. What that means is as much as getting advice can be abundantly helpful, you should always pray to God for which advice applies to you and your child and what doesn't. This also means that you should feel confident to be the mother that your child needs and the mother that brings joy to you and your family's life. Lastly, what that means is you should not judge other mothers and how they show up with and for their children; their children are uniquely made, as well. The best thing we can do is show up for our children and other mothers with love, just as Jesus would.*

WHAT IF WE ALL REPLACED JUDGMENT WITH *love*?

There's so much truth here. I love that last bit the most…What if we all replaced judgment with love?

Alyssa is in her 30s, with four young to school-age children. She shares: *During COVID, I struggled with envy. I was envious of those who didn't have four children and a business to juggle. We were in survival mode. I didn't feel bad for a soul other than those who were deeply lonely. You get to go on a nice, quiet walk every day? You get to work uninterrupted? You get to learn a new skill? They're all gifts! My children and practice were even greater gifts, so I kept my mouth shut and rolled my eyes at the world. I struggled with how my husband would just walk out the door every morning, and nothing changed for him. I was barely treading water with a newborn, two three-year-olds, and a kindergartener, and if I got an afternoon to work in silence, I would feel "lucky."*

I know this mama's heart well, and I love how she openly shares with us here. This mama is hard at work for God! She studies Him and longs to do His will for her life. Again, no one is exempt from the temptations of comparison and envy! Temptation is part of our humanity, but we can overcome it with God!

This next statement may sound ungrateful (especially since we struggled with infertility), but please know that's not my heart/intention. This is a safe, nonjudgmental space, so here it goes… I have felt envious of mamas of "singletons." My motherhood journey has often felt chaotic, like an unending game of (non-violent!) whack-a-mole. Of course, there are many sweet moments every day with my kids, together and individually, but sometimes my heart wonders what having one baby at a time would be like. There. I said it. *Now, please hear my heart, Lord. I love our children and am so grateful You blessed us with them. Help my heart to be grateful and content with the family You've blessed me with as I trust and rejoice in Your plan for my life. Help me not to compare my children to each other. While it's hard to parent twins, I'm so glad I have You from Whom my strength comes.* As President Theodore Roosevelt said, "Comparison is the thief of joy."[10] *Lord, I know the joy of the Lord is [my] strength (Nehemiah 8:10). Lord, may the thief of joy leave my heart and be replaced by You alone. Thank You for the special moments I get to have as a twin mom! Also, Lord, please send extra blessings to every mama with triplets.* (Oh. My. Goodness.)

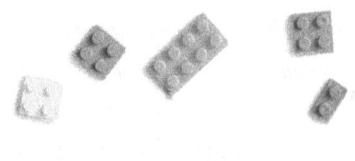

Bible Verse

"Don't compare yourself with others. Just look at your own work to see if you have done anything to be proud of. You must each accept the responsibilities that are yours" (Galatians 6:4-5 ERV).

Prayer

Lord, help us to use the special gifts, talents, and passions You gave us to glorify You in the process of helping others. Instead of comparing and "labeling" our kids, help us to best support their special gifts, talents, and passions in Your plans for their lives. We pray You help us to compare, judge, and envy less. Lord, help us to replace judgment for other mamas with love for them. May we also, instead of envying, be filled with gratitude for the blessings in our own lives, Lord. Help us to pray for other mamas instead of judging or envying them. Thank You for our joy and strength that come from You. We love You. Amen.

Reflective Questions

1. Reflect on the gifts God has given you. How do these gifts show up as you serve and raise your children and honor God?

2. Reflect on a time you've judged another mama. Ask God to forgive you, to soften your heart, and to help you to love and pray for her and other mamas instead.

3. Reflect on a time you've been envious of another mama. Ask God to forgive you and to fill your heart with so much gratitude for how He's blessed you that there's simply no room to envy another.

Week Sixteen

God's Grace for Us Mothers

We're entering a three-week series on grace. Praise Jesus! I'm excited, and I hope you are, too. Looking ahead, next week, we'll talk about God's grace instead of a mother's perfection. The following week, we'll hone in on showing our humility and God's grace to our kids. The Oxford Dictionary defines "the Christian belief" of grace as "the free and unmerited favor of God, as manifested in the salvation of sinners and the bestowal of blessings."[11] As Christians, we believe in the resurrection of Jesus Christ, a demonstration of His forgiveness and grace for believers in Him.

When we were blessed to become mothers and to care for God's children here on earth, I think God extended us a special form of grace… Because let's be honest, we mothers need it! Raising tiny (and I imagine, not so tiny) humans is hard, important work. Motherhood can be messy; God's grace meets us right in the thick of it. Motherhood can be unpredictable; God's grace is available to comfort us. (We'll touch on that more next week.) We will most definitely make many, many mistakes in motherhood. God's grace forgives us and redeems us. Thank God we have Him to guide us and give us His graces throughout our journey in motherhood... Especially when we call on Him!

Alyssa is in her 30s, with four young to school-age children. She shares: *He will give us sufficient graces to accomplish His will. We will find an oasis in Christ so that we can pour out from an overflowing spirit. We won't last long white-knuckle surviving. I have truly found some balance once I started practicing the Sabbath.*

That first sentence alone, gives me so much peace. When we lean on Him, He provides for us according to His will, which is the best laid-out plan, much better than our own plans. **(See: WEEK TWENTY-SIX: Mothering within God's Will and Perfect Long-Term Plan for Our Kids.)** When we spend time with the Lord, He equips us with more than any parenting book, mom group, or form of self-care out there. We need soul care; we need Jesus. We need His grace in our lives, especially when life is hard. And friends, motherhood is hard! We need Jesus and His grace in motherhood. When we seek Him, He provides us with grace and peace! **(See: WEEK FORTY-SEVEN: Christ's Peace in Our Mama Hearts.)**

Amara is in her 30s, with two young (earthside) children. She shares: *Be patient and give yourself grace over and over and over again. Keep leaning on Him.*

> BE PATIENT AND GIVE YOURSELF *grace* OVER AND OVER AND OVER AGAIN. KEEP LEANING ON HIM.

I truly appreciate how she mentions having patience here, because like we've talked about, while God's grace is always abundant and available for us, oftentimes there's a process that needs to take place in our hearts, through God, before we experience the benefits of God's grace and subsequent peace in our lives. We need God. We need to lean and rely on Him constantly. When we do this, over time, again and again, His grace provides everything for us as humans and as mothers.

Bri is in her 30s, with two young to school-age (earthside) children. She shares: *Jesus has SO much abundance of love and kindness to give us! His grace is abundant, and it doesn't run out. He wants us to ask Him for more because He loves giving His children more, just like we love doing for our kids. Don't forget about your eternal position as a child of the King while you're acting as a parent for your own children during our time in this temporary home.*

Did you need this reminder today, too? Oh, thank you for your heart, mama! Thank you for this reminder of the true abundance of God's grace and for the reminder that He wants us to seek Him so He can extend His graces to us. Just like our own children, we are children of God. You, mama, are God's precious child. He loves you. He wants to care for you, through His grace, as you care for the children that He's given you to raise here on earth. His love, kindness, grace, and peace never run out. Let us seek Him over and over again so He can provide His graces to us over and over again!

Beth is in her 60s, with three adult children. She shares how God's grace provided for her and her family after the sins of this world tried to penetrate deep (the story to follow in **WEEK TWENTY-NINE: The Influence of Society/Peers and Their Sin on Our Children**). She shares: *Although I would not wish this experience on any parent, it was a season of such growth, trust, faith, and grace from which we learned so much.*

When life goes from the everyday overwhelm to a hard parenting challenge of sin and evil in our families, God's grace becomes more meaningful than ever. Sometimes, it feels like it's all there is, but truly, it's all we ever need.

Beth goes on to say: *Put Jesus first and listen to Him. He wants this time with you to feed you, guide you, and nurture your motherhood journey in His quiet, loving grace and mercy. I still begin my day early with Jesus laying all before Him, waiting upon His wisdom and abiding in His grace.*

We'll end this week with this reminder to spend time with the Lord. Our lives are busy, yes. But time with the Lord is never a waste of time! Time with the Lord is necessary to experience and be a mother within His grace. We never think eating or drinking for the good of our body is a waste of time, do we? A thousandfold, God's graces become alive and available in our lives when we take the time to be with Him, praying, praising, listening, and waiting for our Lord and Savior to provide for us. And He always does, perfectly.

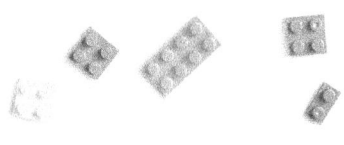

Bible Verse

"But by the grace of God I am what I am, and his grace toward me was not in vain. On the contrary, I worked harder than any of them, though it was not I, but the grace of God that is with me" (1 Corinthians 15:10 ESV).

Prayer

Lord, hear our mama hearts. We know we need You. Help us to call on You and Your graces for us as humans and as mothers. Without You, we cannot live a life worthy of Your death on the cross for our sins. Without You, we cannot mother our kids how You would like us to. Remind us that Your way is always the best way, so we need to constantly be connected with You in prayer to experience Your graces and to raise our kids according to Your will for their lives. Thank You for being a grace-filled God. Thank You for always being available for us. Tug on our hearts, Lord, to call on You when times are tough in motherhood. As we read parenting books or blogs and work hard to learn how to be the best mothers for our kids, remind us that only You can sustain us with Your abundant love, kindness, grace, and peace. Thank You, Lord! We love You. Amen.

Reflective Questions

1. Think of a time when you experienced the grace of God in motherhood… His forgiveness, His blessings of peace, His kindness. Reflect on how receiving God's grace felt in your body and soul. If you're new to faith or nothing readily comes to mind, spend time with God and see what happens! (I'm excited for you!)

2. It can be hard to have patience, but our Lord's grace and teachings are worth the wait. Consider a time when you knew the Lord was molding you. How did He provide for you during that process? How did His grace show up in the process and beyond? What did you learn about God through this experience?

3. Do you believe in God's perfect will for you and your children's lives? Do you believe God is your number one resource in motherhood? Pray about this, either thanking God or asking Him to change your heart and belief in Him, as you carve out time every day to pray.

God's Grace Instead of a Mother's "Perfection"

Do you struggle with perfectionism or control issues, too? I remember being told that I'd need a C-section. While I knew, especially with twins, that a C-section was certainly possible, it was not part of my ideal plan. Things were simply out of my control! Then, after the newborn screenings, we learned my son's thyroid levels were off, and it was up to us, not the doctors, if we wanted to start him on medication or not. I remember feeling pressed to make the right decision for my infant son's short and long-term health, and since the providers were putting the choice in our hands (control I didn't want), I felt completely out of control. And then, I got postpartum hives. Oh, man! My skin was purple with bruising from all the itching! I had turned into an absolute rage-monster from the additional pain and discomfort. Just as my milk was coming in, I was told I could take a steroid to help with the hives, but I was so concerned about what it would do to my milk. I had told myself I wasn't going to pressure myself about nursing my babies, but there I was, stressed about how imperfect my milk would be with steroids running through it!

Things could have been even more out of control, but that was just some of my introduction to motherhood. Perfection and control were nowhere to be found. In all of my careful planning and nesting, a C-section, congenital hypothyroidism, and postpartum hives weren't on any of my myriad of lists and charts. Looking back now, though, what else was missing from my list was Jesus. Have you ever felt so out of control that you forgot to pray? I think I literally forgot about God until my kids were three weeks old! Well, thank God, He didn't forget about me! Thank God I've remembered that I don't have to be perfect, and I don't have to be in control because God is. I realize this is easier to write and read than to believe and live. I'm not perfect at this, and I never will be! And neither are you. But we can pray to the God Who is! His perfect love, grace, and peace are better than any attempt we could ever have at perfection, control, or planning. I have experienced this, and I pray you do, too.

Jill S. is in her 60s, with three adult children. She shares: *Perfection in motherhood is not required, nor is it realistic. God's grace is real.*

Lord, help us never forget this simple but life-altering truth! Because sometimes, I do. Maybe I'll paint it in big black letters on the cream-colored cabinets in my kitchen, where it feels like every one of my attempts at perfection or controlling a situation in motherhood occurs! The thing is, we care about our children so much. That can manifest into wanting to be a "perfect" mother and wanting to control every situation for their good. But God cares for us and our children even more. We must learn to rely on and trust in His perfect grace. I repeat: Perfection is not required. Perfection is not realistic. But God's grace is *real! More of He, less of me! Let go and let God! The Cross before us, the world behind us.* Come on, mama, say it with me! *Help us remember this powerful truth, Lord!* **(See: WEEK THIRTY-SEVEN: Motherhood and Our Children: Idols?)**

THE *Cross* BEFORE US, THE WORLD BEHIND US.

Kacie is in her 30s, with three young to school-age children. She shares: *Giving myself the space to know I have made mistakes and the grace to understand that Jesus and my children love me and forgive me has been so impactful.*

How great is this? When we repent, God forgives us and He made our kids capable of forgiveness, as well! Since we're not perfect and since we're actually not in control (even though I still constantly try to be), making mistakes and sinning and then repenting and receiving God's forgiveness and grace becomes a critical lesson to model for our kids. (More on this next week; see also: **WEEK FORTY-EIGHT: Sin and Spiritual Health in Motherhood**.)

Kacie goes on to say: *You are enough, and you are the perfect person for this job. God made you with your current situation in mind and in His perfect timing.*

The One who doesn't make mistakes has entrusted YOU with your specific children. Through His grace, we imperfect mothers become what our children need through our Heavenly Father's perfect and controlled graces.

Pam is in her 50s, with five school-age to adult children. She shares: *At the end of the day, we do the very best we can. If we fail at something, it means we are human, and we get yet another day to get it right! And that, my friends, is a work in progress.*

Imagine, for a moment, how weird and boring life would be if we always got it right and never had anything on which we could improve. No growth, no teachable moments. What if our children were born knowing everything, perfect and controlled newborns. How weird would that be? What would the purpose of being a mother even be if we didn't need to grow and teach our children from what we've learned? Thankfully, that's not the case. Thinking about that makes me feel differently about my mistakes, failures, and sins. Only Jesus is sinless, and so we must lean on the grace He freely gives us after He died on the cross for us and our imperfect, sinful nature. We were made imperfectly. Our best comes from our loving God; our failures come from our humanity. We truly are constant works in progress! Through prayer, we can make progress over our attempts at perfection by looking to God for control rather than within our imperfect selves.

Her Prayer for Peace

Lastly, thank God for this: Julie is in her 60s, with four adult children. She shares: *Sometimes you'll just blow it. You are not a failure. No parent is perfect. God's love for us and His love for our children covers a multitude of missteps.*

Bible Verse

"For we do not have a high priest who is unable to sympathize with our weaknesses, but one who in every respect has been tempted as we are, yet without sin. Let us then with confidence draw near to the throne of grace, that we may receive mercy and find grace to help in time of need" (Hebrews 4:15-16 ESV).

(You may also review 2 Corinthians 12: 9-10 ESV from **WEEK TEN: Reflection; Miracles in Motherhood (Vol. I).**)

Prayer

Lord, help us remember that only You are perfect and only You are in control. I pray we turn to You more, so that Your perfection can guide our steps in life and in motherhood. Life gets really hard without Your forgiveness, guidance, grace, and peace, Lord. Help us remember that You are the King of perfect plans and perfect timings. You are the King; You are in control. Help us trust You more and rely on our imperfect selves less. Lord, help us not to forget about You in hard, hectic times! Help us rely on and trust in Your grace and guidance even more when we need it even more. When we feel panicked and want to control a situation, help us pause for You, Lord! Help us remember You are always available, waiting for us to rely upon and benefit from Your perfect graces, rather than relying on our desire to control a situation in life and in motherhood. Your perfect love and grace are better than any attempt we could ever have at perfection or control. Remind us, Lord, that You do not make mistakes, but when we do, forgiveness is possible through You and Your grace. Help us draw near to Your throne of grace, that we may receive mercy and find grace to help us in times of need. Thank You! We love You. Amen.

Reflective Questions

1. Whether it was your first few days of motherhood or another time, have you ever been so stressed that you forgot to pray? What did that feel like? How did it feel when you finally sought God and His perfect graces?

2. Do you tend to struggle with perfectionism or control issues? Take a moment and remember a time in motherhood when you found yourself fighting against your innate inability to be perfect or in control. How did that feel? When you finally *let go and let God*, how did that feel in comparison?

3. Prayerfully consider God's perfect love and graces for your children. How does it make you feel that this power extends to them, too? Have you seen this play out?

Week Eighteen

Showing Our Humility and God's Grace to Our Kids

Do you struggle with asking for help because of pride and perhaps a lack of humility, too? **(See: WEEK FORTY-SIX: When a "Helper" Needs Help.)** These words might seem a little harsh, but in doing so, we may be attempting to be the god of our lives rather than allowing the holy, living God to provide His perfect help, guidance, grace, and peace. This is when our God becomes a "jealous God" (Exodus 34:14). When we don't let Him in because we think we can do it better, faster, etc., on our own, this pride and lack of humility makes God lovingly, jealously "oppose" us. (See this week's Bible verse: James 4:6 ESV.) **(See: WEEK THIRTY-SEVEN: Motherhood and Our Children: Idols?)** But mama doesn't know best; God does!

Hear this: God never rejects us but He calls us to humble ourselves. And in doing so, we get to receive and benefit from His blessings and graces! Equally exciting is when our kids see this process in our own lives and in our own hearts; they soak this up like they learn any learned behavior! But likely even more so, as surely the Spirit of God is in this process, guiding our hearts to "train up a child in the way he should go…" (Proverbs 22:6). This way is submitting to God and His perfect will for our lives, which again blesses us and covers us in His perfect grace. When we love and live for Jesus over and over again, our children likely will, too.

Angela is in her 40s, with two school-age children. She shares: *I am here to do my best as a human mother to raise them for Jesus. Thank God He is also a forgiving Lord. I am far from a perfect mother.*

Hear this humble mama's heart! In admitting to doing our best, we know we're imperfect, we know we'll make mistakes, and thankfully, our God is indeed a forgiving God! We talked about this last week and in **WEEK TWO: Raising Kids for Jesus,** but consider this simple instruction: We must humbly raise our kids with Jesus to raise them for Jesus!

> WE MUST HUMBLY RAISE OUR KIDS *with* JESUS TO RAISE THEM FOR JESUS!

We cannot and should not raise our children with our prideful human hearts, as if this huge responsibility rests on our shoulders alone. If you've been in this space, ask for God's forgiveness right now. Ask Him to meet you in your kitchen while you're parenting your kids. Ask Him to bless you with His perfect grace so your children can see Him move in you. When our kids see Jesus in us, they want Him in their own lives, too.

Alyssa is in her 30s, with four young to school-age children. She shares: *So, no one is perfect. The older I get as a mom, the more I realize that so many things I care about don't matter. What am I telling my children if I'm tending to my house over spending time with God? I think it's great for our kids to learn that they aren't perfect, aren't expected to be, and that they should put God first. We are able to build little lovers of Christ. Will they consume themselves with love the way Christ did for us? Not if we aren't boasting in the Holy Spirit when the Lord is good to us. Not if we don't turn to Christ in our suffering to show them to turn in, too! These little eyes and ears take it all in.*

This is humbling for me because I know for a fact that my children see me cleaning my home more than they see me spending time with God.

Much of my time spent with God happens before they're awake or while they're at school because it feels like I can actually focus on Him then. But this is God we are talking about! We pray together before every meal and before bedtime, but this contributing mama has inspired me to bring God's grace into even more moments of my children's lives through the blessings and the hard moments of my own life! He can help us do this. My toddlers love to find the sunshine, watch the leaves change, hear the rainfall, and watch wildlife run around our yard. God created it all. I can share this truth with my kids every day! I'm reminded here of breath prayers, as well. Remember that our children can tell when we're stressed. Breath prayers typically happen in more of a whispered exhale (which is great and helpful), but while I benefit from whispering breath prayers, my children may benefit more if they hear me humbly cry out to the Lord in times of need and blessing. Our kids watch us; they learn from us. How sweet might it be to witness your children cry out to the Lord when they're both joyous and suffering because they saw you boast and rely on His grace first!

A note on our kids not being perfect, either: We all need God's grace, our children included. It's easy to think that when our babies are brand-new, sleeping in our arms most of the day, that they're "just perfect." But they were born imperfectly, just like the rest of us. They need God's grace, too. It's up to us to show them what relying on God's grace looks and feels like, practically and spiritually, in this life on this earth. What a relief for us and our children to not have to try to live up to perfection constantly, an unobtainable threshold for humanity! Only Jesus is perfect. Jesus and His perfect will and grace are what is available for us when we cry out to and rely on Him in faith. *Thank You, Jesus, that when You died on the cross for our sins, our children were set free, too!*

Janette is in her 30s, with three young to school-age children. She shares: *In each hard season of parenting, focus on extending grace and love to your child to show them a glimpse of their Heavenly Father. Use naughty moments to teach them about God's grace and point them to the work of Jesus on the cross instead of instructing behavior. By doing this, we take some of the pressure off ourselves and let God's grace do the work in our children's hearts.*

This share beautifully wraps up our three-week study on God's grace. God's perfect grace is for us as mothers and for our children. When we experience the truth of God's grace, we can more easily show and share it with our children. Mama, together, let's take the pressure off of aiming for perfection and trying to take control. Instead, let's put the pressure on our Lord and Savior. He can handle it. He *wants* to handle it as we pray and trust in Him. Mama doesn't know best; God does!

Bible Verse

"But he gives more grace. Therefore it says, 'God opposes the proud but gives grace to the humble'" (James 4:6 ESV).

Prayer

Lord, help us to seek and experience Your grace instead of striving for perfection and control so we can truly share Your grace with our kids. Humble our hearts for You, Lord. Help us to be humble and seek Your blessings, particularly Your grace, so our children will do the same. As You know, it's in our nature to sin. But through Your grace and through our faith, You've saved us all from our sins! May we humbly ask for Your forgiveness and Your guidance as we parent our children… Your children, that by Your grace, with whom You've blessed us. Help us to teach our children to do the same. Thank You, oh gracious God, for saving our children, too, when You died on the cross for our sins. Help us personally experience this truth and Your grace, Lord. Help us die to ourselves and live for You, Lord! Your perfect will and grace, for us and our kids, are much better than our attempts at perfection, control, and our pride. Remind us of this daily and help us to serve as an example for our kids as we share Your example of love and perfect grace for us all. We love you. Amen.

Reflective Questions

1. Is there a particular area of your motherhood in which you haven't let God's grace affect you? Prayerfully consider circumstances that stress you out, perhaps because of pride or because you are taking on too much yourself. Pray that God creates a space in your heart for Him to help you by offering His grace.

2. Do your children know you love Jesus? Do they see you praise Him for His blessings and seek Him in your suffering? (And, do you actually do this regularly?) Pray right now for this to be true.

3. Identify three ways you can bring the grace of Jesus into your home and into the lives of your children. How can you humbly boast of Him? How can you openly seek Him in sufferable, stressful times? Pray the Lord works in your heart to do this, and do this openly so your kids can learn from Him, through you.

Week Nineteen

Motherhood after Infertility; Secondary Infertility

Personally, I only know motherhood after infertility. (Secondary Infertility is when a couple struggles to have a baby after they have already birthed a child.) Two other mamas who contributed to this devotional also experienced infertility. One didn't mention it in her answers at all. She and I met on Facebook in the Christian Infertility Support Group.[12] We prayed for each other and cried for each other, and after years, within a few months of each other, those desperate tears turned into joyous tears for each other. She was actually the very first person I told about my first-ever positive pregnancy test! I was home alone, and I needed to tell someone who could truly appreciate the exact feelings I was experiencing. Community… It's so important, especially during shared suffering. **(See: WEEK FORTY-TWO: Trials and Struggles in Motherhood Can Grow Our Faith.)**

Kari is in her 60s, with three adult children. She shares: *I believe that God meant for my children to be here, especially after all the years of infertility we had gone through.*

Whatever your journey to motherhood has looked like, even during hard periods of waiting (for your husband, for a positive pregnancy test, for your baby to be born healthy, etc.), as Christians, we must believe in God's plan. We simply must! No matter what our hearts want, we must believe what God wants is what's best for us, and, in the end, that's what will be. In the thick of any struggle, it's natural to want to ask God, *Why?* I definitely did while we experienced infertility! But I recently heard someone share (interestingly, in regard to her secondary infertility) that when we're tempted to ask the question, *Why?*, we must instead fervently trust in the *Who*. Like many things in regard to faith, this is all easier said than done. But with prayer and intention, it is possible. Especially in hindsight, I can now say, every time we're tempted to ask *Why?*, we must tell Jesus we trust Him and in the hope He provides. Over and over again.

So, here's my own share of infertility. This is how I answered question number one: *Please share a time/season in your life when your Christian faith was tested as a result of motherhood. How did Jesus care for you and draw you back during this time?* (I tried to answer as if another mama had asked me, not like I was writing for a devotional I was authoring.)

I always wanted to be a mother. I didn't marry until my mid-30s, so we started trying just three months after our wedding. After some time, we were diagnosed with "unexplained infertility." There wasn't anything identifiably wrong, but we weren't conceiving within the average timeframe. There were lots of tests and lots of tears. Almost every single day, I cried in the shower singing, "It Is Well" by Bethel Music, Kristene DiMarco.[13] *Worship music was huge for me during this season. As the months passed, I grew angry with God. Sometimes, I couldn't even pray, but I could listen to and benefit from worship music. He was there all along.*

We were doing all the testing and procedures through my regular OB clinic but had consulted with a local fertility clinic. We decided to move forward with an IUI (intrauterine insemination). The process was much simpler at my regular clinic, and even though the fertility clinics boasted much higher rates of *success, I felt a sense of peace around continuing with the simpler process. I think that peace came from God. Our first IUI was a failure. I had so much hope going into this procedure; I thought for sure God would bless us then. The month after our first IUI, I was completely apathetic. I couldn't bear to experience my emotions anymore. While I felt numb with sadness, I told God how angry I was with Him. I never stopped believing in Him, but I was definitely confused and angry with Him. Just like I had been doing, and like I'd done right after the first IUI procedure, after our second IUI procedure, I listened to "It Is Well" right there in the doctor's office. After the procedure, I remember laying down, trying not to move a muscle, but hearing this familiar song, tears streaming down my face, audibly hitting the white paper cushion cover, praying, Lord, please give us a baby. (*I have to interject here quickly: Our successful IUI occurred three years ago today, as I write this. *God, let us never forget how powerful You are. Nothing You do happens by accident or by coincidence. We trust in You, Lord.)*

I continued to feel apathetic during the two-week wait following the procedure but also continued to listen to "my" song. Just 11 days after our second IUI, I felt called to take an early pregnancy test. I wanted to make sure I could safely drink a glass of wine at Thanksgiving dinner! And there they were, my first ever two pink lines! I remember saying, "Oh my God, oh my God, oh my God" (not in vain, but in praise!), with tears of joy streaming down my face. We later learned that God had blessed us with not one but two babies... A boy and a girl! Waiting to become a mother was the hardest time in my faith journey. I learned God loves us through all our emotions, and staying connected to Him, even through a single song, was enough for me to know how much He loves me, cares for me, and wants to bring me joy!

YOU ARE NOT ALONE.
God LOVES YOU.

If a mama is reading these words who is currently experiencing infertility of any kind, my husband and I pray for you every single day. You are not alone. God loves you.

From my own personal perspective, I've included some thoughts on what to say and what not to say to a mama going through infertility, found at the back of the book. I can nearly guarantee you know someone going through this heartache right now, so please take the time to read what I have titled, "Things to Say or Not Say when it Comes to Infertility." Please also pray for these women and couples.

For the mama who doesn't feel at peace with the size of her family, I hear your heart, too. **(See: WEEK FORTY-FIVE: How to "Know" when Your Family is Complete – Biologically or through Adoption.)** Infertility of any kind is an incredibly hard journey. I pray you feel the peace of Christ deep within your soul, every time your heart longs for another child. I also pray you hold on to God's hope. I hope that it's in His plans to expand your family. We must also have hope for the eventual future of all Christians… in Heaven. In Heaven, suffering does not exist! We have everything we could ever want: blessings galore! Hold on to hope, mama. And, I pray you experience trust and peace in God's plans for your life.

Infertility is a very personal thing. I'm grateful for my husband, friends, and family, but most importantly, I'm thankful to God. Even though I felt angry with Him throughout our journey, I believe He blessed me with a song that kept me connected to Him and to His promises. Our God does not want us to hurt. But He knows that hurt is part of humanity. May we listen for Him and hear Him in expected and unexpected places. He wants to connect with us. He wants us to rely on Him and cry out to Him. Even when–*especially when*–our hearts are hurting, God loves us so, so much. That one song gave my soul the smallest amount of hope that I needed to feel God's presence in my suffering. And so, when the blessings of our children came, we named our daughter Hope so that we would always remember that no matter what we're going through in this life, God is always present, and He is always the God of hope.

Bible Verse

"Not only so, but we also glory in our sufferings, because we know that suffering produces perseverance; perseverance, character; and character, hope. And hope does not put us to shame, because God's love has been poured out into our hearts through the Holy Spirit, who has been given to us" (Romans 5:3-5 NIV).

Prayer

Lord, we thank You for our children. This week, we are ever-reminded that they are blessings from You, and we thank You for them. Thank You for finding ways to stay connected to us, especially if we don't feel like we can or want to face You because our suffering is so deep. Help us to trust You more. Lord, I pray for the woman longing for a child and for the mama longing for another child. Find a soft spot in their hearts for You, Lord. Let them know how much You love them and help them to feel Your eternal hope. Please also bless them with a community, even one other person, with whom they can be on this journey, Lord. Let them never feel alone. I also pray for every spouse and extended family of someone experiencing infertility. Give them the words to say and the support and love to give, Lord. We love You. Amen.

Reflective Questions

1. Please reflect on your own experience/exposure to infertility, whether it be personally or through a friend or family member. Ask God to meet you and guide you around this topic.

2. Consider a time in your life when your suffering may have pulled you away from God. How did He stay connected to you? "When the world pushes you to your knees, you're in the perfect position to pray."[14] (While not a Christian, I do appreciate the visual of Rumi's quote.) If you can't think of a time when you may have wanted to pull away from God, reflect and praise God for bringing your heart right to His in times or seasons of suffering.

3. At the back of this book, please review the page titled, "Things to Say or Not to Say when it Comes to Infertility." As these are simply my own personal thoughts, please also do a little research on how you might support someone going through this heartache.

Reflection; Miracles in Motherhood (Vol. II)

Yippee! You made it to week 20, mama! Go YOU and go GOD! We've covered a variety of topics in the past nine weeks, and my hope, again, is that you've been in prayer, in action, and in rest with the Lord. God is on the move in our mama hearts! He's helping you hone in on your prayer life. He's met you in your expectations and comparisons. He's shown you His grace.

Take some time to reflect on the last nine weeks:
1. How has God's love and peace for you changed you and impacted your family since you started this devotional, specifically in the last nine weeks (weeks 11-19)?
2. What have been your three biggest takeaways in the last nine weeks (weeks 11-19)?
3. Is there a week you'd like to re-read this week?

4. Is there a mama you thought of in weeks 14, 15, or 19 but you forgot to pray for or reach out to her? Now is your opportunity! Don't let this week go by without praying for her or connecting with her.
5. Do you find yourself seeking, trusting, and relying on God for peace, wisdom, and guidance in motherhood, even 5-10% more than you did nine weeks ago?

Let's pray. *Lord, thank You for the mama reading these words right now. She has been seeking You, Lord. She has been working on relying on You to help her love and raise her children, children who are Yours first. She loves You, Lord. Show her Your love for her right now, Lord. Surround her with Your abundant love, grace, and peace for her. Continue to be present with us, Lord, as we continue week after week, yearning to be with You as we mother our children. Protect the time we carve out to be with You, to honor You, and to be guided by You in this journey of motherhood. Lord, thank You for each mama whose contributions have made up this devotional. Please bless them and their families, Lord. Help me use their words to bring honor and glory to You. I pray this devotional blesses the mamas reading it. Thank You for blessing us with motherhood. We love You. Amen.*

This week, I'll share a miracle of God – from Annette, a mama in her 40s, with one adult child. She shares: *I homeschooled my son, so he came with me to the office all the time. One particular day, we drove 90 miles one way for me to work in the office, and then we headed to Bible study/youth group after work. I finished with my last client and walked out of the room. The receptionist looked at me and said, "I thought you had left. Your car is gone." I looked at her, and then I asked, looking around, "Where is my son?" He was 14 years old, and he had decided to take my car! He would not answer his cell phone. I called my dad and asked him to look at where he was going to have youth group, and he wasn't there. I called the police and reported him (only for his safety and others). I tried calling my pastor's wife, but it went to voicemail. I tried again and again until, finally, I got a text from her saying they were trying to nap before heading over for youth group. I responded with, "My son took the car, and I don't know where he is." She called me right away. I was so beside myself I felt like I could hardly breathe. I went into a treatment room to pray, practically hyperventilating, and came out calmer. This happened several times. I had total peace even though I did not know where my son was. Just as my pastor's wife and I were hanging up the phone, she asked me, "Do you have a red car?" I said, "YES!" She said, "Your son just pulled into our driveway." Her husband drove him and my car to my office, where a police officer was waiting to talk to him. We set up his punishment, and I praised God that he (and everyone else) was safe.*

What is so amazing is that my son told me that he drove and drove and drove and then realized he didn't know where he was and he was scared. But he was also too scared to call me, so he asked God to show him the way, and he found his way to the pastor's house, 40-plus miles away. Knowing that we don't need to know the details but that we can sit down with the Lord to get His directions and peace is the best way to navigate the unknowns.

This story of God's miraculous peace and guidance amazes me. I'm trying to put myself in the place of this mama, and I don't think anyone would describe me as calm under those circumstances! Only the peace of Christ can calm the heart of a mama with a missing child. Only our most powerful God can guide a lost car, driven by a young teenager without a license, to a trusted Christian's home (the exact person's home whom this mama had called in her time of need) without a scratch on him or anyone else. Let's pause in the awesome protection and grace of our God! One additional thing to note: This particular mama is one of the most spiritually-connected people I know. She goes to God for everything. He rewards her reliance on Him, and she hears from Him. She is a faithful servant, and I'm so glad to have her Christian influence in my life (and now your life, too!).

I hope this reflection week has blessed you. Some of the topics in this devotional are hard. Some we can relate to more than others. A week where we pause to review and reflect can be really helpful. And hearing a story about the gift of God's incredible grace reminds us how great our God truly is! It's also a reminder to ask God to protect our families, to be weak and vulnerable, pleading for God to keep our children healthy and safe. In place of fear for our children's safety, we can ask the Lord to give us His peace. If tragedy happens, we can still pray to the God Who loves us.

> IF TRAGEDY HAPPENS, WE CAN STILL *pray* TO THE GOD WHO LOVES US.

This week's Bible verse sums this up well, along with many of the topics we've read about so far:

"The LORD is good, a refuge in times of trouble. He cares for those who trust in him,…" (Nahum 1:7 NIV).

Week Twenty-One

God Leads Mamas of Children with Medical Needs

As mothers, we want the very best for our children! While my son's hypothyroidism is treatable (I've been medicated for this also since my diagnosis 27 years ago), it still stings that my son has a chronic disease. As I've shared, if I'd allowed God in more during Johnny's initial diagnosis, I have no doubt I would have had more peace during that trying time. From Congenital Hypothyroidism to a stroke to imperfect body parts, God leads mamas of children with medical needs... Especially when we completely trust in Him!

Amara is in her 30s, with two young (earthside) children. She shares: *My daughter was a very hard child to parent, especially the first three years. She had a sensory sensitivity to loud noises and would really act out as a result... I felt like God was guiding me through it, but I had a really hard time leaning on Him like I did after we lost our first child. I felt like it was so challenging, and it was so much harder not to understand who my daughter was and how I should be parenting her. But once I prayerfully got guidance from medical professionals, and as she got older, I felt like God was teaching me things that were really hard for me to do, but I knew He was making me grow in motherhood.*

This mama is one of the most patient mothers I know. Her daughter is gregarious, inclusive, and sweet. She speaks in such a loving, peaceful voice when she redirects her daughter's behavior. God is in them both! I'm glad she mentioned seeking professional guidance in her share as well. We did this when, at 15 months, John wasn't even standing by himself, and Hope was literally walking in circles around him. God gave us all gifts we're to use to glorify God as we serve others! There is nothing wrong with receiving help. I repeat: *There is nothing wrong with receiving help!* We've talked about this in the context of letting God in. Rather than feeling like we need to control and do everything on our own, how about letting other people, such as the medical professionals whom God created, help us by using the gifts He gave them? **(See: WEEK FORTY-SIX: When a "Helper" Needs Help.)** Our next mama shares examples from both her children: Prayer and medical guidance supported their family well.

Heather is in her 40s, with two school-age children. She shares: *Jesus has guided and taken such beautiful care of me over the years on my journey through motherhood. One example is when my daughter was 15 months old. She was in the third percentile for weight, sick constantly, and struggled with eating and sleeping. We were at the doctor's office more times than I could count, and I was so fearful for her health. I prayed each day that God would guide me through this adversity, and He certainly did. After my daughter and I had visited the pediatrician one day, sleep-deprived and confused about what to do next, I went to my amazing Christian chiropractor. During my adjustment, we, out of nowhere, started talking about my daughter's health journey, and he asked if it would be okay if he examined her. I said absolutely. I was open to anything that would help her. After careful examination, he told me that her mid-back was out of alignment. The mid-back, he explained, is directly linked to digestion. He adjusted her so gently, and she was really happy afterward. After just two adjustments, she started eating and sleeping better and was rarely sick. My daughter is now nine years old and is healthy and thriving. I never take that for granted for a day and praise God for her healing.*

Regarding her son, she also shares: *One of the best examples of perfect peace and guidance was when my son was diagnosed with ADHD. My son is a first-born rule-follower. He's active but not hyperactive. He really started struggling with school in first grade. His teacher was so patient with him and arranged the extra help he needed at school, and we hired a tutor for the summer. Unfortunately, by second grade, he really started falling behind, despite his teachers commenting on how creative and smart he was. By early spring, his teacher recommended that he see his pediatrician to rule out ADHD. After being examined, our pediatrician concluded that my son did have ADHD. He recommended starting a low dose of medication to help with my son's focus.*

My husband and I are firm believers in a healthy lifestyle and only taking medication when absolutely necessary. That night, we read up on all the possible side effects and prayed that God would guide us in making the right decision. After sleeping on it, we both had the most incredible peace in the morning and agreed that he should try the medication. My son was so brave with taking the medication, and he was blown away by the results. When anyone asked him how he was doing, he'd say, "I'm great. I just started taking this pill, and it's helping me focus so well!" This journey has definitely had its extreme highs and lows, but God has guided us through it with incredible peace and wisdom. His guidance has been absolutely life-changing for our family.

Dianne is in her 40s, with three school-age children. She shares: *At six weeks, my youngest started stacking up the doctor appointments for torticollis, possible tongue tie, and more. This was not life-threatening; it was not compromising her well-being at that point, but it could happen in the future, and it was something we needed to address. I was simply overwhelmed as each medical professional told me, "Just make an appointment." This is where Jesus met me, right in the middle of being overwhelmed by all the appointments. He kept my perspective on how this was not as serious as it could be, and it would just be for a season. So, instead of being constantly overwhelmed, I felt God offer peace to my mind, reassurance to my heart, and wisdom on our next best steps. It was like Jesus was our guide more than me and that our*

> GOD OFFERS PEACE TO MY MIND, REASSURANCE TO MY HEART, AND *wisdom* ON OUR NEXT BEST STEPS.

Her Prayer for Peace

steps ahead would be accompanied by the One Who offers us wisdom when we ask. When I look at her healthy body today, or I see her little bitty helmet in my closet, I think back to that season that was hectic, full, and exhausting. It's a reminder that God met me not once but every single time I needed Him. That's His promise to do that each day forward, too. And not just in the overwhelming seasons.

I remember when Hope and John had their lip and tongue tie revisions at about six months old. I was so stressed! I pray we let God lead us if/when our families face challenging medical issues. Chronic or acute, no matter the severity, God cares for us, and He wants to guide us, relieving us of the stress in situations like this. Remember, He cares for our children even more than we do! *May we never forget this truth and always remember to trust in You, Lord.*

Brianna is in her 30s, with one young child (and one on the way). She shares: *My son had a stroke at some point very early in his life and now has cerebral palsy as a result. My faith was tested by constant worry. Worry about not doing enough; worry about what path to take for him to get the best care. I had to spend time in the Word and finally release all my worries on God. I had to realize that He cares more for my son than I ever could. In the end, everything worked out thanks to great therapists and trusting God. I know He will continue to help us through this journey. We just have to "be still." Actually, just the other night, I was flipping through the Word and crying, desperately seeking answers on what to do for my son's next level of care. I constantly landed on verses about trusting the Lord, and as I sat there, I literally felt God saying to me, "I've got this." All worry left me, and I felt a supernatural peace that only God could provide.*

The peace from our Father, His Son, and the Holy Spirit is a peace like no other. We experience it when we bare all our worries and fears unto the Lord. He holds us in that place, replacing our worries and fears with His supernatural peace. I've been there… It's what prompted me to write this devotional, asking questions of other mamas about how they experienced God's peace, wisdom, and guidance in motherhood. God shows up for us mamas when we bare it all to Him, when we're open to receiving what He has for us instead of worrying and trying to do things our own way.

When we, as mothers, experience Christ's peace, our families benefit as well. **(See: WEEK FORTY-SEVEN: Christ's Peace in Our Mama Hearts.)**

Christine is in her 30s, with three young to school-age children. She shares: *With one of my twins, it has been the peace I have had through her whole medical journey and my belief that no matter what, Jesus has her in His hands. I truly believe that our children are a gift that God lends to us. They are ultimately His, and we are given the privilege to be a part of their God-designed journey.*

This mama didn't go into detail here, but the fact that her one daughter is walking and communicating is an absolute miracle of God. They are very prayerful people. Their daughter has had multiple surgeries and medical attention, literally from her head to her hips and from her fingers to her toes. She is such a joyful child, and she brings so much joy to my friend. *God, You are so good. Thank You for supporting this family with Your guidance and peace.*

Bible Verse

"And the peace of God, which surpasses all understanding, will guard your hearts and your minds in Christ Jesus" (Philippians 4:7 ESV).

Prayer

Help us to be still for Your guidance and leadership regarding our children, Lord. When our children deal with health and medical issues, help us bring it all to You so You (and You alone) can replace our worries and fears with Your perfect, supernatural peace. A peace that helps guide our hearts and leads us to professionals who You created to help us. Help us,

Lord, to have thankful hearts. Even when it's hard, help us to praise and thank You! You are a healing God, a God Who has a perfect plan for each of us. We trust You, Lord. We love You. Amen.

Reflective Questions

1. How does this week's topic land for you, mama? Have you been in a situation similar to these mamas? Did you bare your heart to the Lord or try to white-knuckle through? How might you handle a situation like this now or in the future? Pray about this. Ask God to help you rely on Him more.

2. If a mama and her child came to your mind this week, spend some time in prayer for her and her family. Reach out to her if God calls you to do so. Be thankful for them and for your own family.

3. How have you experienced the peace of Christ in your heart and mind in terms of the health of a loved one (if not your child)? Reflect on the circumstances, blessings, and lessons you learned from this experience.

Week Twenty-Two

Worry in Pregnancy

Whether you're pregnant now or it's been 30 years since you've been pregnant, I pray this week you experience how much God cares for you, especially when we're going through something new in motherhood. I'm not sure there's anything newer and more uncharted than pregnancy. With all the changes to our bodies plus the relatively imminent, lifelong addition of another human being into our lives, our gestational months of motherhood can be filled with joy but also worry. A general worry of the unknown, and specific worries about the health of our tiny, growing baby plus the delivery and nursing… I could go on.

As a triple high-risk pregnant mama–advanced maternal age (thank you for not calling us "geriatric" anymore), multiples, and also my hypothyroidism–I was automatically put into a category in which my worry felt legitimized by the very label of being "high-risk." Plus, after years of infertility and hearing so many heartbreaking stories of loss along the way, I remember being filled with real-tempered joy and tangible worry. I spent a lot of my pregnancy very worried and very fearful.

One particularly worrisome time was when we learned that my son had an issue with his umbilical cord/placenta connection that prevented him from getting all the nutrients I tried so diligently to provide for my babies. I'll also never forget the scan when my son's femur was measured at just the eighth percentile, an indication of how tall he'd be as an adult. I remember getting home from that appointment and going right to Google for a solution. I relied heavily on Google to help me manage my erratic hypothyroidism in pregnancy, too.

Mama, I wish I had gone directly to God for His guidance, leading me to peace. I wish I'd relied heavily on God instead of relying heavily on Google. I wish I'd laid my worries down at the foot of the cross and trusted the Lord to take care of the three of us, trusting His perfect plans for all our lives. I remember feeling a huge sense of relief when medical science told me my babies were viable. I only wish I'd prayed for His peace from the very beginning of this uncharted territory of the beginning of motherhood. That's my prayer this week: Whatever unknown you're going through right now or will be going through in your future, I pray you replace a sizable portion of your perhaps automatic inclination to worry with absolute trust in our powerful, all-knowing, and loving God.

Dianne is in her 40s, with three school-age children. She shares: *Being pregnant for the first time felt like uncharted territory, watching my body change and knowing that a baby is growing, and I really wasn't doing much to make that happen. As my body changed and dreams for my baby grew, so did the worry and anxiety. Some things seemed worthy of worry, like how will a baby change our family. Or will my baby need to be in the NICU after birth? Or is this baby going to flip? Other worries seemed less worthy of worry like what color should the nursery be? Or what do I wear today that fits? In the midst of this worry, it is right where Jesus met me.*

Worry is spoken of really clearly in the Bible... God will take care of me; He loves me more than the birds of the air, and He takes care of them (Matthew 6:26-27). *It was the test of giving back to Jesus things that aren't mine. That was my worry. When worry arrived and overwhelmed me, that was the Holy Spirit's reminder to pray. He reminded me to pray for those who are in the midst of what I worry about, to pray for other mamas who are also pregnant, and to pray for the truth that God's got me and this sweet baby growing inside. When I prayed, that is when the calmness and peace of Christ fell over me, and I would feel it, know it, and then feel good I had prayed for other mamas. It took the focus off me and onto Jesus, the One Who overcomes the worry. Anytime I begin to worry, I pray for wisdom and other mamas as we move forward in peace and confidence in the truth Jesus shared with us, that He's our best caregiver.*

I love how this mama, in her most worried and overwhelmed state in pregnancy, felt the Holy Spirit's call to pray. Oh, I think that is so beautiful! I also love the peace that praying for others can provide us. *Thank You, Jesus, that when we pray for others, You give us peace and confidence in Your truth. You are our best caregiver, Lord. You are the One that overcomes our worry. Your calmness and peace are available to us when we pray, and You save us from our human worries, anxieties, overwhelms, and fears. Thank You, Jesus.*

Kacie is in her 30s, with three young to school-age children. She shares: *The pregnancy of my third child was the most difficult thing that I've gone through as a mother. I felt extreme anxiety, obsessive and intrusive thoughts, and paranoia. Meeting with my pastor to discuss my feelings literally saved me. God knew exactly what I needed to hear and that I needed to feel loved and not ashamed. He provided that through a pastor at my church.*

I remember hearing this mama's heart as she experienced these feelings one morning at our women's Bible study. My heart hurt for her so much! I knew she was prayerful, but let this be a reminder to seek outside help and to counsel one another by the power of the Holy Spirit. We each have the Holy Spirit within us. Whether it's a Christian friend or your pastor, we are called to be there for one another – in Christ! **(See: WEEK FORTY-SIX: When a "Helper" Needs Help.)**

Jan is in her 70s, with three adult children. She shares: *Each of my pregnancies were so difficult that I had to be hospitalized. What a big job and a big blessing when you let Jesus in, trusting Him to guide you.*

I'm reminded again of the phrase, *more of He, less of me.* Relinquishing control and letting Jesus in can seem really hard to do until you do it, and then the reward of His peace is truly endless! Whether pregnancy is physically hard on us, hard on our baby, or emotionally hard on us, God hears our cries. Through Him or through trusted counsel, He provides for us when we call on Him in trust.

Alyssa is in her 30s, with four young to school-age children. She shares: *The Holy Spirit was a crutch when I was pregnant with twins. At 32 weeks, I was measuring 40 weeks, and I was ordered to be no less than 10 minutes away from the hospital as Baby A's cord was presenting, and if I dilated even a half centimeter more, she could die as her blood supply could be cut off. In addition to this anxiety and exhaustion, I had to start relying on my mother and mother-in-law to provide care for our 2½-year-old daughter for six weeks! (My husband was harvesting, so he wasn't an option.) Oh, my heart has never been so strained, physically, emotionally, and spiritually. Only seeing my daughter on the weekends while experiencing contractions every five minutes for all but five days and trying to practice law remotely took everything out of me. I had to have Jesus. I was alone, but I had Him. Then, after praying and praying and praying for relief, Baby A pulled her little feet out of the birth canal, the cord lifted, and her little buns were presenting breech! I stopped having contractions. I spent days with our daughter, who was overwhelmed and couldn't express how much the distance hurt her, but you could see it in her eyes. And I cried in thanksgiving like a little baby as each of those big, healthy twins entered our world.*

Jesus met this mama in such a physically and emotionally dire time in her pregnancy and in her life. Her body and heart were hurting, yet she endured by trusting the Lord. He is worthy of our trust. He is strong when we are weak. I remember getting to the hospital at 37 weeks, two days, and learning that John's heart rate had dropped after a cervical sweep. We had to stay and monitor them until they were born. Thirty hours later, we headed into our unplanned C-section. I was scared, but I also felt a strange sense of calm. I wouldn't go as far as to call it peace, but there was a calm sense of trust there amidst all the craziness. While the emotions, physical discomfort, pain, and hormones ran high, I think Jesus knew my heart. While I don't remember actively praying,

> HE IS *strong* WHEN WE ARE WEAK.

I know Jesus was there, comforting me and keeping us all healthy and safe… Just as if I was actively praying for that.

Bible Verse

"The LORD is my rock and my fortress and my deliverer, my God, my rock, in whom I take refuge, my shield, and the horn of my salvation, my stronghold" (Psalm 18:2 ESV).

Prayer

Lord, help us depend on You more. You created us, and You created our children who grew within us. Let us experience You as our Rock. And I pray that in doing so, we pray, trust, and take refuge in Your strength when times are especially challenging, when we feel alone, and in uncharted territory in motherhood and in life. Lord, I pray for the pregnant mama right now. May she know You are always with her. May she feel Your love for her and the baby with whom You've blessed her. When we care so much, and there's so much newness and so many unknowns, may we and every pregnant mama cling to what we know about You, Lord. You are worthy of our trust; You are our stronghold. Find our hearts, Lord, and give us Your calmness, comfort, and peace. Thank You for being our Deliverer while we deliver(ed) our babies.

Reflective Questions

1. Reflect on your own experience(s) of being pregnant. Pray about a time when you could have received Christ's peace more readily, and also thank God for when you felt Him with you while you are/were pregnant.

2. What's one thing you learned about Christ and Christ's followers this week?

3. If you know a woman who's pregnant right now, please pray for her. If you feel comfortable doing so, please reach out to her with prayerful words from Jesus. Otherwise, spend time in prayer for all pregnant women. Pray for their bodies and their hearts, and pray that they rely on Jesus' strength to overcome any worry in their pregnancy.

A Mother's Hope in Christ when Little Lives are at Stake

God's grace and miraculous healings are worthy of our hope and faith in Him. The raw emotions this week, the cries of these mamas as they prayed for their children's lives to be spared and restored, put so much into perspective as we live our everyday lives. I pray we are filled with absolute thankfulness for the relative health and vitality of our children. As we help our children to eat, sleep, and poop every day, may we truly praise God for their overall health and well-being. Even if our children's health isn't "perfect," may we be thankful for every day we have with our kids. Each day to be their mama is a gift, a blessing from God. I'm so thankful these mamas shared these tender times in their lives and their children's lives with us. *Thank You, God, for healing these children and for supporting these mamas who trusted and relied on You during these most challenging moments in motherhood.*

Kari is in her 60s, with three adult children. She shares: *When my triplet daughters were born early at 28 weeks, I was so scared and worried. I spent as much time as possible in the NICU, sitting by their incubators, worrying about and praying for my babies. I knew that there were many people praying for them, which gave me hope, strength, and peace. I also believed that God meant for them to be here, especially after all the years of infertility we had gone through. Every little milestone while they were in the NICU and later in the Special Care Nursery filled me with gratitude and helped to strengthen my faith. I felt so blessed to be a mom to these three beautiful little miracles, and I was continually filled with wonder and amazement at how God had knit each one together in my womb with such distinctly different personalities and traits.*

My heart aches for every mama whose baby has had time in the NICU. A quick Google search tells me that, thanks to today's medical professionals and science created by God, most babies survive at 28 weeks. Still, I can only imagine how helpless this mama felt watching her three tiny babies in the NICU week after week after week. Feeling worried and praying at the same time is so raw, so honest. I'm glad this mama had so many people praying for them too. That God gave her some hope and peace that her babies were meant to survive and thrive! It is truly a wonderful thing how our children grow inside us and come to be born and thrive on this earth. Again, let us be so thankful for the health and well-being of our children!

Billie is in her 60s, with four adult children. She shares: *My third daughter was hit by a car when she was two years old, in a very freak accident. They didn't think she was going to live. They kept her in a drug-induced coma due to the swelling in her brain. I was on my knees for days, praying for a breakthrough and for God not to take my baby girl. I had wondered if this was a punishment for not watching her closely enough to ensure this didn't happen. Through all my prayers and when there was no change in her condition, I really felt challenged in my faith. I was building anger with God as to why He wasn't healing her. I asked Him why He would take a child from their mother. It was a very hard and challenging few days. Then, one morning, as the sun rose and shone into the ICU, she came to on her own. She opened her eyes and smiled. Again, I was on my knees, this time thanking God for hearing my prayers.*

It was all in His time, not mine, and not the doctors. The doctors were amazed at her recovery; I knew it was He who had healed her.

Having two two-year-olds myself, I'm reminded of how many "freak accidents" we likely avoid every day. Praise God! And while we do the best we can to protect our children, we are not perfect. Only God is perfect, and whatever He allows to happen is due to His perfect reasons. We must trust Jesus with our lives and our children's lives. This mama shares a whole gambit of emotions I could relate to if under these same circumstances. But God does not *punish* us in this way. Nor does He just take a child from their mother. I can definitely relate to feeling angry with God, especially in times of waiting. We don't always get to know why things happen the way they do; we must simply trust in God's plans. God and His plans are never late and never wrong. When things do work out according to our prayers, we must express our sincere thankfulness. In addition to this mama being undoubtedly thankful for her child being healed, her faith was undoubtedly strengthened, as she knew it was He who had healed her. That is a huge blessing as well. **(See: WEEK FORTY-TWO: Trials and Struggles in Motherhood Can Grow Our Faith.)**

> GOD AND HIS *plans* ARE NEVER LATE AND NEVER WRONG.

Pam is in her 50s, with five school-age to adult children. She shares: *My lowest point in motherhood was when my third child was a senior in high school. He was depressed and suicidal. I prayed to get him the help he needed! He's almost 25 now and life is better, and when he struggles, he knows how to ask for help.*

My heart hurts so much for this mama. And, I can only imagine the state of God's heart when one of His children wants to end their life here on earth. I'm so thankful God's hopefulness and healing supported all of our families this week!

We talked about this in **WEEK THREE: Losing a Baby/Child - Miscarriage, Stillbirth, and the Loss of a Child,** and also during weeks 10, 20, 30, 40, and 50 (our weeks of reflection and stories of God's miraculous grace). But if you are a mother who has lost a baby at any age, for any reason, I believe your child is healed, whole, and in Heaven with our God, Who loves them more than we can even comprehend. The pain of losing a child is something I pray we never know. But if you have, please also know how much God loves you. He cares for you, and He knows the pain in your heart. I pray you feel God's love for you and also God's love for your child in Heaven. I pray He strengthens your spirit, gives your heart peace, and blesses you abundantly. Mama, together, we pray for you right now and for the hope you have to be with your child once again eternally.

Bible Verse

"…but those who hope in the LORD will renew their strength. They will soar on wings like eagles; they will run and not grow weary, they will walk and not be faint" (Isaiah 40:31 NIV).

Prayer

Lord, I thank You for every moment we have with our children. Help us keep things in perspective, and no matter what craziness the day brings, help us to be grateful to You for our children. They are a gift to us from You. Thank You for healing our kids who've been sick or injured. Help us to always hold onto Your hope and feel Your peace in life-altering times, Lord. Meet us in the waiting, Lord, and strengthen our faith and trust in You. Lord, I pray once again for the mama who has lost a child. May she know her child is safe with You, and may she live in Your hopeful promise of seeing them again when she sees Your face in Heaven. However long Your perfect will has our children in our earthly lives, we praise and thank You, God. We love You. Amen.

Reflective Questions

1. Have you been in a life-threatening situation with your child? Whether you have or haven't, reflect on your or these other mama's experiences from this week. How was the hope and peace of God experienced?

2. From where do you believe our hope comes? What does it mean to you to be hopeful, especially in life-altering times and times of waiting?

3. Please pray for a family whose child is sick or injured or whose child has gone to be with God. As you pray, ask God how you can best pray for and support this family.

Week Twenty-Four

Our Children are God's Children First; He Loves Them More than We Do

We've talked about this a lot so far, but this week we'll focus on it. We love our kids more than anything in the world. The effort we make to feed them, keep them clean and comfortable, socialize them, and teach them right from wrong is evidence of our vast love for and our duty to our children. Yet, in truth, these people we call "ours" belong to the same God to Whom we belong. Our Heavenly Father Who created us all; we are all His. And He loves us more than words can describe. As much as we love our children, God loves them infinitely more!

Let's really sit with this for a moment. Sit with and experience the love we have for our kids, a love that would bring us to do anything for them. *Thank You, Jesus, for the love we have for our children!* Now, multiply that love by infinity. That's how much God loves us and how much He loves our kids! He, in fact, through His son, died for us and for our kids. Perhaps you've heard of "agape love." It's God's perfect, unconditional, sacrificial, and pure love for all His people. Agape love is the "highest kind of love."[15] As humans, we are not perfect, but because God is perfect, only He can and does love us in this way. This week, we'll hear from several mamas who have found peace knowing that our children are God's children first and that He loves them more, and cares for them better, than we can.

Angela is in her 40s, with two school-age children. She shares: *While I was pregnant with my first son, my husband and I attended a Baptismal preparation class at our local church for our baby's upcoming Holy Sacrament. The priest who was leading our lessons said something that I will never forget. His Words resonated with me in a profound way. He reminded all of the fully grown adults, expecting parents in the room, that we are all God's children. He told us that the babies in our expectant wombs only feel like a new life we created with our partners when, in fact, our bodies are merely vessels. This vessel is God's way of creating more of His own children, more of His own believers and followers. The baby in my belly, and those in all other awaiting mothers, is another one of God's children. As parents, we are given the job of raising Christian followers for God. Blessed with the gift of life into our families, we are given a great assignment directly from our Lord: To parent God's babies on Earth for Him. While these gift-children did come from God through my body, they are, in fact, His.*

We are to raise our children to be followers of God. **(See: WEEK TWO: Raising Kids for Jesus.)** Since our children are God's first, He guides us in this endeavor. Our children also have the Holy Spirit within them, so just as we feel God's presence and peace, so too can our children. I have put a lot of pressure on myself to mother well and model faith for my kids. And while God-willing, I want to do my best for them and also for God, it does provide me with some relief to know God is on this journey with us. Like we've talked about in earlier weeks, we are not to mother our *gift-children* alone. Connecting with God the Maker, along with other members of our family and other Christian mamas, allows us to mother with our perfect Maker and the community with whom God has blessed us... *Lord, thank You for loving our kids so well and for gifting us them and also our community.*

Kari is in her 60s, with three adult children. She shares: *As a new parent, the responsibility of caring for this new little human and the desire to protect him or her from all the bad things out there can be overwhelming. Trust that God loves your child even more than you do and that He is watching over them. You may be limited in what you can do, but God is omnipotent and omnipresent.*

Amen. We are not perfect, so despite our best efforts, we are limited in what we can do for and how we can love our kids. Again, we love them so much, so that may be hard to hear, but thankfully, our Maker has supernatural powers! Through the Holy Spirit, some of that power is in us all, but we must also trust in God's perfect, agape love and His omnipotent plans for our lives and our families' lives.

Jan is in her 70s, with three adult children. She shares: *It was during a challenging time that brought me the revelation that this child was not "mine" but a gift from God. God entrusted me to be her advocate while she grew. The more the world did its thing, the more Jesus guided me toward wisdom and peace in motherhood.*

Debi is in her 60s, with three adult children. She shares: *When we were being investigated by social services for homeschooling (it was not accepted as legal when my kids were little), I was very fearful. But God showed me He loved them more than I did. I realized He may be putting us through this for a reason, although I didn't understand. My husband and I went to the altar and surrendered our kids to His will.* **(See: WEEK TWENTY-SIX: Mothering within God's Will and Perfect Long-Term Plan for Our Kids.)**

Every day, motherhood is full of joys and challenges. But when something extraordinary happens to our children, when we trust in God and truly yield our children to God's will, He will grant us the wisdom and peace our mama hearts need. **(See: WEEK FORTY-SEVEN: Christ's Peace in Our Mama Hearts.)**

Dianne is in her 40s, with three school-age children. She shares: *Our children are Jesus' first. They are gifts from Him. We may have to give them back to Him sooner than we ever expected or intended. Sometimes we don't. But if we remember they are on loan to us, there is a confidence that Jesus is watching over them when we can't, He loves them more than we ever could, and He's making up for our shortcomings as parents. These sweet babies are on loan from Jesus, a gift from Jesus; they are His first. He's entrusted you to care for and raise them earthside and then give them back to Jesus.*

> THESE SWEET BABIES ARE ON LOAN FROM JESUS, A *gift* FROM JESUS; THEY ARE HIS FIRST.

As Christians, we are to trust Jesus in all circumstances. When we don't know the outcome, we are to seek His guidance and trust in Jesus' short and long-term plans. This trust is the confidence that this mama shares. Because we trust in Jesus' infinite love, resulting in His will for our lives and our children's lives, we can be confident in His love, protection, and plans.

Bible Verse

"For as high as the heavens are above the earth, so great is his steadfast love toward those who fear him; as far as the east is from the west, so far does he remove our transgressions from us. As a father shows compassion to his children, so the LORD shows compassion to those who fear him" (Psalm 103:11-13 ESV).

Prayer

Thank You, Jesus, for the gift of our children. They are Your children first. Help us trust You to help us raise them for as long as is Your plan. Remind us of Your perfect, agape love and omnipresence while we raise our children for You, Lord. Help us and our motherhood be guided by You every day. We pray for Your peace, Lord, as we trust in You and Your will.

Thank You for Your vast love for us all, Lord. We trust You with our lives, and the lives of our/Your children. We love You. Amen.

Reflective Questions

1. Is it hard to think of "your" children as a gift and an honorable responsibility from God, that they are actually His children (as are we)? Ask the Lord to meet you here, finding true gratitude that we are all His. Meditate on what this means for you and for "your" children.

2. Is it hard for you to believe that God loves "your" children more than you do? Again, ask the Lord to meet you here. Ask Him to reveal the power of His love and how we and our children benefit from this agape love.

3. How does/would accepting God's peace, wisdom, and guidance in motherhood allow you to experience His love for you and "your" children more fully?

Week Twenty-Five

When Our Kids Hurt, We Hurt, but God's Provision is True

This week, we're focusing on mothering within God's provision for our children. Next week, we'll discuss mothering within God's will for our children's lives. These topics are related and build on each other, so we'll devote two weeks to really glean from what other mamas have learned. Plus, we'll study about the provision and divine destiny as it relates to motherhood. Let's go!

The Oxford Dictionary defines provision as "the action of providing or supplying something for use."[16] To put this in terms of God: God will provide for our needs for tomorrow at exactly the right moment, not a moment early, and not a moment late. So, we have nothing to worry about! God's provision will ensure that His will will be accomplished on earth as it is in Heaven. With God's provision, He supplies us with something for use and does so in His perfect timing, according to His perfect will.

We've talked a lot about worry during motherhood (and we're not done yet), but when we believe in God and His true provision for our lives and the lives of our children, there is simply no use in worrying! I've talked about this as well, but in hindsight, in the moments when I was full of worry early on in motherhood, I also felt furthest from and, therefore, relied the least on God. When motherhood fills me with worry, there is simply no space for God; I feel myself turning ignorant to God's provision. There is a direct correlation to how much we worry and how much we benefit from an intimate, trusting relationship with God and results in His peace. I pray we learn from our contributing mamas this week and that we prayerfully ask God to help us worry less and trust in His provision more.

Megan is in her 50s, with four young adult children. She shares: *I feel Christ's peace most often when my kids come to me with a problem, and I hold back for a minute to let them work things out before I jump in with my own opinion or perceived wisdom. It's hard to see my kids in emotional pain or confusion, but the Holy Spirit reminds me that this is part of their own growth process. If I offer a solution too quickly, I may be aborting the growth, resilience, and wisdom God wants them to discover for themselves! As they get older, Jesus reminds me to listen and ask as many questions as possible to help guide them in their own self-discovery. I also invite them to pray about things so they can experience God's voice and answers for themselves. I ultimately want them to learn and experience God's provision for themselves.*

Biblically, women are helpers. Eve was indirectly called "a helper" (Genesis 2:18). As mothers, we are to help, care for, and raise our children. So, when our children come to us with a problem, our innate gut reaction may be to help them with a solution. Depending on the problem, we may find ourselves worrying about the solution as we care for our kids. My own kids are toddlers, so their day-to-day problems basically revolve around (not!) sharing with their sibling. Still, this mama of older kids discovered how to trust God's provision through prayer and obedience when her young adult children have more profound problems. *Lord, I pray I remember this 15-20 years from now, and even now!* As this mama shares, it's so hard to see our kids hurt emotionally, but God's wisdom, therein, His provision is available if we trust in and allow Him to work with our kids through the Holy Spirit.

My mom and dad did an amazing job raising my two older sisters and me. As I sit here, though, I'm trying to think of a time when, as a teenager or young adult, I encountered a problem, and instead of worrying about a solution, I simply trusted what God was up to while embracing the growth He wanted me to experience. Further, did I ever truly trust the result of His provision and perfect will for my life? I hope we can all follow this mama's example: She absorbed God's wisdom by trusting Him, so she worried less, and so God provided for her children through His provision. This, mama, is how Jesus wants us to help and raise our children (within His wisdom and provision)!

Julie is in her 60s, with four adult children. She shares: *When our kids are struggling, what do you do? Do you avoid the situation, try to take control by speaking up or otherwise intervening, or do you let it play out and stay out? It's a lot to work through, but you seek advice from trusted friends and relatives; you help each child through whatever struggles they face; and you let the child face and work through the situations, and that is how they grow. You also pray a lot, you encourage, and you do your very best to have your kids face everything with their relationship with God and good character as priorities. Watching this play out and seeing God's care and provision drew me close to Jesus.*

I love this last part so much. By stepping back, we are able to see God's provision play out in our children's lives. And in turn, our faith in God increases! My faith in God naturally lessens when I try to control everything or worry about everything. God is much more trustworthy and faithful than me in my lack of experience and, well, complete lack of supernatural power! While we take care of and support our kids in times of trouble, we must also pray for the wisdom and strength to let God take the reins. As this mama says, this process can be *a lot to work through*. Trusting God is simple, but it's not

Trusting GOD IS SIMPLE, BUT IT'S NOT ALWAYS EASY!

always easy! This is where prayer comes in. Mama, let's pray God helps us help our children benefit from His care, provision, and will for their lives.

Pam is in her 50s, with five school-age to adult children. She shares: *When my kids struggle, I struggle, but I also try to be their best advocate when they need me.*

Of course, we are sad when our kids are sad. And that sense of advocacy is special coming from us, mamas! As a Christian family, part of that advocacy is reminding our kids to see God's wisdom and goodness within every struggle. When our kids see us modeling this, they're more likely to naturally or prayerfully do this themselves. They're also more likely to heed our advice when we lovingly remind them to do something we actually do (and benefit from) ourselves.

Bible Verse

"And my God will meet all your needs according to the riches of his glory in Christ Jesus" (Philippians 4:19 NIV).

Prayer

Lord, so much of motherhood is growing and trusting in You, and raising our children to do the same. We're so grateful for Your provision, Lord. Thank You for providing everything we need exactly when we need it. And thank You for growing us and our reliance on You in the process. Lord, we ask You to help us help our children within Your perfect care, provision, and will for their lives. Take our worry from us, Lord, and replace it with confidence and trust in You, in all Your perfection. We love You. Amen.

Reflective Questions

1. Can you think of a time when you relinquished control as a child, a young adult, or even recently, in exchange for waiting on and trusting in God's provision? Is there something in your life right now that you could pray for God to help you do this?

2. Prayerfully identify a struggle for your children right now. How have you dealt with and supported them with this struggle so far? Have you left any room for God's provision and perfect will? Pray for this now.

3. What is your biggest takeaway from the shares this week? Pray the Lord applies this to your motherhood journey and to your children, especially in seeking, trusting, and modeling God's provision in your own life.

Mothering within God's Will and Perfect Long-Term Plan for Our Kids

Parenting classes, parenting books, this philosophy and that philosophy, even this very devotional... There are so many resources about motherhood and mothering our kids! And, while there's nothing wrong (there's a lot that is right!) with asking your Christian neighbor her opinion about something or being in a Bible study with other Christian mamas, I pray we remember our number one source of guidance in motherhood is God, and to trust in His long-term, divine destiny for us all! That doesn't mean we just throw in the towel in motherhood and simply let God do His thing because, as we've already learned, our growth and peace in motherhood equate to our faith and reliance on God. And that is what He wants! So how do we lessen our desire to control, come to grow and rely on God more, while also experiencing the space for God's will in our lives and in the lives of our children? Let's learn from these mamas, from what Jesus has taught them.

Megan is in her 50s, with four young adult children. She shares: *While "let go and let God" is not realistic, there is a bit of truth hidden within this cliche. Over the years, I have found that nurture is important, but encouraging my kids to live out their God-given nature is the best thing I can do for them. Yes, we lean in, listen, and guide. These are our primary responsibilities as moms! But I would encourage all moms to relax a bit and let God guide them as they mother their child. God created them, so He knows what's best. The more I release my need to "control" my kids, the more they realize they have the freedom to develop their own voice and can choose for themselves. This can be scary at times because the consequences of "bad choices" can be devastating, but ultimately, they are amazing learning experiences. I pray that I will decrease and God will increase in their lives in order to lead them into their divine destiny – whatever that is!*

Oh man, so much goodness here! I can definitely speak to feeling the need to control things in motherhood. Every worldly resource about mothering multiples discusses the importance of having a firm schedule. And so, that's what we've had! I was just talking to another toddler mom who complained that her daughter doesn't want to ride in the stroller anymore. Eek! My kids don't even know walking around at the zoo is an option because we just always have them in our double stroller (for their safety, but also for my sanity… and control). This is a simple example, of course, but it makes me think about the choices I could more prayerfully provide for my kids. Choices that create space for, and honor, God's provision and His will for their lives. I don't think riding in a stroller at age two or three affects God's will for their lives, but it's definitely got me thinking! As they get older, there will undoubtedly be plenty of opportunities for me to pray about being less controlling (even if it seems like something's for their safety), to pray for ease as my children learn from their mistakes, and to trust that God knows what's best. He will lead our Hopey and Johnny toward His perfect plan for their lives.

Julie is in her 60s, with four adult children. She shares: *At this point in my life, looking back and trying to recall the struggles of parenthood, it is easy to see that God has a long-term plan (see Jeremiah 29:11), and I am only a part of His workings in the life of each of my children.*

Her Prayer for Peace

I've said it before, but shares like this help relieve some of the pressure I unnecessarily put on myself to raise my kids perfectly. *Why is my inclination to control everything when it comes to raising my kids, Lord? Help me to believe in and trust in Your long-term plan, Lord, about everything, including the lives of each of the children with whom You've blessed me here on earth.*

Cassandra is in her 50s, with six school-age to adult children. She shares: *God has already predestined everything in your life and the lives of your kids, so ease some of your stress and trust God!*

Oh, the truth in this! Mama, we have a God Who immeasurably loves us and our kids. Whatever His plan for them, whatever His provisions along the way, God's plan for every life is absolute perfection! I pray we believe this, and in doing so, I pray we loosen our grips, create more space for God's power, and truly enjoy the blessings that are our children!

> WHATEVER HIS PLAN FOR THEM, WHATEVER HIS *provisions* ALONG THE WAY, GOD'S PLAN FOR EVERY LIFE IS ABSOLUTE PERFECTION!

Before this week ends, I want to add a little practical theology about God's will. God makes His will known to us in at least three ways. Being aware and mindful of these ways may help us stay true to our desire to control less and trust in God more as we mother our children within God's will. Pastor Chuck Swindoll shares how we can be more aware of God's will:

1. through His Word, as we stop and study the Bible;
2. through circumstances, as we look within and sense what He is saying to us; and
3. through the counsel of others, as we listen carefully.[17]

I know you're busy, mama. But remember that spending time with God is never a waste of time. As you have your quiet time with the Lord, while you study His Word, ask Him for more trust and for you to hear what He has to say to you, particularly about your children. Pray about developing a true friendship with our Father, His Son, and the Holy Spirit. He wants to help and guide us. He wants what's best for us and our children. When we spend time with our Maker, He helps us trust Him and gives us His peace. Christ's peace is a true blessing when we want to mother within God's long-term plan for our kids. **(See: WEEK FORTY-SEVEN: Christ's Peace in Our Mama Hearts.)**

Bible Verse

"'For I know the plans I have for you,' declares the LORD, 'plans to prosper you and not to harm you, plans to give you hope and a future'" (Jeremiah 29:11 NIV).

Prayer

Thank You, Lord, for Your plans for our children. Help us trust these perfect plans and nurture our children accordingly. When we feel inclined to control a situation in motherhood, help us turn to You for peace, wisdom, and guidance. Help us teach our kids through our own actions as we trust in You. Help us stick to our role as our children's earthly mothers. Relieve the pressures and stress we may put on ourselves as mothers, Lord. Help us have more fun in motherhood as we rely on You and Your perfect provision and perfect divine destiny! We love You. Amen.

Reflective Questions

1. What does your heart tell you about God's will for your life as a mother? Spend time in prayer for more of His perfect insight.

2. Consider your biggest challenge in loosening your grip and lessening your control when it comes to motherhood. Pray for God to bring you clarity, instruction, and subsequent peace.

3. Prayerfully ask God for one practical way you can mother according to His will today.

Week Twenty-Seven

Mothering and Marriage

This topic could be an entire devotional in and of itself. While we focus so much of motherhood on our children (as is reflected in the answers of the 33 women who contributed to this devotional), God is clear that our marriage relationship is to be held in higher regard than our relationship with our children. God instructs our marriage relationship to be second only to our personal relationship with Him. That said, a God and spouse-honoring marriage is incredibly beneficial for our children!

One quick note about this: Next week, we'll talk about divorce and stepmotherhood. While a few mamas share about their marriages, one briefly shares about her divorce, and a couple of mamas talk about stepmotherhood. I pray no one feels judged by myself or any contributors to this devotional over the next two weeks. When I say that a God and spouse-honoring marriage is beneficial for children, I do not mean, in any way, to judge a mother whose marriage is struggling or whose marriage has ended in divorce. God's love for every mama and every child is greater than any spousal issue and divorce! I also pray that every mama, no matter the current state of her marriage, benefits from the shares this week and that we each personally pray for our marriage and our spouse, even if you're no longer (or you never were) married. Let's start with a short, simple, yet very profound testimony!

Jonnie is in her 40s, with two young adult children. She shares: *Nothing has tested my faith like marriage, and both my faith and my marriage ended up stronger along the journey.*

This is all this mama said regarding her marriage and faith in Jesus, but it's very thought-provoking! Being in love with and married to someone and then parenting with them, can bring out different issues and feelings toward each other. If your spouse was raised very differently than you, to their benefit or their detriment, having children and parenting may become a source of conflict in your marriage and in your motherhood. This mama has an incredibly strong faith. Whatever she and her husband endured due to marriage and parenthood were seemingly God's way of strengthening their faiths, and their marriage. I will remember this mama's words as my children grow and my husband and I face hard marital and parental issues. God can strengthen our faith and our relationships in any circumstance when we stay focused on Him.

Gina is in her 30s, with four young to school-age children. She shares what she heard the Lord tell her: *I will do it with you. It's not your job. Let go and surrender to me so I can lead you, your marriage, and your children.*

> LET GO AND *surrender* TO ME SO I CAN LEAD YOU, YOUR MARRIAGE, AND YOUR CHILDREN.

God wants to lead us in everything! We cannot (and should not) do life alone. By being open to God's leadership in our lives, in our marriages, and in motherhood, we benefit from the love and care of our Maker. He created us, our husbands, and our children. He wants us to love and serve Him and others well and to glorify Him in all we do. It's hard to do any of this without His wisdom, patience, and perfect leadership! *Lord, please open our hands to be led by You in our marriages and in motherhood!*

Alyssa is in her 30s, with four young to school-age children. She shares about priorities and prayer for your spouse: *My husband has always been a faithful believer. As we are all aware, we have peaks and valleys along our faith journey. I used to struggle with my husband's lack of priorities for God, marriage, and family. At this point, I was well aware that getting mad at him could change an afternoon, but not his behavior. I started to pray that my husband would have a deepened relationship with God so that his priorities would straighten out. Imagine if we could both have God, marriage, children, and then work, etc., ordered correctly as a team? That became my dream.*

In 2021, I resolved to listen to the Bible in a Year with Fr. Mike Schmitz. My husband is a huge audiobook and podcast listener as well. At that time, he was primarily listening to content about his interests and vocation: physics, environmentally friendly farming practices, healthy living, and chemistry. The whole family became tired of my husband spending what little time he had in the house sharing his newfound knowledge of what was killing us, what we are doing to the earth, what we couldn't eat, and seeing him just so anxious about it all. My husband is not an anxious man. After talking it over with my mother-in-law, who was also on the back nine of Bible in a Year, and attending the first Bible study with me over Advent, we decided that our beloved needed to immerse himself in something healthier for him and for us all. The Word of God transformed both of us that year beyond our wildest dreams, and we knew it could be something that my husband could immerse himself in, too. He agreed to listen to the Bible in a Year in January of 2022. He started coming into the house saying different things like, "We (meaning the human race) never learn, do we?" Or, "Those Proverbs were for me today." The anxiety disappeared. He was calm. He didn't sweat the small stuff. God is so good!

In July of 2022, we went on our 10-year anniversary trip. We attended Mass, and it was one of those beautiful moments in life. We experienced the realities of life, death, Heaven, and Hell in the same fervency as one another; we were both more rooted in Christ. During that homily, we were truly bonded in Christ as husband and wife. (It was a great homily, too, which can be listened to on the "Padre's Points" podcast by Fr. Mattingly from the first week in July 2022.[18]*) That marked a whole new level in our marriage. Since then,* *we can engage in discussions of Scripture, study, and belief in a deeper and more meaningful way. We can also discuss questions of faith in a sophisticated manner and can pour out love better. We have experienced this deepening consistently ever since, and undoubtedly, every marriage would be better for it. In turn, our parenting has improved, too.*

I'm excited to touch on some of this mama's other points, but the last sentence she said is so valuable! When we, as individuals and married people, spend more time in God's Word and more time praying (together), we are changed by God. And when God changes us, we become better, more God-aligned believers and parents.

I want to go back to this mama's initial two concepts: Our priorities as parents and praying for our spouse. Our livelihood is important! We need to be able to afford to feed and provide for our children. Many occupations take up at least eight hours of our day, half of our average waking hours. (I know this mama's husband works many hours more than this as a farmer.) All this said, it can be easy to feel and actually become consumed by our occupation. But that's never been God's intention for us. Yes, we are to work, we're to serve others, and we're to do so with good attitudes. But our work, interests, and desires should always honor God first. This includes our husbands and our children, mama! **(See: WEEK THIRTY-SEVEN: Motherhood and Our Children: Idols?)** While we and/or our husbands may spend much of our time working, our God-given priorities are to be God first, then our spouse, then our children, and ultimately our occupation. (Shout-out to all the stay-at-home mamas here!) When our priorities are in this correct order, our relationship with God and our marriages are stronger. As a result, our role as mothers becomes more supported and more aligned with God's design for the family.

Lastly, we must pray for our husbands and for our marriages. So much of my prayer life automatically involves my children, and I also pray for myself as their mother. I pray for my husband, but I know I can do so more often and with more intentionality. Praying for our spouses creates a tender intimacy with them, through God (the best way!). Whether we're praying for God to rearrange their priorities, to lead our family's prayer life, for their jobs, their health, and/or their hearts, by praying for our God-given life partner, we're also thanking God for the gift of our husbands in our lives. The intimacy and thanksgiving this creates affects our children and our entire family dynamic.

Bible Verse

"Therefore encourage one another and build one another up, just as you are doing" (1 Thessalonians 5:11 ESV).

Prayer

Lord, help us honor our husbands by first honoring You. Help us to best care for our children by honoring our husbands more than we honor motherhood. Grow our faith in You as our love for our husbands grows through You, Lord. Help us to know that we need You, Lord. Lead us in our marriages first and in parenthood second. Lord, guide us as we pray for our husbands. Help us prioritize praying for them over praying for our children. Create an intimacy between us and our husbands that is rooted in prayer with You, Lord. Realign our hearts every day with who and what You say we should prioritize. We believe this alignment with You and our husbands will benefit our children. We love You. Amen.

Reflective Questions

1. Consider how your relationship with God has changed since you got married and had children. How has your relationship with your husband changed since you became parents? What's one aspect of each relationship that you'd like to see improved for the benefit of yourself, your husband, and, as a result, your children?

2. How might you allow God to lead you in your roles of wife and mother?

3. Consider your personal priorities in life. Do they align with what we know God wants us to prioritize? Do you prioritize praying for your husband within your prayer life? Spend some time praying for your husband right now!

Week Twenty-Eight

Mothering after Divorce and in Stepmotherhood

While I don't have personal experience with divorce or stepmotherhood, I know I can still learn from and pray for the mamas who do have these experiences. As a reminder, God loves us and our children, no matter the logistics of our families! These are some brave mamas we'll hear from this week. Even if you can't relate to their life circumstances or family dynamics, we can always glean something from another Christian mama.

Kari is in her 60s, with three adult children. She shares: *When my first husband (my girls' father) decided he wanted a divorce, I was heartbroken that my children would now be products of a broken home. I never anticipated being a single parent nor having to deal with someone who did not want to co-parent with me. Despite the emotional and financial difficulties of that time, I knew in my heart that God would take care of us (and I actually saw evidence of this many times along the way). I re-dedicated my life to Christ shortly after my divorce was final, as I had hit rock bottom emotionally, and I took great joy in raising my children to know and love God. There were many parenting decisions over the years where I needed to trust God to show me the right way. When my girls would spend time at their dad's, I was allowed no contact, so I also learned to trust that God would take care of them. I knew that He loved them even more than I ever could.*

Oh, the faith of this mama! She mentions her children being products of a "broken home," but that is just a human, earthly term. There is nothing we can do, no circumstances that can happen, that will separate us from the love of God and the home and family we have in Jesus Christ! Through single-parenthood, this mama trusted God. He cared for them and provided for them. After all the emotions of this mama's divorce and single parenthood, she knew she needed Jesus more than ever. This is by His design. When life on earth is full of burdens, our gracious God wants to come to our aide. He wants us to cry out for Him. I can't imagine my children being somewhere without me having access to them (even once, let alone regularly). But while this mama wasn't with her children, God was still with them, when they were at their dad's house. God was also within this mama's heart, giving her strength and peace as she trusted Him. God loves us and our children more than we can even comprehend. Whether we see our children every day or not, we must always trust in Him to guide and protect them according to His perfect plan for them.

Tamara is in her 50s, with one adult stepchild and one young adult biological child. She shares: *God's grace and wisdom came on the scene when I called on Him at the time I was getting married; my husband had a six-year-old son, and I became an instant mother. I asked for wisdom on how to be a great mom by studying James 1:5, which says, "If any of you lacks wisdom, let him ask God, who gives generously to all without finding fault, and it will be given to him."*

The humility of this mama inspires me. She knew she needed God's grace and wisdom as she became a wife and a stepmother. James 1:5 states that we only need to seek God's wisdom, and He will give it to us. The book of James is filled with verses like this. It's one of my favorite books of the Bible. It can certainly be confronting, but the truths and wisdom therein are true gifts from God. I can only imagine, especially if your children are not biologically yours and if you haven't known them their whole life, how the Lord's wisdom, guidance, and His peace are the best tools in a stepmother's toolbox! Said another way, when neither nature nor nurture play a part in your role as a mother, the importance of trusting in God's perfect plan and His wisdom are especially crucial.

Karissa is in her 30s, with two school-age stepchildren. She shares: *We are a blended family. The 13-year-old has always been closer to her mother, while the 10-year-old has always been closer to my husband, their father. Sometimes circumstances can feel unfair, almost like things are being fed to my stepdaughters by the other household (their biological mother's home). My husband and I have both felt directionless at times. I found my faith has pointed me in the direction of starting with kindness and understanding. I also deal with the deeply hurt feelings of my partner. He has felt betrayed and hopeless in many ways and also a bit defensive. Again, my faith has pointed me in the direction of truth and kindness. With a teenager, things aren't personal! Our family structure is just different. It can often feel so hard like we are being observed, and that if we don't do things right (or as the other house wants it), then the children could always choose not to come to our home. I think, in this case, my faith has helped me create some distance from the deep personal hurt.*

If Jesus could forgive the people who crucified Him, then we could certainly take the high road and not stay mired in anger, hurt, and resentment toward our daughters' mom. I think the biggest gift has been learning to trust my gut and intuition. Realizing that the knowledge and wisdom of what to do was already inside me. Or if I lacked knowledge, there are so many resources to tap into, including books, videos, and other parents I respect who have been in the same place. So often, prayers aren't answered in a bolt of lightning fix but in being pointed to all of the tools already around us. Turning to my community has been one of the things that have helped me the most. Hearing stories from others and what they had gone through made me feel less alone.

> IF JESUS COULD *forgive* THE PEOPLE WHO CRUCIFIED HIM, THEN WE COULD CERTAINLY TAKE THE HIGH ROAD AND NOT STAY MIRED IN ANGER, HURT, AND RESENTMENT.

It helped us realize that there are ups and downs in parenthood, but our ability to stay calm and loving no matter what is what matters the most.

Knowing the type of teenage girl I was, I feel for this mama as she takes on stepmotherhood! I love how she talks about emulating characteristics of Jesus, like kindness, understanding, truth, and forgiveness. Every mother would benefit from more of these traits, but especially when family dynamics include additional elements like those in a blended family. I also love how this mama has become so in-tune with the gifts and wisdom God has given her. And also, we cannot forget the gift of community! As she said, sometimes, God leads us to tools and other people here on earth when we pray to Him. This allows us to care for each other, teach each other, and pray for each other.

No matter the family dynamic, emotions can run high. But if we can face every situation with love, drama doesn't stand a chance! Love comes from God, so if we struggle with this, it's something for which we can pray! Plus, Jesus was part of a blended family! Joseph was, of course, not Jesus' biological father. Stepmama, you are not alone. In fact, you are in the best of company! Seek Him, and He will guide you in stepmotherhood, and also through divorce.

Bible Verse

"For this reason I bow my knees before the Father, from whom every family in heaven and on earth is named, that according to the riches of his glory he may grant you to be strengthened with power through his Spirit in your inner being, so that Christ may dwell in your hearts through faith–that you, being rooted and grounded in love,…" (Ephesians 3:14-17 ESV).

Prayer

Lord, thank You that every type of family is rooted in You. We pray for the mamas whose marriages have ended in divorce. Please guide them in Your special ways, especially if they're single mothers. Please heal any hurts in their hearts and help them to trust You more. We pray every single mother knows she has a partner in You, Jesus. Please also give her children peace and love from You, the source of all good things. For stepmothers, provide them with every confidence in You to love and raise their stepchildren well. Help them to turn to You! May their stepchildren have Christ-like patience, acceptance, and love for their stepmothers. Lord, please bless these relationships and these families. May the mamas of divorce and those in stepmotherhood trust entirely in You, Lord, for wisdom, discernment, compassion, and peace. We love You. Amen.

Reflective Questions

1. What's one thing you learned from a mama who shared about the impact of her divorce, being a single mother, and/or her stepmotherhood on her faith life?

2. Do you regularly ask God for wisdom in life and in motherhood? I highly recommend studying the book of James to help facilitate this.

3. If you are a divorced mother, single mother, or stepmother, have you sought out a community of people with similar family dynamics? If not, spend some time praying, asking God to lead you to a community that could support you and speak God's truth to you. If you know someone who's been divorced, is otherwise a single mother, or is a stepmother, reach out to them with prayerful words of encouragement before the end of the week. If you have no personal experience or knowledge of someone who's been divorced, is otherwise a single mother, or is a stepmother, spend time in prayer, generally, for those mamas.

Week Twenty-Nine

The Influence of Society/Peers and Their Sin on Our Children

As a mama of toddlers with hundreds of words in their vocabulary, I get a little annoyed when my kids revert back to "baby talk" because there's a new 16-month-old in their class who doesn't have the ability to use words yet. That said, I am not oblivious to the real, much more serious influence of society and peers. While sin is naturally a part of Hope and John, and part of them learning about cause and effect within their current, narrow exposure to the world, they're a couple of years behind sin being a real teaching point for them. I'm so grateful for the Christian mamas who've gone before me whose kids are older and (unfortunately) have experienced the real influence of society, their peers, and, therefore, the sins of the world. Listen up, mama of littles and also the mama in the thick of this! We're about to learn how God guides mamas in the fallen world in which we live.

Angela is in her 40s, with two school-age children. She shares: *Being steadfast in rearing children to live by the precious commandments and messages from God, with the hurts and daily delusions inflicted on my sons by their peers, feels like an impossible goal. "Kill them with kindness" and the "turn the other cheek" mentality are all too often lost while also teaching my boys to stand up for themselves and be strong leaders and good friends. It is a delicate dance. Jesus is my ever partner. Sometimes, my dance moves lead me down a more unforgiving and malicious train of thought, thrusting me into mama bear mode as I see my boys harmed by the colorful ways Satan presents himself in school-aged children. Then Jesus moves in with His beautiful steps to redirect me. I can literally feel Him take over and guide me back to peace, love, and a more understanding place. It is then that my sons and I pray for peace and love to enter the hearts and minds of these bullies who are inevitably found in so many aspects of daily life. When we pray for those who torment us, rather than retaliate, the presence of Jesus in prayer turns our anger, frustration, and pain into compassion. It is miraculous. Little miracles, they are so powerful – so are hugs.*

Mama bear mode is a real thing. Our fierce love for our children can be a good thing, but it doesn't always look like the love of Jesus. I know this is a minor example, but when my John pulls my Hope's hair, there is not an ounce of patience within me. Naturally, I usually scream and sprint over to them with an angry, impatient scowl on my face. And that's toward (and for) my own child! I sympathize with this mama's immediate, human reaction to other children bullying her own sons. But I also love the peaceful transformation that takes place in her heart when she allows Jesus into the process. Holy Spirit conviction can be a wholly tangible experience, as this mama describes it.

I also love the example she sets when she and her boys pray for the bullies, and in turn, God transforms their hearts to be more like His compassion-filled heart. *God, You are so good! Thank You for working in this mama's heart and in the hearts of her young sons!* Like this mama shared weeks and weeks ago **(See: WEEK TWO: Raising Kids**

GOD TRANSFORMS THEIR *hearts* TO BE MORE LIKE HIS COMPASSION-FILLED HEART.

for Jesus), there are not many other Christian families in her community. *Oh, I pray You change this, Lord.* Conversely, our next mama and her family have many other Christian families in their community. She shares about sin, confession, and forgiveness uniting their own family among other Christian families, and that also aligns their hearts with the heart of Jesus.

Alyssa is in her 30s, with four young to school-age children. She shares: *I need these four little people to ask us what temptation is. I'll never forget when I realized how important it was to show my oldest that I screw up and sin. When she was preparing for First Communion, it was during this turning point in our marriage that we truly deepened our relationship with Christ, as it was an expectation to model for our kids. We were to be a part of various stations to prepare for the Sacraments of Reconciliation and the Eucharist. We had not been to confession since before COVID; it had been years. We sat at home and went through the Ten Commandments, and she adorably struggled to think of a time she hadn't honored her father and mother (ha!). I went with her for her first reconciliation.*

I went in along with many of the other parents. It was so good for ME to see other parents faithfully repenting and examining their consciences. We don't get to see that much in society, do we? Oh, that faith formation is good for us, too! I made my list on my phone so that I wouldn't forget anything, made a humbling confession, and when I walked out, I saw my little girl, wiped clean of sin, in a state of grace, with the most horrified look on her face. Her eyes were as big as lightbulbs. I sat down, and she leaned in, raised her single eyebrow, and said out the side of her mouth, "Mom, you were in there a looong time." I immediately laughed and told her, "I better get to saying my penance, huh?" These moments together, seeing them pray without prompting in times of distress, is God working in them. I pray she listens to the call of Jesus when she carries on with her days. Christ is with them when they are in school, on the bus, talking to adults, lying in bed at night, playing their sport, taking a test, attending faith formation, and sitting in our car.

The influence of society/peers can be unfortunate, but it can also be a good thing! Christ is always with us, and He's always with our kids. When our kids are bullied at school, we want them to think, *What would Jesus do?* If they see us doing the same thing, then they have a Christlike example to follow. Showing them how we (and other members of society) rely on Christ during challenging times, allows our kids to follow suit. When our kids are surrounded by other Christians, especially Christians who know they are sinners too, it's invaluable for them to see forgiveness from Jesus Christ, especially as a community in greater society. This next share hurts my heart so much, but as we see, Jesus can heal every societal/peer hurt!

Beth is in her 60s, with three adult children. She shares: *When our youngest, our son, was a young pre-teen, there was a boy a few houses down who we welcomed into our home almost daily. This boy was from a very tough home situation, and our son took him under his wing, witnessing to him, bringing him to church with us, and having him over for swimming, lunch, dinner, etc. I was very clear that no sleepovers at their home could occur for our son's safety, and yet we witnessed to this boy constantly in hopes of bringing Jesus into his heart and home. Unfortunately, this boy ended up exposing our son to pornography. By the time we figured this out, he had drawn not only our son into this but three of our son's friends from church as well. Talk about shock and devastation! Even with our close monitoring, this happened.*

My husband and I immediately stepped in and severed all contact with this family on a daily basis. We hit our knees along with our son, who, by this time, was scared of something he now could not erase from his mind and heart. As parents, we met with his parents and had a hard, honest conversation, which was NOT received well. This young man was invited to participate, with his father and the four other fathers from our church, in a weekly Bible study about growing your faith as a young man and staying strong and pure of heart and mind. They chose not to participate, which meant there would be no friendship allowed moving forward.

For a complete year, we wives prayed over and for our sons and husbands as these four dads met weekly with and mentored our boys back to strong faith and purity of heart and mind together as a group. As parents, we all felt the Lord leading us daily and lifting us up as we stepped one foot in front of the other, trusting in Him to guide us. He literally gave us Bible verses daily to pray over our son and with our son. We steeped ourselves and our son in His Word daily, speaking His Word aloud over our son, asking for the Lord's love, strength, guidance, and deliverance. We felt full of His peace and watched our son not only grow in his wisdom and trust in the Lord, but in his desire to lead other young men in their faith walk, too. Now as an adult, our son is a leader of young men, mentoring youth in their walk and encouraging young men to remain pure and strong of heart, mind, and body. Although I would not wish this experience on any parent, it was a season of growth, trust, faith, and grace from which we learned so much.

Oh, my heart. Oh, the faith! Only God (and faithful parents) could turn this situation around like this. Our children's lives are/will be full of situations that make the mama bear in us want to come out. Some situations make us drop to our knees and plead to the Lord. Just because we're Christians doesn't mean our lives or our kids' lives will be easy. You already know this. But as Christians, we thankfully always have the Lord our God with us and with our kids. **(See: WEEK FORTY-EIGHT: Sin and Spiritual Health in Motherhood.)**

Bible Verse

"Even though I walk through the valley of the shadow of death, I will fear no evil, for you are with me; your rod and your staff, they comfort me" (Psalm 23:4 ESV).

Prayer

Lord, thank You for living in the hearts of these mamas. Thank You for helping us live, and for helping us teach our kids to live, for You in this fallen world. Lord, I pray for self-control and reliance on You when we face sinful societal/peer circumstances in our families. Help us teach our kids how to prayerfully react to and how to pray for sinful peers. Protect our kids, Lord, according to Your will. We trust You. When our kids get hurt, create in us, and in them, even more reliance on You, Lord. Please also create compassion and trust in our hearts as You guide us in managing tough situations like we read about this week. Lord, let our kids see that we, too, are sinners. We are sinners who need a forgiving and compassionate God. Help us be forgiving and compassionate to others, Lord, even when they do us wrong. We love You. Amen.

Reflective Questions

1. After this week, how might you react if your child is bullied? Be sure to pray about this.

2. Do your children know that every person is a sinner, capable of being forgiven, including you and also them?

3. Have you ever experienced Holy Spirit conviction when battling the sins of others in this world? Journal and pray about this.

Reflection; Miracles in Motherhood (Vol. III)

We're over half way there! Go YOU and go, GOD! We've covered a variety of topics in the past nine weeks, and my hope continues to be that you've been in prayer, in action, and in rest with the Lord. God is on the move in our households, mama! He cares for us and our children. He has a perfect plan for our lives. He guides mothers in different family structures.

Take some time to reflect on the last nine weeks:
1. How has God's love and peace for you changed you and impacted your family since you started this devotional, specifically in the last nine weeks (weeks 21-29)?
2. What have been your three to five biggest takeaways in the last nine weeks (weeks 21-29)?
3. Is there a week you'd like to re-read this week?

4. Is there a mama you thought of in weeks 21, 22, or 28, but you forgot to pray for her or reach out to her? Now is your opportunity! Don't let this week go by without praying for her or connecting with her.
5. Do you find yourself seeking, trusting, and relying on God for peace, wisdom, and guidance in motherhood, even 5-10% more than you did nine weeks ago?

Let's pray. *Lord, we are so thankful that You are a God Who cares for us and our children to an infinite degree. It's hard here on earth sometimes! But through every tough time, You are there to care for us, to guide us, and to fulfill Your perfect will for every life on earth. Whatever Your will is and in whatever circumstances we find ourselves and our family, help us to trust You more, Lord. Help us to hear Your still, small voice within us as we navigate motherhood in a worry-filled, sinful world. And help us be beacons of Your light for others, Lord! Bless us with Your confidence to bless others in knowing You and Your love for us and our families. We love You. Amen.*

> HELP US TO HEAR YOUR *still, small voice* WITHIN US AS WE NAVIGATE MOTHERHOOD IN A WORRY-FILLED, SINFUL WORLD.

This week, I'll share a miracle of God – from Julie, a mama in her 60s, with four adult children. She shares: *An instance of God's protection occurred when our family was coming home from an event in two vehicles. My youngest daughter was probably between one-and-a-half and two years old. I had pulled the car into the driveway of our little raised ranch home, shut it off outside the closed garage door, and was unloading kids and things through the walk-in door. I don't remember what I had in my hands, but I put her right inside the door to the garage and closed that exterior door to keep her from going back outside while I ran the item up to the kitchen. I was setting the item in the kitchen when I heard the garage door open and the car start. My husband had gotten in my car and was pulling the car into the garage, not knowing that our daughter was right there. I ran screaming down the stairs, and there she stood just fine. I grabbed her and melted into tears. She could so easily have been run over.*

I bet most of us know a scenario and a feeling like this. As Christians, we praise God for His care and grace at times like these. We praise Him for the health and safety of our kids. And we're reminded how precious their little lives are and how grateful we are to be their mama. There are days when I can't wait to drop my kids off at school. There are nights I can't wait for a babysitter to come "close." (The fact that my husband and I kiddingly, but not really, call the end of the night "closing" is pure evidence of how being a parent is a real, and hard job!) But as we raise our kids to know and love Jesus, we must remember that through the ups and downs of motherhood that grow our faith life, this most important job ever, motherhood, is not one we are meant to do alone. As mothers, we nearly always have our hands full of toys, groceries, or laundry, but God always has our children in His hands, according to His perfect plan.

I hope this reflection week has blessed you. Some of the topics in this devotional are hard. Some we can relate to more than others. A week where we pause to review and reflect can be really helpful. And hearing a story about the gift of God's incredible grace reminds us how great our God truly is! It's also a reminder to ask God to protect our families, to be weak and vulnerable, pleading for God to keep our children healthy and safe. In place of fear for our children's safety, we can ask the Lord to give us His peace. If tragedy happens, we can still pray to the God Who loves us.

This week's Bible verse sums this up well, along with many of the topics we've read about so far:

"For he will command his angels concerning you to guard you in all your ways; they will lift you up in their hands, so that you will not strike your foot against a stone" (Psalm 91:11-12 NIV).

Does Motherhood Ever Get Easier?

If you've been a mother for more than, let's say, three to six months, how would you answer the question, does motherhood ever get easier? As a mama of two-and-a-half-year-olds now, I'd be inclined to say, "Yes." But that's not because my children are really any easier. Perhaps they are in some aspects, but in others, they are definitely not! I think I've gotten better at being a mom. Indeed, this comes with experience, but there is also a direct correlation between my level of trust and reliance on God and how hard motherhood is for me. This is something I'm mindful of and grateful for every day, and I hope you are, too! This week, we'll hear from one wise mama whom the Lord has blessed and equipped with wisdom, patience, and peace.

Gina is in her 30s, with four young to school-age children. She shares: *At the beginning of motherhood, if I wasn't serving with my body, I was serving emotionally or mentally. As my kids grow, I now experience the shift from physical service, where I am my children's sole source of food, safety, and ability* to use the bathroom, to a different form of service as they age, one of emotional and mental service. But truthfully, it feels total.

Every now and then, I can tell I'm shedding a new layer in motherhood. **(See: WEEK ONE: Losing Yourself in Motherhood.)** But it's not so much about what I am shedding as it is what I am putting on in its place. Now, as a mother of four, I often have new moms ask me, "Does this ever get easier?" with their eyes eager for me to reassure them that it will. I can assure them that shedding is never easy, but if you let Him, the Lord will replace everything you shed with beauty. He replaces control with trust, anxiety with peace, pride with surrender, vanity with self-love, and your dreams with new dreams that are better than you could have ever made for yourself… so much better because motherhood is for the mother.

Ian Murphy is a Christian author who describes the journey of faith as a cyclical journey up to the summit of a mountain.[19] We return to the same place on the mountain often, but we are up a little higher where we can see better and have a new perspective from when we began our journey down below. I like to think of motherhood in this way. It doesn't get easier, but I can easily recognize this place as somewhere I have been before. Only now, I have a little more trust, peace, surrender, and self-love that He clothed me with the first go-around. I'm still working, sweating, and crying, but now I know the purpose.

Now, when I feel my arms being stretched and my head bent to the side in exhaustion, I give it over to Him. I know that to Him, I am not a mom. I am His daughter. He cares deeply for all of me: my health, dreams, anxieties, and my mother's heart. Self-discovery comes from a gift of self. A total gift of self… That word total is hard. It's one I pray about often. It doesn't mean I am a total gift of self to my kids, though many times, they are my means of service. Instead, I am a total gift to the Lord. When I give myself to Him totally, He helps me find balance in motherhood. **(See: WEEK NINE: Balance in Motherhood.)**

This balance means setting healthy boundaries and sometimes setting aside my needs for others. It's all done in prayer because I trust Him to lead me forward. Sometimes, it's forward into something that will hurt because, well, shedding hurts. Back to the main question. Does it ever get easier? "Easy" isn't the right word. It sells a mother's total transformation short. And no, she's not transforming into a mother; she is transforming into a more authentic version *of herself, into the daughter of the King. He makes all things new. Motherhood is our journey to Him.*

Amen. Can you relate to her very last sentence in particular, too? I've been a Christian my whole life, but it took motherhood to feel this reliant on and this connected to God. When I became a mother, I eventually found out how much I truly needed God in my life. Mama, I read so many books about pregnancy, birth, and infancy. I even read about potty training when I was still pregnant! I wish I'd sought God instead of Google to drown out my anxiety and fear of the unknown. Of course, God knew how it would all play out. He knew I'd seek information to suppress my anxieties about pregnancy and the upcoming birth of our twins. He knew my worry and fear in my first 18 months of motherhood would distance me from Him, the God of peace. He knew I'd eventually hit my knees for Him, laying it all at His feet. As a result of the newfound peace in my life, Christ's peace, He knew this devotional would come to be. If you feel called to share this devotional with another mama, even a newly pregnant mama, I pray you don't ignore it. As our sharing mama this week said, it's a journey, just like life. And while I wouldn't change how things have turned out, I know my relationship with Jesus is more meaningful than all the knowledge I no longer have about, let's say, the 31st week of gestation! Motherhood isn't supposed to be easy; it's what's hard that draws us closer to Him. *Motherhood is our journey to Him.*

> MOTHERHOOD IS OUR *journey* TO HIM.

Bible Verse

"For this is what the LORD says: 'I will extend peace to her like a river, and the wealth of nations like a flooding stream; you will nurse and be carried on her arm and dandled on her knees. *As a mother comforts her child, so will I comfort you;...'"* (Isaiah 66:12-13 NIV, emphasis added).

Prayer

Lord, we need You. Our children need us to need You. You've blessed us with motherhood, knowing it is not easy. Knowing our hearts would break for our children like Your heart breaks for us. I pray for every mama, reading these words, that she exposes herself to You so that You may fill her with Your wise, patient, and peaceful Spirit. I pray we seek You more and more in this journey of motherhood, Lord. Let us never think we have our fill. I pray we always seek You because as long as we are mothers, we will always need You. Help us to serve You and our kids well! Thank You that You replace control with trust, anxiety with peace, pride with surrender, vanity with self-love, and our dreams with new dreams that are better than we could have ever made for ourselves. We love You. Amen.

Reflective Questions

1. How did you initially answer the question/this week's topic: Does motherhood ever get easier? What are your thoughts now?

2. Think about a time in motherhood when you sought Him, and He made things easier for you. Conversely, is there a hard part of motherhood you're trying to handle on your own right now? Pray to God about this right now.

3. Please pray for a pregnant or new mama this week. If it comes up, be real about how hard motherhood can be! But if you've had a similar experience as I have, share what the hard looked like before and after you (continuously) let God and His peace in. Gift this devotional to a new mama if you feel God tugging at your heart to do so.

Week Thirty-Two

Extreme Anxiety in Motherhood

This is one of those weeks where it may be hard to hear the hearts of our contributing mamas, but it's so good to hear how the God of light shows up for us in our darkest moments. To this day, my wife/mama-mind still takes me places I know aren't from God. I'll hear my husband running down the stairs, and the fearful thought of him falling comes barreling into my mind. I worry about him driving in dangerous weather and getting hurt or even dying. Much of my anxieties and intrusive thoughts involve my husband, but sometimes my children, too. These thoughts started when I was pregnant. I'll share with you the simple prayer I pray to make these evil, terrifying images of my family hurting dissipate... *Jesus, Jesus, Jesus.* I repeat His name until He takes the images away, filling me with His love and peace instead. *Thank You, Lord, for helping us mamas lean on You for the care of our minds and our hearts, especially when our hearts ache with unnecessary worries and anxiety for our families.*

Gina is in her 30s, with four young to school-age children. She shares: *I recall the beginning of my motherhood journey being filled with* many extremes. *I was overwhelmed with joy, love, and fulfillment, along with anxiety, fear, and even anger. Over time spent in prayer, I learned how He replaces control with trust and anxiety with peace. Now, when I feel anxious, I give it over to Him. I know that I am His daughter. He cares deeply for all of me: my health, dreams, anxieties, and my mother's heart.*

I love the journey this mama shares here. After years of motherhood, she still gets anxious, but now she knows to bring her anxieties to God as quickly and completely as possible.

Dianne is in her 40s, with three school-age children. She shares: *As my body changed and dreams for my baby grew, so did the worry and anxiety.*

The brief memory of this mama during her pregnancy is so relatable to me, even now. While the newness of pregnancy and infancy is filled with all kinds of emotions, as our children grow, our anxieties may grow with them. As they have more experiences, exposures, and developments, we may find ourselves more and more worried and anxious. In order to stop this cycle, we must continue to deepen our faith and prayer life.

My own share: *I was filled with worry and fear. I knew fear came from the enemy and not from God, but I struggled to overcome all the stresses and unknowns of motherhood. I'd had therapy early on postpartum, which was helpful. Still, it wasn't until I started really talking about my struggles with other Christian mamas and asking them to pray for me that I started to experience some relief.*

Sometimes, talking to other faithful people can be just as helpful (and sometimes seemingly more accessible) as praying to God. Try it! While our goal is to go vertical for help, before going horizontal, keep asking God to bless you with Christian mom friends!

Kacie is in her 30s, with three young to school-age children. She shares: *I have felt extreme anxiety, obsessive and intrusive thoughts, and paranoia. Meeting with my pastor to discuss my feelings literally saved me. God knew exactly what I needed to hear and that I needed to feel loved and not ashamed, and He provided that from a pastor at my church.*

If not, other Christian mamas, church affiliates, and also medical professionals are there to help us. Pray for God to lead you to these helpers when you need them.

Jonnie is in her 40s, with two young adult children. She shares: *The concept of death and Jesus' resulting resurrection has impacted me in more ways than I'll understand. The fear was always the worst when I was traveling. I was afraid my kids would die, get hurt, etc. I even had intrusive thoughts of seeing them dead while I was gone. God showed up over and over. Most frequently, they tell me that even if they died, it is not the end but a beginning for them, and not a forever separation for me.*

Personally, I am so glad this mama shared her struggle and God's truth with us here. Because I do struggle with intrusive thoughts sometimes, reminding myself that death leads us closer to God seems to lessen the fear behind my anxieties around death! So, when the enemy plants a seed in my heart about illness, pain, or death within my family, the truth of Jesus having conquered death knocks the fear and anxiety right out. *Lord, I pray this truth is fully experienced the next time any mama or I fear for our family's life.*

Christine is in her 30s, with three young to school-age children. She shares: *With each of my children, there have been different times in their lives that I have felt Jesus' true peace and wisdom. With one of my daughters, it has been in the moments where her anxiety flares, and I know that I can help her walk through this. God has given me so many different periods of anxiety/depression, and what I have learned I will share with her to help ease her experiences.*

We are our children's best example of Christian living. If we have gone through something especially hard and then experienced the grace and peace of God, we can walk the journey alongside our children. While praying to the Father, Son, and the Holy Spirit, or talking to other followers of Christ (whether lay people, church affiliates, or medical professionals), modeling for our children how God has helped us conquer our own anxieties is a blessing for them.

Our church did a sermon series on mental health. The first message was about the church and mental health.

> MODELING FOR OUR CHILDREN HOW GOD HAS HELPED US CONQUER OUR OWN ANXIETIES IS A *blessing* FOR THEM.

It was incredibly insightful and supportive. If you struggle with extreme worry, fear, and anxiety, I encourage you to check it out.[20]

Bible Verse

"'Have I not commanded you? Be strong and courageous. Do not be afraid; do not be discouraged, for the LORD your God will be with you wherever you go'" (Joshua 1:9 NIV).

Prayer

Lord, help us to live, breathe, and model Joshua 1:9. Thank You for being with us wherever we go. Deepen our trust in You and all You command of us. We care for our children so much, Lord. You know our hearts for our kids. Please calm our hearts with Your peace. Lead us away from evil, away from anxiety and darkness, toward You and Your powerful loving light for both us and our children. Help us be there for each other, Lord. Help us remind each other of who You are and who we are to You. We trust You. We love You. Amen.

Reflective Questions

1. Take a moment to be in prayer with the Lord. Let Him into your heart, where all your deep emotions live. Ask Him for protection and peace over any intrusive and anxious thoughts you may have.

2. Consider your personal thoughts on death. Are you fearful of your own death or the death of others? Pray about this, asking God for His truth and peace.

3. Please spend time praying for a mama you know who struggles with anxiety. If no one specific comes to mind, pray for the anxious hearts of mothers as a whole. Pray they come to rely on God and Godly people in motherhood, especially in times of fear and angst. His peace is real!

Week Thirty-Three

What Might You Share with a New Mom Who's a Believer in Jesus? (Vol. I)

From Mamas in their 30s

Especially after last week, I hope you're ready for three weeks of goodness, mama! The number 33 is Biblically special because Jesus was likely 33 earthly years old when He was crucified for our sins and resurrected three days later. (How cool that exactly 33 Christian mamas contributed to this devotional, too!) So, over the next three weeks, we'll focus on the third question I asked our contributing mamas: *What might you share with a new mom who's a believer in Jesus?*

For comparison, I've grouped the tips and advice into the ages of our contributing mamas (in the random order in which I received their answers). We'll start this week with mamas in their 30s and end in three weeks with mamas in their 70s. There are some repeated lines, some stories you've read before, and duplicate topics you'll notice throughout the next three weeks. If something jumps out at you (again), particularly if you recall it from when you initially read it, I encourage you to pay special attention and heed what these Christian mamas collectively share with us. I'm excited to learn from our mamas over these next few weeks. I hope you are, too!

1. *Be patient and give yourself grace over and over and over again. Keep leaning on Him.* – Amara, with two young (earthly) children.

2. *Motherhood is our journey to Him.* – Gina, with four young to school-age children.

3. *I started answering this question with so many practical parenting tips. Still, then I realized that when you boil it all down, there is one main mission of motherhood if you follow Jesus: To make lifelong Jesus-followers. All of the other advice and hard seasons of parenting fade away in comparison to our calling to teach our children about Jesus and how to walk with Him. So here is my best advice: In each hard season of parenting, focus on extending grace and love to your child to show them a glimpse of their Heavenly Father. As they grow, use every hard moment with your children as an opportunity to turn their hearts and attention to the Lord. Use naughty moments to teach them about God's grace and point them to the work of Jesus on the cross instead of instructing behavior. Make sure they understand that we as parents aren't God, that we serve someone much higher because we, too, sin and need a Savior! Make your home a place where they can learn about Jesus, ask questions about Jesus, and, God willing, choose to follow Jesus themselves.* – Janette, with three young to school-age children.

4. *I would say people are serious when they say, "It takes a village." So, utilize your village!* – Kary, with two young to school-age children.

Her Prayer for Peace

5. *You are enough, and you are the perfect person for this job. God made you with your current situation in mind and in His perfect timing. The most important thing you can do is share the love of Jesus with your children... Everything else can follow.* – Kacie, with three young to school-age children.

6. *Schedule Jesus at least once a day. Your schedule isn't always yours, so find it when you can or in the midst. Find your thing. Ask Jesus to help you figure out that time and to spend your time doing whatever Jesus wills you to do. Remember that being married is a vocation. Being a mom is part of that vocation. He will give us sufficient graces to accomplish His will. We will find an oasis in Christ so that we can pour out from an overflowing spirit. We won't last long white-knuckle surviving. I have truly found some balance once I started practicing the Sabbath. That doesn't mean a day without doing... Sabbath is active! Yes, laundry is included in that as time for listening to God. It's time to go out in our community, serve the poor, serve our church, host or attend Bible study, do something with our hands instead of just sitting at a desk, play a sport with our kids, and go out to eat. My time is from noon on Saturday to noon on Sunday. Trust that God can do more in six days than we can do in seven.* – Alyssa, with four young to school-age children.

> HE WILL GIVE US SUFFICIENT *graces* TO ACCOMPLISH HIS WILL.

She also shares: *We'll never feel like we're giving enough to our children, spouse, self, and in the way we serve others. Isn't one of the best things about God that He tells us that we're not supposed to be enough? He will give to us faithfully and abundantly, and we are to share it. The gifts of others around us and the omnipotent, omnipresent, and everlasting God are more than enough. Pray, Jesus, I trust in You. Jesus, help me to do Your will today. Lord, keep me from the things in my day that do not glorify You. Help me. Strengthen my relationships. Whatever those other things are on my mind, those things must be worldly. Even if they are "good," if they aren't glorifying You today, help me to avoid them so that they will not diminish the way I live to be sanctified by You. The world lies. Keep your eyes and confidence up, sister!* – Alyssa, with four young to school-age children.

7. *God has created each individual uniquely. That means that your children are unique, and so are you. What motherhood will look and feel like for you is different than that of ANYONE else. What that means is as much as getting advice can be abundantly helpful, you should always pray to God for which advice applies to you and your child and what doesn't. This also means that you should feel confident to be the mother that your child needs and the mother that brings joy to you and your family's life. Lastly, what that means is you should not judge other mothers and how they show up with and for their children; their children are uniquely made, as well. The best thing we can do is show up for our children and other mothers with love, just as Jesus would.* – Christine, with three young to school-age children.

8. *Breath prayers are so helpful. They are quick, few-word prayers that are spoken with an exhale. I often say, "God, give me patience." These have helped me get through the toughest moments when I am about to lose my cool!* – Chelsea, with four young children.

9. *Jesus has SO much abundance of love and kindness to give us! His grace is abundant, and it doesn't run out. He wants us to ask Him for more because He loves giving His children more, just like we love doing for our kids. Don't forget about your eternal position as a child of the King while you're acting as a parent for your own children during our time in this temporary home.* – Bri, with two young to school-age (earthside) children.

10. *Stay in the Word. Always seek God. When you feel too busy or overwhelmed to find the words, God knows your every thought and feeling, and the Holy*

Spirit intercedes for you. – Brianna, with one young child (and one on the way).

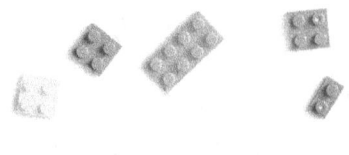

Bible Verse

"A generous person will prosper; whoever refreshes others will be refreshed" (Proverbs 11:25 NIV).

Prayer

Lord, thank You for every mama who contributed to this devotional. She took time away from her own family to bless and refresh every mama/family reading these words. May we prayerfully review this advice from other Christian mamas this week. Lord, show us which tip is most meant for us in our current season of motherhood. Thank You for blessing us with our kids, Lord. Help us to remember how powerful You are and how much You love us and our families. We love You. Amen.

Reflective Questions

1. After reviewing these ten tips from our Christian mamas this week, spend time with the Lord in prayer. Ask Him to show you which tip(s) to focus on, to pray about, and with which to trust Him the most. On the other hand, in which piece of advice are you currently thriving? Thank God for that!

2. Check in with your prayer life over the last week. Are you having an especially busy week? Have you spent time praising and praying to God today? Ask Him to meet you where you are right now.

3. Please pray for the mamas who contributed to this devotional. Please also share at least one of their tips with at least one other Christian mama you know.

Week Thirty-Four

What Might You Share with a New Mom Who's a Believer in Jesus? (Vol. II)

From Mamas in their 30s (continued) & Mamas in their 40s & 50s

Welcome back, mama! We'll hear tips/advice from 13 more Christian mamas this week. *Lord, thank You for the wisdom You've given these mamas and for their courage to share with us. Open our hearts to hear from You as we read their words this week.*

11. *Motherhood may challenge you multiple times every single day. Sometimes, I literally do cry over spilled milk. I'm learning, however, to ask Him to help me, mold me, teach me, and remind me that He's always with me! When I spend time with the Lord, leaning on Him before anyone else and trusting in His love for my children, I feel His peace as He guides my actions with my children. God's people are the second-best resource. I encourage you to*

join The MomCo or a small group of mothers at your church. – Monica, with two young children (my own share).

12. *For all those who have lost a child, know that there is beauty that is initially hidden amidst the devastation. God is good. Your child in Heaven is happier than you could ever imagine, and they are in a paradise more incredible than our brains can fathom. They will only ever know joy and happiness since they are in the presence of God for eternity. You, your spouse, and any other children you might have now, have their very own guardian angel to watch over you and pray for your family. You will see many "pearls of God's goodness" throughout the experience and for years to come.* – Emma, with two young (earthside) children.

13. *Realize that you are going to feel like you are failing. You are going to have that dread in your gut that you're just not good at this, and it is just too much. Trust your wise friends who have been there before. Pray when things get overwhelming. Look around you for resources that resonate with you and realize how supported you really are. Also, please be kind to yourself. Nobody who is a decent parent feels like they are nailing parenthood. It's just too important of a job to mess up, and that feels like a lot of pressure. Realize while you aren't doing motherhood perfectly (and because you're not Jesus, it isn't possible to do it perfectly), you are doing the best you can, and that is plenty good enough.* – Karissa, with two school-age children.

From Mamas in their 40s

14. *Knowing I have our Triune God in my corner gives me peace and strength as I do my very best with the ever so flattering–but oh so challenging– assignment of motherhood. I'd remind mothers who believe in Jesus this and hope they, too, take the role seriously but also enjoy the ride Jesus chose to put you on!* – Angela, with two school-age children.

Her Prayer for Peace

15. *I'd tell her: Remember, these sweet babies are on loan from Jesus, a gift from Jesus. They are His first. He's entrusted you to care for and raise them earthside, then give them back to Jesus.* – Dianne, with three school-age children.

16. *As parents, we often parent from fear and not faith. We think we shape and affect our children far less than we actually do. We are to shepherd them and encourage them toward the Lord. God created us to experience bliss and peace. That is our role as parents, to let their little lives unfold, teaching them faith in God, meditation, and to live according to His Word. Then God helps them to become who He created them to be... blissful and peaceful, too.* – Jonnie, with two young adult children.

> *Pray* EVERY SINGLE DAY THAT GOD GIVES YOU WHAT YOU NEED TO BE THE BEST MOTHER TO YOUR CHILDREN.

17. *Pray every single day that God gives you what you need to be the best mother to your children. It's so much easier to do life with God's guidance versus going at it alone.* – Heather, with two school-age children.

18. *Have a set of minimum standards that you always exceed, but the minimum is a line you do not cross. Also, make sure you have something that is just done for you, even if you share it with your kids.* – Valerie, with two adult children.

19. *Having your children see you spending time with the Lord with your "I'm sorry" and your "I'm so happy," and all the in-betweens is the one way to "Train up a child in the way he should go; even when he is old, he will not depart from it" (Proverbs 22:6). Knowing your peace comes from God and NOT from your child's behavior is a huge and beautiful place to be. God is so very faithful and loves to give us parental advice, along with all the other life advice there is to give.* – Annette, with one adult child.

20. *Pray daily, learn to ask for help, and let go of control.* – Teresa, with two school-age children.

From Mamas in their 50s

21. *Trust, trust, and trust! Sometimes, it's hard to trust and keep the faith when life is so busy and there is barely time for yourself. Step back and allow yourself just 10-15 minutes to be thankful and grateful for everything that is going on around you, as crazy as it may be at times. Trust me, before you know it, the "crazy" is gone, and your time to parent, teach, and mold your children is gone. And that is when you really do have to TRUST and have FAITH that you did your job as a mom! As parents, we need to be reminded that our children are not ours; they are GOD's, and He trusted us to love, teach, and care for them while they are young so that when they do go off on their own, they do so with the faith, knowledge, and confidence we instilled in them.* – Jill J., with two adult children.

22. *While "let go and let God" is not realistic, there is a bit of truth hidden within this cliche. Over the years, I have found that nurture is important, but encouraging my kids to live into their God-given nature is the best thing I can do for them. Yes, we lean in, listen, and guide. These are our primary responsibilities as moms! But I would encourage all moms to relax a bit and let God guide them as they mother their children. God created them, so He knows what's best! The more I release my need to control my kids, the more they realize they have the freedom to develop their own voice and can choose for themselves. This can be scary at times because the consequences of "bad choices" are great, but ultimately, they are amazing learning experiences. I pray that I will decrease and God will increase in their lives in order to lead them into their divine destiny – whatever that is!* – Megan, with four young adult children.

23. *My advice comes from my mom. Always one day at a time, a new day, a new slate; stay persistent and consistent with your parenting even when it's hard. Turn to trust in God and faith for the things you are grateful for as well as the things you struggle with. Prayer is powerful. You may not always get the answer in the way you had hoped, but sometimes, it arrives in the way you need. Always be patient. Sometimes, on the outside, it looks*

so easy for the mom next door, but we all have our struggles… Sometimes, we hide them well. At the end of the day, we do the very best we can. If we fail at something, it means we are human, and we have yet another day to get it right! And that, my friends, is a work in progress! To my knowledge, these littles do not come with a perfectly laid-out handbook! Lean on The Big Guy upstairs when you're struggling… it's a thing! – Pam, with five school-age to adult children.

Bible Verse

"As iron sharpens iron, so one person sharpens another" (Proverbs 27:17 NIV).

Prayer

Lord, thank You for every mama who contributed to this devotional. May we prayerfully review this advice from other Christian mamas this week. Lord, show us which tip is most meant for us in our current season of motherhood. We love You, Lord. We want to be close to You. We want to learn from You. Infiltrate our hearts, Lord, so we can better hear Your words of wisdom and love for us and our families. We love You. Amen.

Reflective Questions

1. After reviewing these 13 tips from our Christian mamas this week, spend time with the Lord in prayer. Ask Him to show you which tip(s) to focus on, to pray about, and with which to trust Him the most. On the other hand, in which piece of advice are you currently thriving? Thank God for that!

2. Check in with your prayer life over the last week. Are you having an especially busy week? Have you spent time praising and praying to God today? Ask Him to meet you where you are right now.

3. Please pray for the mamas who contributed to this devotional. Please also share at least one of their tips with at least one other Christian mama you know.

What Might You Share with a New Mom Who's a Believer in Jesus? (Vol. III)

From Mamas in their 50s (continued) & Mamas in their 60s & 70s

It's our final week of hearing tips/advice from other Christian mamas. I hope you've been prompted and also encouraged! I believe God was part of the process as I reached out to these women about contributing to this devotional. I believe He was with them when they wrote their responses. I hope you hear from the Lord this week through the words of another Christian mama.

24. *Your relationship with Christ becomes even more significant as you begin your journey as a mom. Learn how to turn to Him for everything, not just the critical or challenging moments. Jesus is truly your best friend! God has*

already predestined everything in your life, so ease some of your stress and trust God! – Cassandra, with six school-age to adult children.

25. *Ask God for wisdom on how to be a great mom.* – Tamara, with two young adult to adult children.

From Mamas in their 60s

26. *Parenting is tough and also rewarding. Our best lessons are going through hard times and walking away on the other side of hard with a positive perspective of the experience. Our kids are not our best friends, nor are we theirs… Jesus is. Always be willing to admit wrongs and ask for forgiveness from your child when you are wrong. It will teach them a valuable lesson. Love without condition. Let your kids make mistakes and learn from them. Go to the Lord with all your requests and listen. His response may not be immediate, but He will respond.* – Jill S., with three adult children.

27. *Teach your kids that it is more important to please God than to please you. You won't always be with them, and one day, their friends or spouse will be a bigger influence than you, but God will always be with them.* – Debi, with three adult children.

28. *As a new mom, I cannot encourage you enough to dig into the Word daily. Start your day early in the morning before your household wakes in the Word with Jesus. Wait upon Him, listen to Him. The day will be busy enough, full enough, and exhausting enough on its own to tire you out, so you won't have that time at the end of the day because a mom's job is never done, no matter how young or old your children are. I encourage you to make a place in your home that is "Mom's prayer corner," where you begin every day alone with Jesus. Don't give that up, not even for a day! Put Jesus first and listen to Him. He wants this time with you to feed you, guide you, and nurture your motherhood journey in His quiet, loving grace*

and mercy. He stands as a gentleman and waits, knocking at the door of your heart. It is your job to open that door, welcome Him in, and sit at His feet and listen.

Even now, with all three of my own children grown, married to wonderful believers, and growing their own households, I still begin my day early with Jesus laying all before Him, waiting upon His wisdom and abiding in His grace. My prayers for my children have grown and shifted as they have grown into adulthood. All of them still remember being young children coming out in their jammies, finding Mommy in the Word, and spending time with the Lord before our family day began. I remember that the days I let that time go, skipping it in order to meet the needs of a hectic day, I would always feel disconnected somewhat, not centered, and not fully present, nor capable of meeting the demands of the day. These early morning times with Jesus are still like air to my lungs. I encourage young moms to embrace this as well. You'll never regret it! – Beth, with three adult children.

29. *Things will be hard. There is no instruction manual that comes with your beautiful child. We do, however, have words of wisdom and guidance from the One Who can answer all questions. When things are hard, breathe, pray, and listen! He will guide you – always. As parents, we feel responsible for our children and try to fix everything. We think that's our job. While that is partially true, God may have other plans where we need to take His guidance, not ours. On the flip side, always remember to thank Him for all the blessings with your child. Be thankful for all the smiles, cries, fingers, and toes. Even for the times they test you to your limit, this is when God can shine brightly through you. God is good all the time, and all the time, God is good.* – Billie, with four adult children.

30. *As a new parent, the responsibility of caring for this new little human and the desire to protect him or her from all the bad things out there can be overwhelming. Trust that God loves your child even more than you do and that He is watching over them. You may be limited in what you can do, but God is omnipotent and omnipresent.* – Kari, with three adult children.

31. *Pray, pray, pray, pray, and trust, trust, trust, trust! Know that God is so very worthy of our trust. In your prayers, tell God that you trust in Him. Have courage. Fear is the enemy of faith. Pray in advance in anticipation of what is ahead. Pray for their future spouses. I pray frequently for all my grandchildren and future grandchildren that they will be healthy in mind, body, soul, and spirit. It's not all about what you do. You are just one, however critically important, but only one of many factors and persons that will impact the lives of your children. Pray for their future role models (and that they will choose good ones). Pray for their future school teachers, church teachers, youth leaders, priests, pastors, coaches, and other leaders. They are so important in their lives.*

Look forward in anticipation of bright surprises. God has great plans for each one. It is interesting and fun to watch the life of each unfold. Love each with fierce love. Each one is your favorite child… Be sure they each know that. Enjoy the journey. Childhood is a journey, not a race or a competition. Don't waste your time or emotional energy quietly or openly competing with your child's classmates, friends, etc. Make sure your child knows they are not the center of the universe. They are part of a family, and they are part of the love and support that is due to each member. Sometimes, it is their turn for the attention, the celebration, etc., but others also should have their moment in the sun. They should also expect to have jobs that they do as part of the family. They should not expect to be paid for things they do for the family. That is part of being in a family. Don't compare your children. Don't say, "He's my smart one," or "She's my (whatever, fill in the blank)." This can take away from the sibling's aspirations and/or confidence in an area.

Encourage, encourage, encourage. Notice what they are doing right. Point it out when you see good effort, behavior, performance, achievements, etc. We all need and appreciate deserved praise. Give them the respect you expect from them. Demand respect in return. What you tolerate, you teach. If you put up with a disrespectful tone of voice or words toward you or anyone else, you are teaching

CHILDHOOD IS A *journey*, NOT A RACE OR A COMPETITION.

them that it is okay. Set reasonable boundaries and enforce them. Follow through. Don't make a promise or threaten a consequence that you cannot or will not make happen.

Sometimes, you'll just blow it. You are not a failure. No parent is perfect. Love covers a multitude of missteps. Don't trust your feelings. You may not like your child at every moment, but you choose to act in a loving way. Whether in your marriage or with your children, love is a decision. Loving feelings will always follow. – Julie, with four adult children.

Lastly, here are some Bible verses this mama shares with us:

"Finally, be strong in the Lord and in his mighty power" (Ephesians 6:10 NIV). *(The whole chapter of Ephesians 6 is valuable for people, especially parents. It talks about the Armor of God.)*

"And pray in the Spirit on all occasions with all kinds of prayers and requests. With this in mind, be alert and always keep on praying for all the Lord's people" (Ephesians 6:18 NIV).

"'For I know the plans I have for you,' declares the LORD, 'plans to prosper you and not to harm you, plans to give you hope and a future'" (Jeremiah 29:11 NIV).

"Fathers, do not provoke your children to anger, but bring them up in the discipline and instruction of the Lord" (Ephesians 6:4 ESV).

From Mamas in their 70s

32. *Have fun with motherhood! What a big job and a big blessing when you let Jesus in, trusting Him to guide you. Kids and life can be messy. Do not doubt yourself. Start every day having high expectations for yourself, even if it means fitting in a nap. Look to Jesus as Lord and Savior. It's a personal relationship that only the two of you share.* – Jan, with three adult children.

33. *I would tell any new or experienced mom that it's really important to make time for Jesus in your life in order to deepen your faith. Just try to carve out*

a few minutes each day of quiet time to either study the Word of God or just pray. And sometimes, I just sit and listen; God speaks to those of us who have quiet time. It's hard to find that quiet time; you have to work really hard at it. Even schedule it like you do other appointments and make it a top priority in your life. – Carmie, with three adult children.

Bible Verse

"So–join the company of good men and women, keep your feet on the tried-and-true paths" (Proverbs 2:20, The Message).

Prayer

Lord, thank You for every mama who contributed to this devotional. May we prayerfully review this advice from other Christian mamas this week. Lord, show us which tip is most meant for us in our current season of motherhood. Thank You for our kids and for equipping us to mother them well for You. We love You. Amen.

Reflective Questions

1. After reviewing these ten tips from our Christian mamas this week, spend time with the Lord in prayer. Ask Him to show you which tip(s) to focus on, to pray about, and with which to trust Him the most. On the other hand, in which piece of advice are you currently thriving? Thank God for that!

2. Check in with your prayer life over the last week. Are you having an especially busy week? Have you spent time praising and praying to God today? Ask Him to meet you where you are right now.

3. Please pray for the mamas who contributed to this devotional. Please also share at least one of their tips with at least one other Christian mama you know.

Week Thirty-Six

Gratitude in Motherhood

So much of Christian motherhood (and Christianity in general) is about how God meets us in the hard times. But thanking God for our children and thanking Him for bringing us closer to Him and closer to other Christian mamas through motherhood is important, too! Gratitude is such a powerful tool in our Christian motherhood toolbox! When we're praising God in gratitude, it's nearly impossible to fully experience our challenges at the same time. One way I thank God is by listening to praise/worship music. Especially songs that really honor Who God is to us. We can also thank God in our everyday language... loud enough for our kids to hear! I love modeling this for my kids by praying out loud, in thanks to God. My kids love to thank God, too. They thank Him for everything: The sunshine, their shoes, their backpacks, and anything else in their sightlines at any given moment, but hey, that's something! Let's hear how some other mamas thank God in and through motherhood.

Jill J. is in her 50s, with two adult children. She shares: *Step back and allow yourself just 10-15 minutes to be thankful and grateful for everything that is going on around you, as crazy as it may be at times.*

Billie is in her 60s, with four adult children. She shares: *Always remember to thank Him for all the blessings with your child. Be thankful for all the smiles, cries, fingers, and toes. Even for the times, they test you to your limit, as this is when God can shine brightly through you.*

Pam is in her 50s, with five school-age to adult children. She shares: *Turn to trust in God and faith for the things you are grateful for as well as the things you struggle with.*

These wise mamas are not oblivious to the craziness, tests, and struggles we go through as mothers. I had no idea how crazy motherhood could be or how crazy it could make me feel! Nonetheless, they remind us to be grateful in spite of it all, and for it all. At the end of the day, motherhood is a gift and a blessing, indeed!

Julie is in her 60s, with four adult children. She shares: *When you pray for God to protect and then you see that protection right before your eyes, you cry because of what could have happened, and get on your knees and thank God from the depths of your being for sparing your child's life, for protection from disability, or for keeping your child free from the suffering or serious illness. I am just sharing the graces I have experienced, for which I am very grateful. I am sure there have been many times that we have been protected, and we were never aware of it.*

Kari is in her 60s, with three adult children. She shares: *Every little milestone filled me with gratitude and helped to strengthen my faith.*

Billie is in her 60s, with four adult children. She shares: *I was on my knees, this time thanking God for hearing my prayers.*

When we praise God, our faith in Him grows! While it's incredibly important to thank God for protecting our children, it's also important to note how gratitude can (quietly) exist among tragedy, as well.

Emma is in her 30s, with two young (earthside) children. She shares her grateful outlook after the loss of her child. *For all those who have lost a child, know that there is beauty that is initially hidden amidst the devastation. God is good. Your child in Heaven is happier than you could ever imagine, and they are in a paradise more incredible than our brains can fathom. They will only ever know joy and happiness since they are in the presence of God for eternity. You, your spouse, and any other children you might have now have their guardian angel to watch over you and pray for your family.*

The quiet gratitude in this mama's heart is a gift from God. In **WEEK THREE: Losing a Baby/Child – Miscarriage, Stillbirth, and the Loss of Child,** this mama further shared how she and her husband grew closer to God in their suffering and how God also made His presence known to others through their faith in suffering. When we suffer with God, our faith in Him can grow. What a gift for this mama and her husband! *Thank You, Lord, for blessing them in this way, even during this devastating time.*

Megan is in her 50s, with four young adult children. She shares: *Eventually, the incessant postpartum sadness subsided, but thankfully, the friendships did not. Some of those women are my best friends today!*

Thank God for Christian mom friends!

Angela is in her 40s, with two school-age children. She shares: *Thank God that Jesus is persistent! Thank God He is also a forgiving Lord.*

This mama is one of the only mamas this week whose children still live under her roof. For us mamas of littles, let us not wait to experience the gratitude we feel for our children and the gratitude we feel for the Maker of our children as He guides us in the early years of motherhood.

Tamara is in her 50s, with two young adult and adult children. She shares how she prays for her children by personalizing verses and thanking God: *Father, I thank You that my sons' steps are ordered by You, oh Lord, that they both are surrounded by Your hedge of protection, according to Psalm 91. Father, I thank You that no weapon formed against them will prosper, according to Isaiah 54:17. Father, I thank You that Your favor surrounds them like a shield, according to Psalm 5:12. Lord, I thank You that You are amazing. Your goodness and mercy follow them all the days of their lives, according to Psalms 23:7.*

I love this: Thanking God for blessings and protection in the present and into the future. This is true faith and trust, in gratitude, for our all-powerful and all-loving God. May we make gratitude to God part of our motherhood and part of our prayers!

MAY WE MAKE *gratitude* TO GOD PART OF OUR MOTHERHOOD AND PART OF OUR PRAYERS!

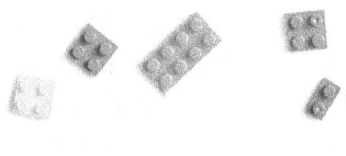

Bible Verse

"Sing and make music from your heart to the Lord, always giving thanks to God the Father for everything, in the name of our Lord Jesus Christ" (Ephesians 5:19-20 NIV).

Prayer

Lord, give us a grateful heart. Sometimes, being a mom isn't fun. Sometimes it is! Thank You for being with us no matter what. Help us to grow closer to You as we thank You for everything about our children, with whom You've blessed us. Help us to cultivate a community and culture where we thank You more. Help us see how much You love us as we mother our children. We trust You, Lord, as we pray and thank You for protecting our children. If and when we encounter suffering as a mother, help us to praise You even then, Lord. You are a mighty God worthy of our praise! We love You. Amen.

Reflective Questions

1. Do you regularly thank God for your children? Even when they're testing your last limits? Pray about this, asking God to give you a grateful heart no matter what motherhood looks like today.

2. How does your heart feel after hearing from the mama who lost her child? What might God want you to learn from her share, faith, and grateful outlook?

3. Prayerfully write a list of at least ten things about motherhood for which you are grateful.

Week Thirty-Seven

Motherhood and Our Children: Idols?

Motherhood was especially challenging for me in the beginning, in part, because I believe I made it and my children my idols. I started to place my value in my motherhood. And by doing so, I tried to do everything "perfectly" and on my own, creating a distance between myself and God, from Whom my value truly comes. Therein entered worry and fear. *Thank You, Lord, for not giving up on me when I tried to do so much of early motherhood on my own. Thank You for reminding me that I need to prioritize You and mother my children with You!* (**See: WEEK THIRTEEN: Modeling Faith to Our Children by Mothering (and Living) with God and WEEK SEVENTEEN: God's Grace Instead of a Mother's "Perfection."**)

The Oxford Dictionary defines an idol as "an image or representation of a god used as an object of worship."[21] When we hear this definition, we may think, *Well, that's not me! I don't worship motherhood or my children!* But what do our day-to-day words and actions as mothers actually sound and look like? What's our prayer life like? Where does God fit into our motherhood? Do we think we have value because God says we do or because we are a mother? Think about these things as we hear from several mamas this week. We'll learn how to prioritize God, not idolize/worship motherhood or our children, while we also love, teach, and model this for our precious kids, as well.

Note: Unconditional love does not equal idolatry or worship of motherhood or our children. We love our children (as) unconditionally (as humanly possible) since there is nothing they can do that will lessen our love for them. But our love is not perfect because we are not perfect. When this is aligned in our hearts, we have more room to rely on the only (perfect) One we should idolize/worship at all, including in our motherhood journey: God.

Billie is in her 60s, with four adult children. She shares: *As a parent we feel responsible for our children and try to fix everything. We think that's our job. While that is partially true, God may have other plans where we need to take His guidance and not ours.*

Karissa is in her 30s, with two school-age children. She shares: *Realize while you aren't doing motherhood perfectly (and because you're not Jesus, it isn't possible to do it perfectly), you are doing the best you can, and that is plenty good enough.*

Bri is in her 30s, with two young to school-age (earthside) children. She shares: *I reminded my daughter of how I try to love her the best I can, but we also need the love of Jesus to satisfy our hearts' cries.*

Dianne is in her 40s, with three school-age children. She shares: *But if we remember they are on loan to us, there is a confidence that Jesus is watching over them when we can't; He loves them more than we ever could; and He's making up for our shortcomings as parents.*

We need to leave a lot of room for God as we mother our children, mama. Being a mother is a huge blessing, with huge responsibilities. But it cannot be our everything! Motherhood or our children cannot be our idols. It's easy to become overwhelmed with the level of responsibility of being a mother.

Motherhood OR OUR CHILDREN CANNOT BE OUR IDOLS.

Still, when we share the responsibility with God and worship and trust Him by asking for His guidance and peace, He helps us to mother well... but still not perfectly. Because we're not Jesus, we, as human mamas who need Jesus, will never get it right all the time. It's His perfection that fills in our human, motherly limitations. When we rely on Him because we know His power is infinite and because He loves our children more than we possibly can, He helps us do this incredibly important job of motherhood in accordance with His perfect will.

Jill S. is in her 60s, with three adult children. She shares: *Our kids are not our best friends, nor are we theirs. Jesus is. This will teach them a valuable lesson. Love without condition. Let your kids make mistakes and learn from them.*

Debi is in her 60s, with three adult children. She shares: *Teach your kids it is more important to please God than to please you. You won't always be with them, and one day, friends or spouses will be a bigger influence than you, but God will always be with them.*

Janette is in her 30s, with three young to school-age children. She shares: *Make sure they understand that we as parents aren't God, that we serve someone much higher because we, too, sin and need a Savior!*

We have been blessed to be mothers. We are to teach our children about the love of Jesus because He is their best friend. We are not. **(See: WEEK FORTY-ONE: Jesus is a Mama's (and a Kiddo's) Best Friend.)** When we teach our kids (especially by modeling this) to honor Jesus above everyone and everything else, including ourselves, we are supporting them in developing the most important and meaningful relationship of their lives. That is, when we choose not to treat motherhood or our children as our idols, we're teaching our kids to always please and worship God first, too. Teaching our kids about how much we need Jesus as people and as mothers is an invaluable lesson for them. Oh, mama, let us be humble. Being a mother is honorable and full of responsibilities, but it should not become our idol. Rather, mothering with His guidance is what serves our loving God, the only One worthy of our worship.

Alyssa is in her 30s, with four young to school-age children. She shares: *What am I telling my children if I tend to my house over spending time with God? I think it's great for our kids to learn that they aren't perfect, aren't expected to be, and that they should put God first, too.*

Annette is in her 40s, with one adult child. She shares: *Knowing you get your peace from God and NOT from your children's behaviors is a huge and beautiful place to be.*

There are three great points here. If we were to ask our children what the most important thing to us is, they hopefully would answer God, Jesus, etc. It definitely shouldn't be them (since before them, it should also be our spouse), and it should absolutely not be keeping the house clean. Trust me, though, I fully understand the magnetic pull that sometimes seems to exist between my hands and any given mess at any given time of day! Then, if our love for motherhood and our children becomes our primary focus of energy, time, and yes even worship, what are we modeling for them? It's twofold. First, it's almost as if we're holding them to a perfection that only God can meet. And therefore, secondly, if they're number one, God is not.

I included the final contribution this week because I just love it so much. It can take intentionality and work to make our lives and our peace not revolve around our children. Everything we need, God provides – peace included! **(See: WEEK FORTY-SEVEN: Christ's Peace in Our Mama Hearts.)** Our children are absolute blessings, but if we treat them as idols, we could start to indirectly communicate unreasonable expectations from them, things that only God can and does provide for us. Mama, let's only idolize, worship, and find our value in God, as we share Him with our children.

Bible Verse

"Set your minds on things that are above, not on things that are on earth" (Colossians 3:2 ESV).

Prayer

Lord, help us live for You rather than for motherhood or our children. Help us remember that we have value because You say we do, not because we are a mother. Help us teach and model for our children to prioritize You, with the love we have for You and for them. Help us make more space for You in our motherhood journey, Lord. Help us to focus on serving You as we mother with Your guidance. Lord, please grow our personal friendship with You! Help us treat You as our best friend so our kids follow our example. Help us model Christianity well for our kids, Lord. Thank You. We love You. Amen.

Reflective Questions

1. Can you think of a time or a season when you idolized motherhood or your children? Said another way, have you ever found more value in being a mother than being a child of God? Meditate and pray about this.

2. What would your children say is the most important thing or person to you? Pray and ask God to align your heart to desire Him more than anything and anyone.

3. Take note to see if/when you might be seeking peace or something similar from your children. Notice too, if you are trying to fulfill any Godly characteristic for them. Ask God to take up all the space in your and your children's souls with His peace and also the value we hold, in Him.

Week Thirty-Eight

Overwhelm in Motherhood

I remember thinking I felt "overwhelmed" before I had kids. Ha! Relationships, my wellness business, personal goals, etc. There are so many variables to life, with or without kids! We know Jesus tells us that life will be challenging, likely even more so for Christians, but that He will always be with us, guiding and supporting us in whatever worldly things come our way. *Thank You, God, that You have overcome the world!*

Because of my background and experience in wellness, I can't help but devote a week to taking care of ourselves. **(See: WEEK FORTY-NINE: Caring for Yourself when You Become a Mother.)** But, the best way to tame overwhelm of any kind is through prayer, connection, and a true relationship with Jesus Christ, and also other believers.

As mothers, we're not only responsible for taking care of ourselves, but we also SHARE in the responsibility of taking care of our children! Thank God for God! Praying to God is our way out of overwhelm, mama. This said, even prayerful people can find themselves feeling overwhelmed. It is okay to have emotional reactions to things life throws our way! God

Her Prayer for Peace

gave us (and our kids) various emotions. But we also need to be in prayer to help us move away from overwhelm before it takes us down and out. **(See: WEEK THIRTY-TWO: Extreme Anxiety in Motherhood.)**

Gina is in her 30s, with four young to school-age children. She shares: *I recall the beginning of my motherhood journey being filled with many extremes. I was overwhelmed with joy, love, and fulfillment, along with anxiety, fear, and even anger. I was constantly serving. I would always run to the Lord in prayer and begrudgingly tell Him about how much this hurt and that this was all too much. I remember one day, in particular, having a breakdown in front of the crucifix and asking the Lord how He could expect me to do this. He gently reassured me, "You can do it because I have done it first. I will do it with you."*

Kari is in her 60s, with three adult children. She shares: *As a new parent, the responsibility of caring for this new little human and the desire to protect him or her from all the bad things out there can be overwhelming. Trust that God loves your child even more than you do and that He is watching over them. You may be limited in what you can do, but God is omnipotent and omnipresent.*

> YOU MAY BE LIMITED IN WHAT YOU CAN DO, BUT GOD IS *omnipotent* AND OMNIPRESENT.

While the beginning of motherhood brings its own type of overwhelm, I think this mama's words ring true for the beginning of any new and different stage of motherhood, too. As our kids grow and change, new and different circumstances come into our families and into our lives. We may start to experience the familiar emotions and the sense of being overwhelmed. This is when we must turn to Him, mama. We must humble ourselves before the Lord and ask Him to help us serve our family. We are limited in how we can serve and support our children, but God is not. We are limited by our emotions, but God is not!

Dianne is in her 40s, with three school-age children. She shares: *When worry arrived and overwhelmed me, that was the Holy Spirit's reminder to pray. This is where Jesus met me. So, instead of being constantly overwhelmed, I felt God offer peace to my mind, reassurance to my heart, and wisdom on our next best steps. It was like Jesus was our guide more than me and that our steps ahead would be accompanied by the One Who offers us wisdom when we ask. And He promises to do that each day forward, too, not just in the overwhelming seasons.*

Karissa is in her 30s, with two school-age children. She shares: *Pray when things get overwhelming. Look around you for resources that resonate with you and realize how supported you really are. Also, please be kind to yourself.*

Brianna is in her 30s, with one young child (and one on the way). She shares: *Stay in the Word. Always seek God. When you feel too busy or overwhelmed to find the words, remember that God knows your every thought and feeling, and the Holy Spirit intercedes for you.*

I love this: When worry and overwhelm arrive, we can train ourselves to hear the Holy Spirit telling us to pray. Talk about a habit to form! When you feel worried: pray. When you feel overwhelmed: pray. Our God is wise and trustworthy. I pray we allow Him to guide us, especially when we're overwhelmed in motherhood. Times of being overwhelmed are great times for breath prayers, too. **(See: WEEK SIX: Postpartum/ The Fourth Trimester.)** God also gives us people in our lives to help and support us. While God always hears our prayers, sometimes looking into another believer's eyes, holding their hands, or hugging each other can be such a blessing! Christian mom friends are a blessing from God! And, God knows our hearts. When the prayers just won't come out or the overwhelm makes us feel low on energy or like we want to isolate, God knows the longings of our hearts. The Holy Spirit can intercede for us! Then, when the overwhelm starts to dissipate, we must praise God for helping us even when–especially when–it was too hard to ask.

My own share: *I'm so grateful for The MomCo. I remember crying to my small group one night, just confessing how overwhelmed with worry and fear I was. I asked them to please pray for me. Prayer works.*

Prayer indeed works, and community prayer is an absolute gift from God. Those mamas and their prayers to our awesome God changed motherhood for me. I am so grateful to be out of my year-plus-long season of feeling completely overwhelmed by motherhood. Sometimes, we pray. Sometimes, our friends pray for us. And sometimes, the Holy Spirit works a miracle in our minds and in our hearts. Overwhelm in motherhood is natural. But just like our kids come to us with their big feelings, we can go to God with ours. Or, God just might come to us!

I've learned so much from our contributing mamas. I hope you have, too! When motherhood is overwhelming, may we try to rely on God to care for us, and do so in front of our kids. When we model Christian behaviors, our kids have the opportunity to do the same. I can't wait for the day when I just barely hear our kids say a breath prayer in the middle of being overwhelmed!

Bible Verse

"From the end of the earth I will cry unto thee, when my heart is overwhelmed: lead me to the rock that is higher than I" (Psalm 61:2 KJV).

Prayer

Lord, we cannot reach the rock of freedom without Your help. When we feel overwhelmed, help us automatically pray for Your peace. Holy Spirit, calm us from within when overwhelm tempts our hearts. Lord, we know the enemy wants us to feel overwhelmed and separated from You. Bring us back, every time, with trust in You and Your care, Lord. Thank You, Jesus, for placing Christian mamas in our lives so we can learn and grow in our relationship with You and one another. Help our kids see You as the number one way we handle overwhelm, especially in motherhood. Help us model this for our kids, too, Lord. We love You. Amen.

Reflective Questions

1. How do you currently handle overwhelm? Is there a set of circumstances in motherhood that usually creates a sense of overwhelm in your heart? With new awareness, ask God to meet you there now and every time after.

2. Mama, do you believe you have emotional limits? Do you believe our God has limitless power? Ask God to fill your soul with this truth. Ask Him to help you rely more on Him, especially when you need extra care.

3. I can't help myself: Consider your closest relationships. Do you have at least one Christian mom friend? Pray about this. Ask God to lead you and your friendships. Also, be the Christian mom friend who, instead of saying, "You've got this!" says, "He's got this!" His peace and care have you in the middle of overwhelm!

Avoiding Mom Guilt as a Working Mom

It's currently the day after Christmas. Happy birthday, Jesus! After a few days off, I'm trying to reorient myself and my family. My husband is back at work, and my kids are overtired and overstimulated after spending time with their cousins at my parent's house. They're still on Christmas break for another week, and I've got several weeks/topics to write before I hand my manuscript off to my editor in just three weeks' time. I've done my personal devotionals for my soul. I've had a protein bar for my mind and body, and just as I sit down in my writing chair, I hear a bang and a cry from one of my children. They're downstairs with one of our favorite sitters. I listen as our sitter addresses whatever happened to whichever child. And then, I close the door. But before I go back to my writing chair (verifying that my phone volume is turned on), I turn on a fan to drown out the sounds of my darling children so I can focus on writing. Oh, oh, here it comes, there it is… And the *mom guilt* smothers me.

And so, I pray, *Lord, please keep my kids happy and safe with our sitter downstairs. Help me peacefully focus on our devotional for the next 80 minutes that I have childcare. Thank You for my children, Lord. As I pay someone (wonderful!) to watch them, remind me of all the ways You help me show them love when I'm not working. Remind me that You've put this devotional on my heart, Lord. Help me complete this work without guilt that I should be doing anything else, even playing with my kids. Calm my mama heart, Lord. Focus my mind to do the work You've given me to complete right now. And Lord, after their nap, please give us a wonderful evening together as a family! Thank You for my husband, Hope, John, my wellness business, and this devotional, Lord. Each is a blessing from You. May this devotional bring You glory!*

This is a big topic, so there's a lot to say this week. I believe the Lord gave me my passions and gifts to serve others while honoring and glorifying Him. But He also gave me my sweet family. My kids need me, and it's a blessing to be needed by them! So where do our passions/our work fit among our family life? Sometimes, when I'm working, I miss my kids. And sometimes, when I'm with my kids, I think about a wellness client or the devotional topic I'll write next. When our work takes us away from our families, mom guilt can surface and even smother us. This week, we'll talk about really being intentional and present when we're with our children, when we're working our jobs, and therein relying on God to help us to be present and grateful in each role we play, at any given time.

Abbie Halberstadt has a chapter in her book, *M Is for Mama*,[22] where she talks about mom guilt versus Holy Spirit conviction. When we're working for our family's livelihood, serving others, and especially when we're glorifying God, mom guilt can be a way the enemy tries to distract us. When we're working, but we've made it more about us than about others; if our kids are suffering, that may be the Holy Spirit convicting our hearts.

Before we hear how God supports working mamas, I've got one final thought: Since we were all uniquely created, each family is also unique. What works for one mama and/or family may not work for another. Remember our week about comparison? **(See: WEEK FIFTEEN: Comparison: The Thief of Joy (Plus Judgement and Envy).)** I pray these examples create space for you to be prayerfully mindful of your own personal and family goals, and that you're also encouraged to develop prayerful habits about how you personally spend your time and resources as a mama.

Dianne is in her 40s, with three school-age children. She shares: *The three littles that I had dreamt of since I was a little girl were now a reality. It also meant three young kids who needed my attention, energy, and efforts while I worked full-time and did all the other "life" things like feeding people, pumping and measuring milk, and planning birthday parties and Christmas gifts. Ages four, two, and newborn were a test all by itself. I loved it and didn't at the same time. God met me not once but every single time I needed Him.*

My takeaway from this share is that it's okay not to always love every aspect of motherhood. After all, we had passions and responsibilities before our children were born! And then, we were blessed to become mothers. While I pray we take the efforts of motherhood seriously and honorably (with the help of God), I also pray we trust our time and energy (inside and outside of our homes) to our Creator God, Who meets us every single time we need Him.

> IT'S OKAY NOT TO ALWAYS *love* EVERY ASPECT OF MOTHERHOOD.

Julie is in her 60s, with four adult children. She shares: *At this point in my life, it is easy to see that God has always had a long-term plan, and I am only a part of His workings in the life of each of my children.*

Our main sitter is a sweet Christian girl. Her stepmom is a good friend of mine! We go on double dates with her dad and her stepmom. Their family and our family go to the same church. She prays with my kids before she serves them snacks or meals and before she puts them down to sleep. Time spent with our sitter is a blessing for my kids! Inviting other people into our kids' lives can initially feel scary, but through prayer, we can trust God to guide us in choosing great, temporary caregivers and teachers. The school my kids attend several hours a week is another example of people I believe are meant to be in my children's lives. I prayed about where to send them to school. When I was just 20 weeks pregnant, a mama who contributed to this devotional shared about where they sent their four children to school. What a blessing to be at the same school as this devout, God-loving family! This mama also reminds us that we need the support of others in our life. While each family's needs are a little different, it's important to recognize that God blesses our children with people other than us in their lives! *I am only a part of His workings in the life of each of my children.*

Carmie is in her 70s, with three adult children. She shares about being a stay-at-home-mom: *Sometimes I just sit and listen; God speaks to those of us who have quiet time. It's hard to find that quiet time; you have to work really hard at it. Even schedule it like you do other appointments and make it a top priority in your life.*

Here's a mama who worked hard to make time for God among the stresses and responsibilities of motherhood. By doing so, she was able to hear His voice for herself and her family. When we make Him, and spending time with Him, a priority, our other responsibilities, including paying jobs and also motherhood, fall into place. There are a million ways to spend our time. Daily prayer and/or quiet time with God is a guilt-free way, every time!

Alyssa is in her 30s, with four young to school-age children. She shares about being a working mama: *Early motherhood was just a season in my life where I learned that staying home and doing that darn laundry was providing for our family's best interests. I didn't like it. Work was the best. When COVID hit, I had teenagers coming over so that I could work in my bedroom. If I had an afternoon to work in silence, I felt like I should feel "lucky." All in all, I was home with our four children for 16 weeks of 2020. That taught me that God has our back, even in the face of major risk. It made me confident that, once again, we could do with "nothing" as far as net income was concerned as He provided, and we remained faithful.*

This mama loves her children. She also loves her work. But most of all, she loves Jesus. And with the love and trust of Jesus in her heart, she's more likely to feel content with how she spends her time between her children and her business. No one is perfect. She may experience mom guilt or even Holy Spirit conviction from time to time. But when Jesus is the priority of our lives, we know we can always seek and trust in His perfect peace and balance with our time – as working moms or stay-at-home-moms.

Valerie is in her 40s, with two adult children. She shares: *I was particular about not wanting my kids to spend more of their waking time with someone else other than me (or my husband, but he was only home half the time because of his job). I worked on arranging my college schedule (and internships/part-time jobs) so that it was only three days a week, and the other four were for my kids. If I could not do something in the three days a week, they were in daycare; then I didn't do it. If I was invited to an adult-only BBQ on the days my kids were home with me, we would not attend. It even led to me turning down a 40-hour-a-week internship because I knew, ultimately, those minimum standards were not what I wanted. Having those standards was harder, but it gave me a starting point of ensuring my minimum standards (priorities) were met and everything else could factor in after that! God kept me engaged at the level I could handle!*

And that's really it: God knows us and our families so well that when we rely on Him, He perfectly balances motherhood and our other responsibilities for us and our unique family. When we're unsure how we should spend our time and energy, He's there for the asking! For the mama who isn't in school or who doesn't work outside of motherhood, you have the same leading responsibilities as moms who work outside the home, as well. That is, to make time for God personally and to raise your children for Jesus, with Jesus. Whether that's done with one person's help for a couple of hours a week or several people's help several days a week, when we ask and trust in God, He provides a plan for us. And nowhere in that plan does it include mom guilt (or shame). So Enemy, be quiet!

Bible Verse

"…let us draw near to God with a sincere heart and with the full assurance that faith brings, having our hearts sprinkled to cleanse us from a guilty conscience and having our bodies washed with pure water" (Hebrews 10:22 NIV).

Prayer

Lord, thank You for helping us release our mom guilt. You bore all guilt on the cross, once and for all, thank You! Help us remember that Your grace is sufficient, and Your power is made perfect in our weaknesses. Help us make You our driving force in, and our reason for, how we spend our time. Guide us and give us peace in this, Lord. Help us pray for other families instead of comparing ourselves to them. Lord, hear our hearts and help us serve You and others (including our families) well and within Your perfect will for our lives. Thank You for each way we get to glorify You! Help us to be present when we're with our children, Lord. Lastly, Lord, if You are trying to reach us with Holy Spirit conviction, I pray You are heard loudly and clearly. If our children are suffering because of how we're spending our time, change our hearts and schedules swiftly, Lord. We trust You. We love You. Amen.

Reflective Questions

1. Prayerfully ask God about any mom guilt you may experience, especially consistently-felt mom guilt.

2. What's your biggest takeaway from this week? Include God in this thought process.

3. In prayer, ask God about any Holy Spirit convictions He may have for you regarding how you spend your family time.

Reflection; Miracles in Motherhood (Vol. IV)

Can you believe we've been together for almost a year now? Go YOU and go GOD! We've covered a variety of topics in the past nine weeks, and my hope continues to be that you've been in prayer, in action, and in rest with the Lord. God is on the move in our hearts and in our households, mama! He's helping us learn from the advice of other Christian mamas. He's worthy of our praise and gratitude in motherhood. He helps us avoid mom guilt and pray about Holy Spirit conviction.

Take some time to reflect on the last nine weeks:
1. How has God's love and peace for you changed you and impacted your family since you started this devotional, specifically in the last nine weeks (weeks 31-39)?
2. What have been your three to five biggest takeaways in the last nine weeks (weeks 31-39)?
3. Is there a week you'd like to re-read this week?

4. Is there a mama you thought of in weeks 32, 38, or 39 but you forgot to pray for or reach out to her? Now is your opportunity! Don't let this week go by without praying for her or connecting with her.
5. Do you find yourself seeking, trusting, and relying on God for peace, wisdom, and guidance in motherhood, even 5-10% more than you did nine weeks ago?

Let's pray. *Lord, we are so thankful that You are a God Who cares for us and our children. We're also thankful for other Christian mamas who've shared things with us that draw us closer to You, our husbands, and our children. Help us see the correlation between relying on You and motherhood being "easier." Help us find things to be grateful for in motherhood and in our children, even in the struggle. Lord, please deepen our prayer life and relationship with You. We know when we're deeply connected to You, there will be less anxiety and overwhelm in our households and less mom guilt in our hearts. Thank You for blessing us as mothers. We love You. Amen.*

This week, I'll share a miracle of God – from Debi, a mama in her 60s, with three adult children. She shares: *When my daughter was away at college, there was a tornado over a mile wide heading for her dorm. She said to me, "Mom, I'm scared. They are saying nothing above ground will survive this tornado." We prayed and lost connection shortly after. I had a peace I knew from learning to trust God in previous crises that even if the tornado hit, if it wasn't her time, God would protect her somehow. And He did. The tornado made a drastic turn two blocks before it hit her dorm.*

To have a peace after praying for your child's life to be spared, and then having communication cut off, is an incredible example of His faithful peace. This mama trusted her child to God and His perfect plans for her life. And in return, God gave her the peace she prayed for in a time of critical waiting. **(See: WEEK FORTY-SEVEN: Christ's Peace in Our Mama Hearts.)** As Christians, at times like these, we praise God for His care and His grace. We praise Him for the health and safety of our kids. And we're reminded how precious their lives really are. Our God is a loving God! This mama is faithful!

I've learned so much about how the heart of God supports mamas who love and trust Him. I hope you have, too. My biggest takeaway so far is that motherhood is "easier" when we include God. When we trust and rely on Him to guide us, He fills us with His grace and peace. God is always extending His grace with open arms to protect our kids (and our mama hearts) according to His perfect will.

MOTHERHOOD IS *"easier"* WHEN WE INCLUDE GOD.

I hope this reflection week has blessed you. Some of the topics in this devotional are hard. Some we can relate to more than others. A week where we pause to review and reflect can be really helpful. And hearing a story about the gift of God's incredible grace reminds us how great our God truly is! It's also a reminder to ask God to protect our families, to be weak and vulnerable, pleading for God to keep our children healthy and safe. In place of fear for our children's safety, we can ask the Lord to give us His peace. If tragedy happens, we can still pray to the God Who loves us.

This week's Bible verse sums this up well, along with many of the topics we've read about so far:

"Let the peace of Christ rule in your hearts, since as members of one body you were called to peace. And be thankful" (Colossians 3:15 NIV).

Jesus is a Mama's (and a Kiddo's) Best Friend

Honestly, it's never occurred to me before to think of Jesus as my best friend. Maybe I'm alone in this! But when I think about it, I do usually treat Him that way! I trust Him with all of my secrets, I call on Him when I'm in need (though I'm working on doing this before I call on anyone else!), and I absolutely know He's always there for me. But I don't remember teachings at church or in my childhood home, where Jesus was referred to as my best friend. My heart would sing if I heard my kids call Jesus their best friend, so I'm thankful these mamas have shared with us about their personal relationship, their best friendship, with Jesus.

Taking this a step further, what kind of friend am I to Jesus in return? I'm pretty sure Jesus doesn't have any secrets. Ha! But when I hear Him whisper for me to do something in His holy name, do I always listen? Do I actually listen when Jesus calls on me? Am I always there for the person on earth who represents Jesus... the hungry, thirsty, stranger, naked, sick, and imprisoned (Matthew 25:31-46)? I know you have a whole household to care for, mama, so I won't go into the friend we are to Jesus (and "the least of these") much more, but it's thought-provoking, isn't it? It's certainly something about which I'm going to pray! Maybe you, too? Alright, let's hear from our wise mamas this week and their best friendships with Jesus.

Cassandra is in her 50s, with six school-age to adult children. She shares: *Your relationship with Christ becomes even more significant as you begin your journey as a mom. Learn how to turn to Him for everything, not just the critical or challenging moments. Jesus is truly your best friend!*

Jesus, You are my best friend! Jesus, thank You for being my best friend! How does it feel to say this to Him, mama? We'll dive a little deeper with this in our reflective questions, but try it yourself. I also agree that our best friendship with Jesus becomes even more significant when we became mothers. We've heard how it takes a village to raise children, but I recently heard how it takes a church! And Christian mom friends are so important, but Jesus is better than any friend and support system we will ever have here on earth! I'm really starting to embrace this now. I hope you are, too. Jesus is always there for us, mama!

Angela is in her 40s, with two school-age children. She shares: *Jesus is my ever-partner.*

"Partner" describes a solid and meaningful relationship. My husband is both my earthly partner and my earthly best friend! However, we have a spiritual, all-knowing best friend and partner Who loves us and our kids more than we could ever love, and He is *Jesus. You are my best friend! Thank You!*

Jill S. is in her 60s, with three adult children. She shares: *Our kids are not our best friends, nor are we theirs... Jesus is.*

Here's our behavior modeling again. When our kids see that Jesus is our best friend, they know He can be their best friend, too. When we have our quiet time, pray before meals, or are in the thick of craziness with breath prayers, we can simply add "best friend" when we reference Jesus. "Mama's going to have some quiet prayer time with my best friend, Jesus." "Jesus, our best friend, thank You for this food, etc." "Jesus, my best friend, give me patience." I'm going to start this today at dinner! Instead, if we act like our kids are our best friends, or vice-versa, that puts a lot of unnecessary, and actually impossible, pressure on them and us. It can also get in the way of discipline, which is part of our jobs as mothers raising tiny, then not so tiny, humans. **(See: WEEK FORTY-FOUR: Disciplining Our Children with the Love of Jesus.)**

I think my biggest takeaway from this week is the reminder that Jesus isn't only our Savior, but we are also in an actual, loving relationship with each other. He is our best friend. Lovingly labeling our relationship in this special way makes me feel closer and more connected to Jesus! It makes me feel even more cared for, and like I want to be as good of a friend right back to Jesus as is humanly possible. I hope you feel a deeper connection between you and Jesus after this week, too!

> JESUS ISN'T ONLY OUR SAVIOR, BUT WE ARE ALSO IN AN ACTUAL, LOVING RELATIONSHIP WITH EACH OTHER. HE IS OUR *best friend*.

Bible Verse

"Greater love has no one than this, that someone lay down his life for his friends" (John 15:13 ESV).

Prayer

Jesus, we know You died for us. Therefore, the Bible says that You are our greatest friend. Help us to see You as our best friend, Jesus! Help us treat our friendship and partnership with You as the most important one we will ever have. Thank You for being our best friend, especially in motherhood, Jesus! Help us experience You as our best friend in our lives and in our homes. Help us model our best friendship with You for our own benefit and for the benefit of our children. May You be their best friend, too! Jesus, help us also treat others as You'd like us to treat them. May "the least of these" (Matthew 25:40), be blessed by You, through us. Thank You, Best Friend! We love You, Amen.

Reflective Questions

1. How does it feel to call Jesus your best friend? How does this loving label impact how your relationship with Jesus feels in your heart?

2. Prayerfully consider your relationship with your kids. Do you sometimes try to be their best friend? Pray about this. Ask God to highlight times you choose anyone, especially your children, to be your best friend over Jesus.

3. Consider ways you can show your kids that Jesus is your best friend. Ask Him to guide you as you strengthen this important friendship by calling it out and growing to further rely on your best friend, Jesus.

Trials and Struggles in Motherhood Can Grow Our Faith

Trials and struggles of any kind create an opportunity to grow our faith. Before we got engaged, I struggled with how long it took my husband to propose. (It really wasn't that long, but it felt long to me!) I prayed and tried hard to trust God and His plan for my life. When Ryan proposed, I was so grateful, and my faith in Christ grew.

Similarly, I struggled and then really suffered with how long it took to conceive (again, many people try longer than we had to, but it felt like the absolute longest time to me). But God provided (times two!) in His perfect timing, even when all I could do was sing His praises. And so, my faith grew again!

In fact, while we were trying to conceive, I tried to cling to my previous experience of struggling in the waiting for my husband to propose. I tried to remember how thankful to God I was when my prayers were finally answered. My struggles in early motherhood and still even now have grown my faith, too (though, thankfully, my joys in motherhood are starting to outweigh my struggles). When I confessed to my fellow MomCo mamas that I was experiencing trials in motherhood, and when I laid my burdens of motherhood at the Lord's feet, the difference in how I felt that next morning, with His incredible peace in my mama heart, drastically grew my faith in Jesus!

When life is hard, we have an opportunity to trust God. With that trust, God provides in His perfect way and perfect timing, and in doing so, our faith in Him can grow. Whether we're struggling or really suffering in a time of waiting, or with a serious issue or concern in our life, or if the daily trials of motherhood are overwhelming us, no matter the outcome of our prayers, God is able to grow our faith in Him when we continue to pray and continue to trust in Him. No matter the outcome, even when it's hard, we must remember that God works all things for good (Romans 8:28). And, while I've shared some answers to some really big prayers in my life, there is one big personal prayer I've been praying for almost ten years. While I wait, I trust the Lord is working all things for good. Because that is Who He is. He is the God of hope; Jesus is the Prince of Peace!

Angela is in her 40s, with two school-age children. She shares: *Christ's peace, wisdom, and guidance show up for me and my family hour-by-hour throughout the day. My boys are sweet, smart, strong, and highly lovable humans who drive me absolutely bananas. As they grow into the men that Jesus wants them to be, the daily trials and tribulations – growing pains of their beautiful minds and bodies, often reveal themselves in temper tantrums, obstinance, and even frustrating fits of rage. Over these short (though often feeling like an eternity) years of my motherhood, I have been working harder than ever before on listening for Jesus' soft and tender guidance during otherwise royally loud and furious times in our home and hearts. This continues to be a monumental challenge for me. Thank God that Jesus is persistent! When I am finally able to calm down and settle my mind, mouth, and heart, I feel His peace, wisdom, and guidance. It is only then that I can help steer my boys through rougher waters of life and teach them to also stop, breathe, and listen to the Lord. For at that time, all felt more reasonable, goals were more attainable, and a larger space for peace and love was opened.*

Jesus is persistent, indeed! No matter the struggle, big or small, our patient God is always waiting for us to seek Him, so He can provide for us in His perfect way and in His perfect timing, so He can hopefully and eventually grow our faith in Him.

Jan is in her 70s, with three adult children. She shares: *Many trials have come my way in life, but through them, my faith stays constant in prayer. My own dear mother set such a strong example. I witnessed her living her life in faith, prayer, and study, showing much strength. Such a blessing! Whether it's your own mother or another woman, seek and be that example of shining faith. A trial that lasts years is exhausting! We have a child with an affliction, which meant symptoms were exhibited without warning. It was important to conduct life normally as a family. Therefore, we continued to go to church, eat out in restaurants, teach valuable manners, and, of course, regularly needed shopping trips. I remember strangers staring and giving me unwanted advice. Our pediatrician gave her diagnosis with suggested practices, but those appointments were not what carried me through those difficult experiences. It was during these times that brought me the revelation that this child was not "mine" but a gift from God. God entrusted me to be her advocate while she grew. The more observers freaked out, the more Jesus guided me toward wisdom and peace.*

This mama touches on two great points. When we have someone after whom to model our behaviors, in this case, we learn to continuously pray when trials come our way. If our kids see this over and over, they are more likely to pray in times of need, too. Secondly, this mama did not feel better about her child's trial because of a medical professional's guidance; but rather, because of how God empowered her with His truth, wisdom, and peace. No doubt, her faith in God expanded as a result of His supportive faithfulness.

Pam is in her 50s, with five school-age to adult children. She shares: *Getting back to your faith and praying keeps you sane along with everything else. It helps give you the strength to deal with hard things.* YES!

Billie is in her 60s, with four adult children. She shares: *This season also brought my daughter so much closer to God and helped to build her faith.*

Do you remember the mama who trusted God with her daughter's drug addiction? **(See: WEEK FOUR: When We Faithfully Obey God, He Can Work against Sin and Evil in Our Families.)** When her daughter gave her struggle with addiction to the Lord, He rewarded her in ways beyond motherly prayers. And so, both of their faiths in God grew!

Emma is in her 30s, with two young (earthside) children. She shares: *Through prayer and reflection, I remembered that, although suffering is a mystery, it is when we are at our weakest that we are more likely to run to God and cling to Him. Through suffering, He gives us an opportunity to draw closer to Him.* Maybe you recall, this is the mama who shared about the loss of her son at 17 weeks gestation. **(See: WEEK THREE: Losing a Baby/Child – Miscarriage, Stillbirth, and the Loss of Child.)** A monumental blessing of this tragedy and subsequent suffering is that this mama will always have this prayerful experience upon which to reflect. No matter the trials she goes through, in life and in motherhood, I know this mama will always remember how God met her in her great suffering and how He grew her faith in Him, even then.

Bible Verse

"Rejoice in hope, be patient in tribulation, be constant in prayer" (Romans 12:12 ESV).

Prayer

Lord, we don't like to struggle or to see our children struggle. Help us remember that trials produce perseverance and are also opportunities to grow in our faith in You. Help us cling to Your hope and peace. Help us be patient in times of waiting and constantly pray to You when we are suffering from (long) trials in life and motherhood. May our automatic response to struggles and suffering be You, Lord. Help us trust You more. Help us lean on You more. Help us get out of Your way so You can work in and with us. Thank You for every blessing, Lord. Remind us of Who You are, our God, Who works all things for good (Romans 8:28), even when we get an outcome that doesn't make sense to us. We love You. Amen.

Reflective Questions

1. Can you think of a time when you experienced trials or struggles in life or motherhood, and when you leaned on God, your faith in Him grew? Thank God and ask Him to help you remember that experience every time you and your family experience trials.

2. Prayerfully ask God to help you identify any barriers you may have in seeking Him in times of suffering. Ask God to help create an automatic prayer response in you when you have trials in motherhood.

3. Write down a list of ten blessings in your life. As you recall the circumstances of each blessing, acknowledge any hard times that came before God blessed you. Try to recall how grateful you were and also the status of your faith life before, during, and after each of these ten blessings.

Helping Our Children in Their Faith and Prayer Life

This week, we will learn how to model our faith and prayer life in front of our children. We'll hear about certain Scriptures, daily practices, ways to act like Jesus in the face of conflict, and how to pray for and serve others with our kids. We'll also hear about how it isn't solely our responsibility to help our children in their faith and prayer lives. Don't forget to include and rely on God, mama! We'll start and end this week with mamas of older children who share the importance of supporting our younger children in their personal relationship with Jesus.

Jill J. is in her 50s, with two adult children. She shares: *Trust me, before you know it, the "crazy" is gone, and your time to parent, teach, and mold your children is gone. As that is when you really do have to TRUST and have FAITH that you did your job as a mom! God trusts us to love, teach, and care for our kids while they are young so that when they do go off on their own, they do so with the faith, knowledge, and confidence we instilled in them.*

Since God trusts us with our (His) children, we can trust Him to guide us in raising prayerful children, especially when that's our own prayer.

Angela is in her 40s, with two school-age children. She shares: *I am teaching my children to love and obey the Ten Commandments and that timeless message that is repeated over and over in the Bible: "Love one another as I have loved you" (John 15:12), and "As you wish others would do to you, do so to them" (Luke 6:31). My sons and I pray for peace and love to enter the hearts and minds of bullies who are inevitably found in so many aspects of daily life. When we pray for those who torment us, rather than retaliate, the presence of Jesus in prayer turns our anger, frustration, and pain into compassion. It is miraculous. It is only then that I can help steer my boys through rougher waters of life and teach them to also stop, breathe, and listen to the Lord.*

Megan is in her 50s, with four young adult children. She shares: *When my kids come to me with a problem, I hold back for a minute to let them work things out before I jump in with my own opinion or perceived wisdom. It's hard to see my kids in emotional pain or confusion, but the Holy Spirit reminds me that this is part of their own growth process. If I offer a solution too quickly, I may be aborting the growth, resilience, and wisdom God wants them to discover for themselves! As they get older, Jesus reminds me to listen and ask as many questions as possible to help guide them in their own self-discovery. I also invite them to pray about things so they can experience God's voice and answers for themselves.*

Alyssa is in her 30s, with four young, school-age children. She shares: *No one is perfect. The older I get as a mom, the more I realize that so many things I care about don't matter. What am I telling my children if I tend to my house over spending time with God? I think it's great for our kids to learn that they aren't perfect, aren't expected to be, and that they should put God first. When my children speak the truth about God, they can ask me huge questions for little people. They can tell me, "Mom, I don't want to go to Heaven because I could be eaten by a whale (Jonah)," and we can have those conversations. We are able to build little lovers of Christ. Will they consume themselves with love the way Christ did for us? Not if we aren't boasting in the Holy Spirit when the Lord is good to us! Not if we don't turn to Christ in our suffering to show them to turn in, too! These little eyes and ears take it all in. I need these four little people to pray the Lord's prayer from the bottom of their hearts. They need to ask us what temptation is. They need to watch cartoons, attend VBS, and go to Mass every Sunday. Christ is home. We can't pretend that Jesus is only at Mass and go on with our week, and neither can they. We have an enormous job to do. He will give us sufficient graces to accomplish His will. It's time to go out in our community, serve the poor, serve our church, and host or attend Bible study as a family.*

Julie is in her 60s, with four adult children. She shares: *You pray a lot, you encourage, and you do your very best to have your kids face everything with their relationship with God and good character as priorities.*

Carmie is in her 70s, with three adult children. She shares: *There are so many obstacles, especially today, that get in the way of our faith life. I see how busy my children and grandchildren are. With little time to deepen their faith because of so many things that are not really that important. I just keep praying, praying, praying. That's the only thing you can do; put it all in Jesus' hands because He will take care of everything. You just have to trust in Him. When my youngest one was at home, in the mornings before he would go to school, we would do Bible study together. There was a children's program at that time that I could just ask him questions and teach from. That was a very blessed time for me. I was studying the Bible with him knowing that he was just soaking up that Scripture. I was very, very happy about that. Bible study fellowship was a lot of work, but I loved every minute of it, and my children learned so much from it.*

> WHEN WE TRUST IN HIM, HE PROVIDES A WAY... HIS *perfect* WAY.

When we trust in Him, He provides a way... His perfect way.

Debi is in her 60s, with three adult children. She shares: *Teach your kids it is more important to please God than to please you. You won't always be with them, and one day, friends or spouses will be a bigger influence than you, but God will always be with them.*

Annette is in her 40s, with one adult child. She shares: *Having your children see you spending time with the Lord is the one way to "Train up a child in the way he should go; even when he is old, he will not depart from it"* (Proverbs 22:6).

Beth is in her 60s, with three adult children. She shares: *All of them still remember as children coming out in their jammies, finding Mommy in the Word, and spending time with the Lord before our family day began.*

Modeling our prayer life is one of the most meaningful ways we can share the love of Jesus with our children.

Pam is in her 50s, with five school-age to adult children. She shares: *I lost my husband suddenly last year, and all five of my kids, from 18 years to 28, have shown grace, resilience, and faith in how they have coped with this tragic loss. In their moments of grief, they are finding ways to continue to honor their dad. I am a very proud mama. You feel like all the things we as parents have done along the way come together, so they get to evolve into people helping and connecting with others. I spent many years praying about this. It is so joyful for me to see this happen in a season of sadness for them.*

I'm so grateful to these mamas for sharing how they support the faith and prayer life of their kids. I'm going to start reading my Bible in front of my kids. They see my daily devotional all the time (*Make a Difference* by Ken Castor[23]), but oftentimes, I study the Bible on my phone. (Including the other daily devotional I love, The First 5 app by Lysa TerKeurst.[24]) Because I work on my phone and have a social life on my phone, etc., the Lord is encouraging me to read my actual Bible in front of my kids every day. With this, I pray their own faith and prayer life grows, so as they grow, they have a firm foundation of Jesus Christ on which to stand.

One thing I'll add is that we pray together before every snack and meal. We thank God for various people and things and ask Him to help keep us healthy and safe. We tell Jesus that we love Him! Oftentimes, my son will loudly clap and cheer when we're done praying! Sometimes, we even cheer, "Go, Jesus, go, Jesus, go, Jesus, go, Jesus!" And then my heart (and I bet Jesus', too) simply beams with love and gratitude for Jesus, my kids, and the love of Jesus. He is helping us foster His love within the hearts of our children. (See: *Raising Prayerful Kids: Fun & Easy Activities for Building Lifelong Habits of Prayer* by Stephanie Thurling & Sarah Holmstrom, referenced in **WEEK TWO: Raising Kids for Jesus**.)[25]

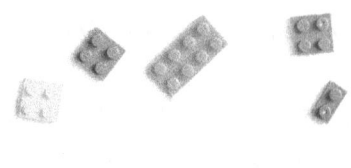

Bible Verse

"How can a young person stay on the path of purity? By living according to your word" (Psalm 119:9 NIV).

Prayer

Lord, please help us live according to Your Word, by getting into Your Word, so we can best model for our children. Help form our own consistent prayer life, Lord. Please help us teach our kids to act how Jesus would in times of conflict. Lord, help us remember to ask You for guidance as we teach our kids about You. Lord, help us to pray for our children. We are so grateful for You, Lord. Help this gratitude seep into our daily lives and so also into the lives of our children. Lord, we pray that our children know You well through us modeling and spending time together with You and them in prayer and study, as well as in serving others. Please soften the hearts of any children who've turned away from You, Lord. We pray they feel Your love for them every day. May our kids know You as their best friend! Thank You, Lord. We love You. Amen.

Reflective Questions

1. What is the Lord encouraging you to do to help support your child's or children's faith/prayer life right now? Spend some quiet time with God so you can hear His wisdom and guidance.

2. How can you and your family serve others in the name of Jesus? Make it happen, mama! (Be sure to teach your children about the example Jesus set first, by serving and caring for all humanity.)

3. Take some time this week to pray for each of your children and their faith/prayer life. Please also pray for at least three other families in the same way.

Week Forty-Four

Disciplining Our Children with the Love of Jesus

I'm not much of a yeller, but I have been called a "feisty Italian" once or twice! As we read this week's topic, mama, let's try to remember how imperfect we are and how we come closer to excellence (but we never reach perfection) only with God's help. That is to say, no mama gets it "right" all the time. While these mamas provide us with valuable insights this week, they don't always get it right, either. We will become unhappy with our children. We will yell! But with the wisdom the Lord has given these mamas, hopefully we will learn and start to specifically pray about how to discipline our children with the love of Jesus, too.

When I became a mom, I learned about something that's not necessarily Biblical, called "restoration." It's about making right or, "restoring" things with our kids when we haven't (re)acted with love and compassion, like Jesus. When I raise my voice or when I'm distracted and so not paying as much attention to my kids as I'd like to, or really anything that could cause mom guilt and especially Holy Spirit conviction, we can and should always restore things with our kids as soon as possible. **(See: WEEK THIRTY-NINE: Avoiding Mom Guilt as a Working Mom & WEEK FORTY-EIGHT: Sin and Spiritual Health in Motherhood.)**

For example, if I've raised my voice, making my daughter even more whiny, sad, mad, etc., once I realize I didn't handle that situation very well, I might say: "Hopey, Mama's sorry. I should not have raised my voice with you. Next time, I'll do my best to speak to you with more kindness. Can you please forgive me?" And then I give her a hug. Our kids need to see that we make mistakes, and that they have the ability to forgive us, too. Maybe there's more Biblical nature to restoration with our kids, after all! We could even pray right then and there with our kids, asking God to help us respond with more love, like Jesus. Now, let's hear how Jesus has guided these mamas in disciplining their children with the love of Jesus.

Janette is in her 30s, with three young to school-age children. She shares: *In each hard season of parenting, focus on extending grace and love to your child to show them a glimpse of their Heavenly Father. As they grow, use every hard moment with your children as an opportunity to turn their hearts and attention to the Lord. Use naughty moments to teach them about God's grace and point them to the work of Jesus on the cross instead of instructing behavior. Make sure they understand that we as parents aren't God but that we serve someone much higher because we, too, sin and need a Savior! Make your home a place where they can learn about Jesus, ask questions about Jesus, and, God willing, choose to follow Jesus themselves.*

Lord, thank You for the wisdom You've given this mama! I pray we all do this more for the benefit of both us and our children.

Christine is in her 30s, with three young to school-age children. She shares: *With my oldest, I make choices for him and our family that others may think are too strict but help him to thrive and be calm. I feel confident and peaceful with these decisions. The best thing we can do is show up for our children with love, just as Jesus would.*

Don't you love how our connection with God and Jesus, through the Holy Spirit, can provide us with confidence and peace? When we're unsure about how to mother and discipline our children, we can pray

> THE BEST THING WE CAN DO IS SHOW UP FOR OUR CHILDREN WITH *love*, JUST AS JESUS WOULD.

for clarity, wisdom, and guidance. The way and peace of Christ can fill us when we rely on Him to help us mother our children, as our Heavenly Father wants us to. And, Amen to loving our children with a Jesus-like love, especially when our sinful human nature might pull us in another direction.

Julie is in her 60s, with four adult children. She shares: *Encourage, encourage, encourage. Notice what they are doing right. Point it out when you see good effort, behavior, performance, achievements, etc. We all need and appreciate deserved praise. Give them the respect you expect from them. Demand respect in return. What you tolerate, you teach. If you put up with a disrespectful tone of voice or words toward you or anyone else, you are teaching them that it is okay. Set reasonable boundaries and enforce them. Follow through. Don't make a promise or threaten a consequence that you cannot or will not make happen. Don't trust your feelings. You may not like your child at every moment, but you can still choose to act in a loving way.*

There's a lot of goodness here! My favorite part of what she shared is that we should praise them when our kids behave well! This will likely make discipline (with love) more effective. I also love how we're to model respect for them by showing them respect first. Respect and love like Jesus! And I'm thankful for the reminder to not always trust my feelings! May we always restore with our kids after our less-than-desirable-(re)-actions. Likewise, we can pray for help (re)acting with love like Jesus, even when our child is doing unlikeable things.

Megan is in her 50s, with four young adult children. She shares: *I ultimately want them to learn and experience God's provision for themselves. While "let go and let God" is not realistic, there is a bit of truth hidden within this cliche. Over the years, I have found that nurture is important, but encouraging my kids to live into their God-given nature is the best thing I can do for them. Yes, we lean in, listen, and guide. These are our primary responsibilities as moms! But I would encourage all moms to relax a bit and let God guide them as she mothers her child. God created them, so He knows what's best. The more I release my need to "control" my kids, the more they realize they have the freedom to develop their own voice and can choose for themselves. This can be scary at times because the consequences of "bad choices" are great, but ultimately, they are amazing learning experiences. I pray that I will decrease and God will increase in their lives in order to lead them into their divine destiny – whatever that is!*

It takes a lot of emotional and physical effort to try to control our kids, likely especially as they get older. While there are specific, important, logistical things we can do as their mother, as the last mama shared, imagine if we allowed God to guide both us and our children with more of the day-to-day issues, especially conflicts with family. Disciplining and mothering our children with less effort and more of Christ's love and trust in Him will allow us to enjoy motherhood more. This will also be so much more helpful for our kids. Ask yourself, "In this situation, what would Jesus–not the imperfect, sinful me–do?"

Kacie is in her 30s, with three young to school-age children. She shares: *The most important thing you can do is share the love of Jesus with your children… Everything else can follow.*

Heather is in her 40s, with two school-age children. She shares: *Pray every single day that God gives you what you need to be the best mother to your children.*

Kari is in her 60s, with three adult children. She shares: *You may be limited in what you can do, but God is omnipotent and omnipresent.*

Mama, as we spend more time in prayer with our all-powerful God, we can better show the love of Jesus to our kids when they misbehave or sin. Getting into the Word teaches us more about Jesus, so we can better imitate His loving ways with our family.

Her Prayer for Peace

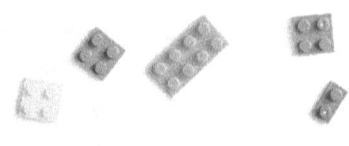

Bible Verse

"Fathers [Mothers!], do not provoke your children to anger, but bring them up in the discipline and instruction of the Lord" (Ephesians 6:4 ESV, emphasis added).

Prayer

Lord, we love our children so much. But our flesh is weak, and our tongues can be sharp, especially in times of conflict. Help us to strengthen our faith and trust in You and Your love, so we can be more loving examples for our children. Help us lead our children with Your example of perfect love. Help us rely on You more, Lord, especially in disciplining our children. We pray for Your peace when we're following You, especially in how we're disciplining our children. You know our children best! May we never forget that. Lord, help us make our home a place where, no matter their behavior, our children can learn about You, ask questions about You, and choose to follow You themselves. We love You. Amen.

Reflective Questions

1. In prayer, reflect on how you normally discipline your children. Without judgment, ask God how to discipline your children in a more loving, Jesus-like (and likely more effective) way.

2. Have you ever prayed for guidance on how to address a particular conflict with your child? Have you then experienced the peace of Christ as He guided you in His loving way? If yes, reflect on this, thanking God. If not, focus on your own prayer life this week while trusting God to help guide you in lovingly disciplining your children.

3. Have you heard of, and do you practice, restoration with your children? Try it out! Ask God to help you remember to restore with your children as soon as you (re)act differently than Jesus would. Bring Jesus and forgiveness into the conversation as well.

Week Forty-Five

How to "Know" when Your Family is Complete – Biologically or through Adoption

We are actually in the thick of this right now. As I've shared, we used science and medicine (and hope and prayer!) to help conceive Hope and John. Praise God for science and medicine! Now, we feel Christ's peace about trying the good old-fashioned way… At least, I think we do! It's also on our hearts to potentially adopt someday. With my background as a child protection advocacy volunteer (Guardian ad Litem/Court Appointed Special Advocate[26]), I know the need for adoptive families is great within child protective services, and otherwise. There are so many children in the world who need a good home!

So, how exactly do we know when our families are complete, if we should try for a biological child, or if a child should be adopted? I'm not going to go into the logistics of age, health, or finances here. But I will share some of the journey we're on right now and also some of my friend Megan's journey. Megan Nilsen is the amazing, God-honoring mama who wrote the book *A Beautiful Exchange – Responding to God's Invitation for More.*[27]

This book study is what provided the way for me to respond to God's invitation to write this devotional! Her story is amazing! I can't wait to share some of it with you.

First, when my kids were almost two years old, my husband and I told each other that if we ever felt strongly about wanting to try to add to our family, we'd be open and honest with each other. Mama, not one week later, my husband said he'd like to try for another child. I felt all the emotions. I was shocked (even though we'd just talked through this possibility), excited, and also terrified. Infertility can cause trauma. While we are very thankful for it, we feel strongly about not using science and medicine to grow our family again. And with a diagnosis of "unexplained infertility," only God knows if we could ever conceive a child naturally. Or maybe He'll bless us with a miracle baby! *Lord, help us trust Your plans for our family.* While I'm still a little scared, I had A LOT of fear when Ryan initially shared with me his desire for a third child. I am 39 years old. As you may know, there are greater risks with pregnancies and births as we age. And also… an increased likelihood of twins…

Fear, fear, fear. What if, what if, what if. Initially, I didn't know that fear was the root of all my feelings. But God showed this to me, so I prayed for Him to deepen my trust in Him. Fear does not come from the Lord. I'm not perfect at it, but I'm praying for God to help me trust His plans rather than be stopped by my fear. My husband and I have the mindset that if it's part of His plan that we have another baby, God will make it happen. And if not, He will make it clear if we should adopt, providing the path for another child through adoption. This is our belief! I'm not going to pretend any of this is easy. It's not. I still worry, and I'm still fearful. Every time I get my period, I am simultaneously sad and relieved. *Lord, give my heart rest and peace. Help me trust Your plans for our family, Lord.* This is what Megan and her family did, too! I'm excited to share some excerpts from her book with you! While her story involves adoption, the principles apply to having more biological children, and really all of life, as well.

Her Prayer for Peace

Megan is in her 50s, with four young adult children (two biological and two adopted). Within excerpts of chapter three of her book, she shares: *God's call of adoption lingered like a sweet perfume over my heart and mind, but for the life of me, I couldn't decide if I really liked the scent. Perhaps adoption was something God intended for* other *people, I reasoned. Maybe it wasn't, you know, for* us. *The thing I had dreamed of for over five years was finally manifesting in real-time action. As we began to proactively explore options and agencies, I didn't know how to integrate my fickle emotions.*

After braving the elementary school drop-off lane with rushed kisses and frantic good-byes, the Holy Spirit nudged me to curtail my plans for the day. A list of errands ran through my mind. I had so much to do. I can't explain it any other way except to say the to-do list felt trite, and a holy invitation leapt to the top of the list. "Scratch your personal plans for the day," *the whisper seemed to say.* "Exchange your agenda for mine and meet with me. I have something for you…" *Instead of turning left and heading to the gym, I turned right and headed home. Despite the strong urge to tidy up, I grabbed my Bible and settled in at our sticky kitchen table. The dirty dishes and mounting laundry stared me down like a bull taunting a matador. Don't get distracted, I commanded myself.* Don't let anything derail your attention. Today is the day to leave it all at the Cross. Dive in and ask Jesus to lead. Only then will true answers come.

> DON'T LET ANYTHING DERAIL YOUR ATTENTION. TODAY IS THE DAY TO LEAVE IT ALL AT THE *Cross*. DIVE IN AND ASK JESUS TO LEAD. ONLY THEN WILL TRUE ANSWERS COME.

I had spent many years asking others and avoiding this type of tender vulnerability with the Lord. If I honestly sought His will for our family, it stood to reason I should spend time pointedly *asking and, more importantly,* actively *listening. Instead of closing my eyes and randomly pointing to a passage of Scripture in a game of darts like I might normally do, I opened up the concordance and referenced the word "orphan." It should come as no surprise to anyone vaguely familiar with the heart of God that His Word is chock-full of messages regarding His heart for the fatherless. The silent hours passed in a flash as my heart and mind flooded with words and thoughts containing one singular revolutionary message:* I was an orphan. *In His tender mercy, God chose to adopt me just has He has chosen to adopt You. In this moment, He was inviting our family to put feet on our faith and go and do likewise. What had previously appeared so complicated now seemed clear and, to be honest, utterly terrifying. I slowly released my fierce grip on our current family status and realized perhaps God was asking us to turn the looking glass of life on its head. Through the power of the Spirit, an indescribable peace rested in our unified hearts. Together, we committed to take one step at a time and trusted the Lord would open and close doors according to His sovereign providence.*[28]

Without quoting her entire book (I highly recommend reading it in its entirety!), just try to guess what happened next. I'll paraphrase: Megan's husband had had a nagging feeling about having FOUR children. At the beginning of this process, Megan had briefly considered adopting a sibling pair but bagged the idea, thinking her husband would never go for it. Megan reached out to her adoption contact and learned that on the EXACT same day she had changed all her plans to spend time in the Word, a mother had relinquished her TWO children for adoption. *Lord, You are the coolest!* And so, Megan and her family ended up welcoming two young children from Ethiopia into their family... Four children in all.

While Megan heard this when she spent time studying and listening for the Lord, I heard: *Write a collaborative devotional for mamas.* Spending time with the Lord is NEVER a waste of time! No matter what's on our hearts, God wants in! If you're wondering if you should expand your family (or anything else), be still, and in prayer with God the Father of us all.

Lastly, I have to mention again, one more amazing Christian book involving motherhood, *M Is for Mama* by Abbie Halberstadt.[29] She talks about a variety of motherhood-related topics throughout her book, one of which includes how, when she was young, she shared how she gave her fertility to the Lord. Then, since she thought this was pleasing to God, she thought she could request that however many children He gave her, she wanted them to come just one at a time. Ten children later, including, you guessed it, not one, but two sets of identical twins (and my heart skips a beat...), she laughs at this sort of deal she tried to make with our most powerful Creator. I'm starting to (nervously) laugh a little, too, since MY plan is to try naturally for another five months and then call it. Oh, how I wish we knew God's plans for us sometimes! It doesn't matter, though, as His plans are always perfect.

While we have our own goals and desires for our lives and our families, this week's take-home message is that we are not in control, so let us instead, spend more time with the One Who is. Some babies are born despite birth control, including natural family planning. While other loving, God-fearing couples struggle to conceive their entire lives. Unexpected blessings and agonizing questions are part of our temporary life here on earth. But our God has the best reasons for everything, including exactly what our families will look like. We must trust Him with our fertility, our families, and our lives, with no strings, caveats, or deals attached. His plans are meant to bring us joy and to further His kingdom. His plans for our families are trustworthy!

Bible Verse

"In their hearts humans plan their course, but the LORD establishes their steps" (Proverbs 16:9 NIV).

Prayer

Lord, we are so grateful for our children and families. Help us trust You and Your will for our lives and our families. Lord, thank You for communicating with us. Help us to take the time to hear Your voice. Help us relinquish control in motherhood and family planning. We trust You, Lord. Guide us and guide our families. Thank You for adopting us as orphans, Lord. Whether through adoption or other acts of service, help us support and pray for the orphans around us. Free us from worldly constraints like fear as we trust You and You alone. We love You. Amen.

Reflective Questions

1. Whether you can relate to this week's topic or not, what do you hear from God? Be still, and listen.

2. Consider an area of your family life and motherhood that you're still trying to control yourself. Pray and ask God to help you give Him control. Trust Him!

3. Prayerfully consider one way you can support the orphans in your own community... They are there.

Week Forty-Six

When a "Helper" Needs Help

Since women and wives are indirectly called "helpers" in the Bible (Genesis 2:18), we will focus on asking for help this week. Throughout this devotional, we've talked about having Christian mom friends and utilizing your village, especially postpartum. Sometimes, we mamas still struggle to ask for help. **(See: WEEK FIVE: Christian Mom Friends: Be One, Have Many.)**

A prayerful friend of mine was just sharing a struggle she and her husband are having with their seven-year-old. I asked her if she'd prayed about it. I could see the lightbulb turn on immediately! (Community, community, community!) Automatically praying about every problem we have takes practice and even accountability. So, why is it so hard to ask for help, especially as a mother? For me, it's usually because of pride, because I like to have a sense of control, or because I'm afraid of burdening others. But sometimes, mama, we *need* the help of others. Whether due to personal situations, like illness or chronic pain, or even a season of needing to focus on one of our children, there comes a time when every mama needs to humble herself by focusing on prayer and then asking for counsel/earthly help from a friend. Just like we can feel blessed to be a blessing when we help others, it is a gift to provide someone else with the opportunity to help us in return!

Teresa is in her 40s, with two school-age children. She shares: *During the last three years, while working full-time, I committed to my personal and professional growth by advancing my education. This required me to sacrifice time with my family and ask for help in different ways. During this time, I worried my children would feel my absence, and that I was not showing up as a parent in full capacity. Daily prayer included asking the Lord for guidance and strength to trust that my children would continue to grow and thrive under our new normal. The greatest peace and wisdom I received from the Lord during this time was the ability to let go of the need for control. I learned how to ask for help and accept the conditions of the help. Letting go of control often created unforeseen circumstances but built resilience for our family. I thank God for my husband and his support and willingness to be present with our children when I could not. Christ's peace was with my children as they grew and gained independence over these three years. They cared for me in ways I felt I should be caring for them. They brought me dinner while I studied, tucked me into bed, and cheered me on when I didn't think I could finish. While I initially struggled with this role reversal, I have realized it was their demonstration of love, support, and faith. Our shared values of faith and love were displayed often, reminding me that Christ's love and wisdom are at our family's foundation.*

By asking for help, this mama was able to accomplish something that would allow her to help many, many other people. But her humility and release of control also ended up serving the people under her own roof. Her husband got to step into her parenting shoes, likely becoming even more aware of all she normally does for their family. But my favorite part is that their children benefitted in so many ways when this mama asked for help! Not only did they get to care for their mama in different and special ways, but they, too, relied on the Lord more! When this mama asked for help, it became apparent to her that Christ's love and wisdom were part of her family's foundation. We can and should model giving and receiving help for our kids. Additionally, to prayerfully give (age-appropriate) kids the opportunity to live this out, helping and serving their mother, is a blessing and gift that will likely benefit her children for the rest of their lives... Not to mention an increase in reliance on their prayer life! *God, thank You for blessing this family in this way!* For parents and kids, when we give and receive help, to and from each other, we can also develop the habit of seeking help from God.

Janette is in her 30s, with three young to school-age children. She shares: *Sleep has been a hard-won battle at our house. We have not (until recently!) slept consistently through the night for six years, thanks to our three children. Two separate sleep consultants and a pediatric sleep doctor helped to get us to where we are today.*

While this mama grew as a believer and a mother, as her kids struggled to sleep, she also learned to ask for help. Mama, asking for help is a strength! God created us to help one another, but this doesn't happen if we don't also benefit from the help of others.

Pam is in her 50s, with five school-age to adult children. She shares: *My lowest point in motherhood was when my third child was a senior in high school. He was suicidal, depressed, and had a horrible friend situation. I just tried to get him the help he needed the LOUDEST way I knew how! He's almost 25 now, and life is better. When he struggles, he knows how to ask for help.*

When we mamas model asking for help, our kids learn to ask for help, too.

Billie is in her 60s, with four adult children. She shares: *My daughter and son-in-law were in rehab and had housing lined up for them and their children. They had a caseworker who was assigned to personally help them get their lives back... Therapy for all, a job for my son-in-law, and much more. I knew only God could have pulled this off. When I finally talked with my daughter, she told me that one cold night, as they were trying to stay warm in their truck, God spoke to her. He told her to get on her knees and give it all to Him. They both did it together. They prayed for forgiveness and help to get clean and get their lives back, and from that moment on, things began to turn around. This season also brought my daughter so much closer to God and helped to build her faith.*

Thank You, God, for working through good people in this world, especially when we ask them for help!

Alyssa is in her 30s, with four young to school-age children. She shares: *God showed me the gift of family and community. None of us are independent. Since then, I have truly appreciated the truths of a "village." I have been a part of the village for others. They have been the village for me. Our family continues to be interdependent. Think about how many people are there to help you deliver that little peanut. It is a lie of the enemy that tells us that we can't trust the good people in our world.*

Karissa is in her 30s, with two school-age children. She shares: *Turning to community has been one of the things that helped the most. Hearing stories from others and what they had gone through made me feel less alone. It helped us realize that parenthood has ups and downs, but our ability to stay calm and loving no matter what matters most.*

> TURNING TO *community* HAS BEEN ONE OF THE THINGS THAT HELPED THE MOST.

Christine is in her 30s, with three young to school-age children. She shares: *God has created each individual uniquely. That means that your children are unique, and so are you. What motherhood will look and feel like for you is different than that of ANYONE else. What that means is as much as getting advice can be abundantly helpful, you should always pray to God for which advice applies to you and your child and what doesn't.*

God first, community second. May we remember to pray for discernment when we get advice from our friends and members of our community.

Valerie is in her 40s, with two adult children. She shares: *My kids were YOUNG for the tragedy of 9/11, and we lived in Rhode Island. My husband was on duty and became the USCG on-site commander for the entire state of RI. We could not see him for several weeks as he was stuck at the station. That day, I went home and turned on the news, found out as much as I could, and then went and picked up my kids from daycare. The television never went off of the Disney channel. Because we were so close to New York, I did not want them to fear for themselves or for their dad. We moved to Virginia in late June of 2002–the kids were four and five at that time–and they had no clue about*

9/11 and what happened. God let them keep their innocence and not be fearful about the what-ifs. He helped guide me and my husband in what and how to talk to them about things. This later proved helpful when he would deploy to combat zones for an average of 285 days per year for about ten years.

This would be so hard. *God, thank You for being our number one helper in motherhood and in life!*

Lastly, if I hadn't sought help and prayers from my MomCo group that night, which led me to prayerfully release control and trust God with my motherhood, this book you are holding may not exist. Mama, let us give and receive help from God and others.

Bible Verse

"Carry each other's burdens, and in this way you will fulfill the law of Christ" (Galatians 6:2 NIV).

Prayer

Lord, help us to carry each other's burdens, both giving and receiving help, just as You command. Humble our hearts and help us allow others to be blessed by accepting their help in our times of need. We know we can always turn to You for help, Lord. We also know You call us to be in community with each other. Guide us in choosing who to ask for help, and then remind us to seek Your guidance in implementing any advice we may get from others. You are our number one source of help, Lord. May we never forget this. Help us to help others, too, Lord. We love You. Amen.

Reflective Questions

1. Prayerfully consider one area of motherhood where you could use the help and support of another Christian mom or an otherwise trusted friend. Pray for the strength and humility to ask for help in this area by the end of the week.

2. Consider a time in motherhood when you (perhaps reluctantly) asked for help but then felt supported and blessed in having done so. Consider a time when you helped another mama. How did it feel in your heart to help her and her family?

3. God brings people into our lives purposefully. Spend time in prayerful gratitude, thanking God for all the helpful people in your life. And be sure to thank them, too!

Week Forty-Seven

Christ's Peace in Our Mama Hearts

The words "peace" or "peaceful" were mentioned in nearly every one of our contributing mamas' answers. That's because it was my prayer for Christ's peace in my mama heart that drove away so much of my worry and fear in my early motherhood. It was His peace in Christian motherhood about which I wanted to hear and learn more. Below are several of the answers addressing the peace of Christ that I received from our contributing mamas (in the order I received them). As you read how Christ's peace affected these mamas and their families, I can't wait for you to better recognize how His peace has been granted in your own mama heart.

Gina is in her 30s, with four young to school-age children. She shares: *He replaces control with trust, anxiety with peace, pride with surrender, vanity with self-love, and your dreams with new dreams that are better than you could have ever made for yourself... so much better. Motherhood doesn't get easier, but I can easily recognize this place as somewhere I have been before, only now, I have a little more trust, peace, surrender, and self-love that He clothed me with the first go-around. I'm still working hard, sweating hard, and crying hard, but I now know what it's for.*

Angela is in her 40s, with two school-age children. She shares: *Then Jesus moves in with His beautiful steps to redirect me. I can literally feel Him take over and guide me back to peace, love, and a more understanding place. Thank God that Jesus is persistent! When I am finally able to calm and settle my mind, mouth, and heart, I feel His peace, wisdom, and guidance. Only then can I help steer my boys through rougher waters of life and teach them to also stop, breathe, and listen for the Lord. For at that time, all felt more reasonable, goals more attainable, and a larger space for peace and love was opened. Knowing I have our Triune God in my corner gives me peace and strength as I do my very best with the ever so flattering–but oh so challenging–assignment of parenthood.*

Dianne is in her 40s, with three school-age children. She shares: *Anytime I begin to worry, I pray for wisdom and other mamas as we move forward in peace and confidence in the truth Jesus shared with us, that He's our best caregiver. So, instead of being constantly overwhelmed, I felt God offer peace to my mind, reassurance to my heart, and wisdom on our next best steps.*

Jonnie is in her 40s, with two young adult children. She shares: *God created you to experience bliss and peace.*

Megan is in her 50s, with four young adult children. She shares: *I feel Christ's peace most often when my kids come to me with a problem, and I hold back for a minute to let them work things out before I jump in with my own opinion or perceived wisdom.*

Jan is in her 70s, with three adult children. She shares: *The more adversities we experienced, the more Jesus guided me toward wisdom and peace.*

Jill S. is in her 60s, with three adult children. She shares: *I have absolutely felt peace, wisdom, and guidance through my faith in Jesus Christ. Some of this was after a challenging time of parenting, and it showed up as the calm of knowing I had held firm on what was right even though it was hard. Sometimes, it appeared as witnessing the lessons my kids had learned from their father and I play out in real-life situations. Most of all, it was in the patience I learned and knowing that perfection is neither required nor realistic, that our true friends and family will accept and love us no matter how messy our house might be after a long week of busy schedules, and that Jesus loves me unconditionally.*

Christine is in her 30s, with three young to school-age kids. She shares: *With one of my daughters, it has been the peace I have had through her whole medical journey and my belief that no matter what, Jesus has her in His hands.*

Heather is in her 40s, with two school-age children. She shares: *My husband, and I are firm believers in a healthy lifestyle and only taking medication when absolutely necessary. That night, we read up on all the possible side effects and prayed that God would guide us in making the right decision. After sleeping on it, we both had the most incredible peace in the morning and agreed that our son should try the medication. This journey has definitely had its extreme highs and lows, and God has guided us through it with incredible peace and wisdom.*

Debi is in her 60s, with three adult children. She shares: *I had a peace I knew from learning to trust God in previous crises.*

Beth is in her 60s, with three adult children. She shares: *We felt full of His peace and watched our son not only grow in his wisdom and trust in the Lord, but in his desire to lead other young men in their faith walk, too.*

Brianna is in her 30s with one young child (and one on the way). She shares: *I was flipping through the Word and crying, desperately seeking answers on what to do for my son's care. I constantly landed on verses about trusting the Lord, and as I sat there, I literally felt God saying to me, "I got this." All worry left me, and I felt a supernatural peace that only God could provide.*

> I LITERALLY FELT GOD SAYING TO ME, "I GOT THIS." ALL WORRY LEFT ME, AND I FELT A SUPERNATURAL *peace* THAT ONLY GOD COULD PROVIDE.

Annette is in her 40s, with one young adult child. She shares: *I had total peace even though I did not know where my son was. Knowing that I didn't need to know the details but sitting down with the Lord to get His directions, to get to peace, is the best way to navigate through the unknowns. Knowing you get your peace from God and NOT from your child's behaviors is a huge and beautiful place to be.*

Billie is in her 60s, with four adult children. She shares: *It wasn't until I heard that I needed to turn everything over to God. I needed to back away and let Him do the work only He can do. This was guidance I had not expected, so with everything in me, I laid everything down. I stopped contact and stopped any further attempts to help. Once I did this, I felt a sense of peace. It was crazy how peaceful I felt. How could this be? With all the trauma, turmoil, and potential disaster that could happen. Once again, God told me to be still and let Him work. I took that step back, even with many others coming at me as to why I wasn't helping. The peace that I had was so hard to describe.*

Emma is in her 30s, with two young (earthside) children. She shares: *My husband and I felt God's presence more clearly than we ever have in our lives. We immediately experienced this during the birth of our son, which was an extremely peaceful and holy experience. There was no doubt that God was wrapping us in His arms and showering us with His mercy and love. We had no doubt that Johnny was in paradise.*

Lastly, my own share: *After more specialists appointments for more body parts than I can remember, four medical/surgical procedures on his tiny little body, then a delay in walking, plus his congenital hypothyroidism and also all he went through in utero, my mama heart was so full of worry and fear for the health and well-being of my son for the first 18 months of his life. That is, until I laid it all down at the Lord's feet, trusting that He would take care of my son, according to His perfect plans for his life. Once I did that, while also sharing with my MomCo group, who prayed for me, I felt the peace of Christ in my mama heart for the first time in motherhood. And, I've come to learn that's from where all peace comes, from trusting the Prince of Peace Himself.*

Her Prayer for Peace

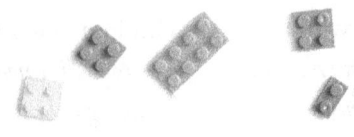

Bible Verse

"I have said these things to you, that in me you may have peace. In the world you will have tribulation. But take heart; I have overcome the world" (John 16:33 ESV).

Prayer

Lord, thank You for hearing our prayers for peace when our mama hearts are hurting. When we believe and trust in You, Your perfect peace is available to us. Thank You for overcoming the world, Jesus! When the tribulations of this world push us to our knees, help us remember to pray to the Prince of Peace. Help us remember that You care for us more than we're capable of understanding. Help us remember that You want to grant us Your peace! Lord, we love our children so much. When they're hurting, help us ask for and rely on Your peace and guidance as we care for them and share Your peace with them, too. We love You. Amen.

Reflective Questions

1. From the shares this week, prayerfully consider your three biggest takeaways regarding Christ's peace.

2. When in your life have you experienced the peace of Christ? Remember as much of the situation as you can, including how you felt before you had the peace of Christ in your heart and afterward.

3. Ask God to help you more readily trust Him and, so, accept His peace for you. Prayerfully consider what might stop you from fully receiving His peace during challenging times in life and in motherhood.

Sin and Spiritual Health in Motherhood

In week 17, we talked about our lack of perfection and our lack of control (in life and) in motherhood. In week 39, we talked about mom guilt. As part of week 39, I mentioned the distinction *M Is for Mama*'s Abbie Halberstadt[30] makes between mom guilt and Holy Spirit conviction… That is to say, sin. This week, we'll dig deep, mama. You might be asking, "What do my personal sins have to do with my motherhood?" Well, especially when it comes to sin, the devil is a tricky guy. He loves to fill our minds with excuses, justifications, rationalizations, and ignorance. This includes you, me, and every other God-honoring mama in the world! But we were also each fearfully and wonderfully made by the God of forgiveness, truth, grace, and peace!

We've talked a lot about modeling our faith and faith life for our kids. And, while we're focusing on our personal sins and spiritual health this week, our sinful nature impacts our kids. Depending on the sin, it could directly or indirectly impact them. Any action, behavior, habit, or otherwise that doesn't align with Who God is can create an emotional space between us and God; sin separates us from God. (This is why we need Jesus!) Because sin is part of our human faith life, our sinful nature provides the opportunity for us to model repentance to, reliance on, and closeness with God as we strive to mother our kids according to His perfect will.

I'm not going to confess any of my personal sins to you this week, of which there are many, but I will share one personal thing with you: In my sin, I feel separated from/not close to God. I might even attempt to hide from God in the midst of my sin. Like when sin entered the world through the Garden of Eden, Adam and Eve tried to hide from God, too. Here's how this lack of closeness, as a result of our personal sin, affects our Christian motherhood: It is incongruent to hide/be far from God as a result of our sin and also seek closeness in order to benefit from His peace, wisdom, and guidance in motherhood. When I sin, when I know I've hurt God's heart in some way, even though this is not the truth, I find myself feeling unworthy of a relationship with God. Said another way, I can (incorrectly) feel that since I've done something bad, I can't seek the help, support, or guidance of Someone good – God. Again, the devil is tricky. He deceives me into thinking that *God* has distanced Himself from *me* when I sin. But that is not the truth, and again, why we need Jesus, Who God sent to die for our sins. It is our *sin* that separates us from God, but through Jesus' death, we can repent (modeling as we do so) to the God Who graciously loves us. And the God Who helps us mother our children well is the same God Who can help us defeat our temptations and Who forgives us of our sins!

Lord, thank You for sending Your Son, Jesus, to die for our sins. As we seek closeness with You, please forgive us of our sins, as we also seek Your guidance in motherhood.

No contributing mamas spoke specifically of their sins either, but a few mentioned sin and forgiveness. As you'll see in the reflective questions this week, my hope is that you start to become more aware of your personal relationship with God when you sin. Taking this a step further, consider how your relationship with God coincides with your desire and ability to seek and rely on Him to help you mother your children in a Godly way.

Lastly, consider how we can model our sinful nature, repentance, God's forgiveness, and our subsequent continued closeness with and reliance on God to our children. We are sinners. We shouldn't try to hide that from our children, just like we can't hide our sins from God. Our first mama shares more about how our sinful nature is an opportunity to show our kids how much we need God our Savior, too.

Janette is in her 30s, with three young to school-age children. She shares: *Make sure they understand that we as parents aren't God, but that we serve someone much higher because we, too, sin and need a Savior!*

My daughter is really into emotions right now. When she's sad, she says, "Hopey is sad." When she's happy, she says, "Hopey is happy!" She will also ask me if I'm happy, most often after she's finally apologized to Johnny for taking his toy and running away with it (for the third time since breakfast). Why is the quicker one always the toy thief, too?! She knows it makes me unhappy when she takes her brother's toy from him. And so, after she's returned his toy and apologized, she seemingly wants to make sure she's made me happy again. "Are you happy now, Mama?" Stick with me; I'm getting to my point: This makes me ask myself, *How do I help my kids do the right things for the right reasons?* That is, and I know my kids are still pretty young, but I want my kids to want to make God happy instead of their sinful mama. And maybe that's just it!

Mama, let's be sure to tell our kids that sometimes we all say and do unkind things to others... that we all sin. And that, thankfully, we serve a God Who wants us to come to Him for forgiveness no matter what. He wants to forgive us because He loves us (*Even more than Mama loves you, Hopey!*). Let us not be too proud to admit to our children that we are sinners. Being open about it, confessing to God and also to our children, allows them to see God's forgiving light erase our sinful darkness. Our lack of perfection and our sins are how we can teach our kids about exactly why we see Jesus on the cross. Again, I know my kids are young, but they think Jesus is up there just sleeping right now! But we know He's not.

> LET US NOT BE TOO PROUD TO ADMIT TO OUR CHILDREN THAT WE ARE *sinners*.

Lord, help us teach our young kids about Jesus' sacrifice to save us from our sins. Help us teach them to love and treat others well because You did this first. But, Lord, we are all sinners. Help us be honest with our kids about our sinful nature and our ability to repent and be forgiven so that our sin doesn't separate us from You, Your love, Your guidance, and Your peace. Thank You, Lord.

Alyssa is in her 30s, with four young to school-age children. She shares: *I'll never forget how I realized how important it was to show my oldest that I messed up. When she was preparing for First Communion, we were to be a part of various stations to prepare her for the Sacraments of Reconciliation and the Eucharist. I made my list on my phone so that I wouldn't forget anything, made a humbling confession, and when I walked out, I saw my little girl, wiped clean of sin, in a state of grace, with the most horrified look on her face. Her eyes were as big as lightbulbs. I sat down, and she leaned in, raised her single eyebrow, and said out the side of her mouth, "Mom, you were in there a looong time." I immediately laughed and told her, "I better get to saying my penance, huh?"*

I love this example of a mama showing her child that she's a sinner and needs a Savior, too. Not only that, but it shows that we can still (and should!) come to God despite our sins. He still loves us and wants us to come to Him, to rely on Him, no matter what. This mama further shares: *I think it's great for our kids to learn that they aren't perfect, nor are they expected to be, and that they should put God first.* If we admit that we're imperfect sinners, our kids will know they're imperfect sinners, too, and that we all need our Savior God more than anyone or anything.

Our last three shares focus on our forgiving God. It's an important reminder for us and an essential lesson for our kids that even though we're all born sinners, we believe in a God who forgives. He forgives us, and we can turn to Him for help in not committing the same sin over and over again, through the power of the Holy Spirit. But if (and when) we do, our God forgives us over and over again. In this, we can give and receive forgiveness with our kids and also teach our kids to forgive one another. When we model God's love and forgiveness, and our kids model us, our kids end up modeling God through us!

Angela is in her 40s, with two school-age children. She shares: *Thank God He is also a forgiving Lord. I am far from a perfect mother.*

Kacie is in her 30s, with three young to school-age children. She shares: *I have made mistakes, and the grace to understand Jesus and my children love me and forgive me has been so impactful.*

Jill S. is in her 60s, with three adult children. She shares: *Always be willing to admit wrong and ask for forgiveness from your child when you are wrong.*

That last share reminds me of the restoration process we discussed in **WEEK FORTY-FOUR: Disciplining Our Children with the Love of Jesus**. When we've made a mistake or sinned and want to restore with and be forgiven by our kids, we can ask God for forgiveness in the same breath. We can show our kids that we are sinners, that we are sorry, and that we seek our Savior's forgiveness, too.

One final thought: I saw an image on social media once that read something along the lines of, "Your kids aren't driving you crazy; they're revealing your sins." This struck me. Maybe I'll share some of my sinful behaviors after all. Immediately, when I think about how I'm feeling and acting when it feels like my kids are driving me crazy, I think of selfishness and impatience. *Lord, help me experience these sins less, especially when I'm with my kids. I confess this to You, Lord. Please heal my sinful heart, forgive me, and help me give my kids my (Your) best. I need Your help to be less selfish and more patient with my kids, Lord! Over and over again!*

Mama, this week was a big week. It took me hours and hours to write and rewrite this topic. I hope it was clear enough for you to get the point! Maybe it was because of my own sin, or maybe because the devil just doesn't want this truth in our mama heart and so also in the hearts of our children. We live in a sinful world. But I pray we focus on the forgiveness of the Cross amidst our sins and the sins of this world, especially for the benefit of our motherhood. **(See: WEEK FOUR: When We Faithfully Obey God, He Can Work against Sin and Evil in Our Families.)**

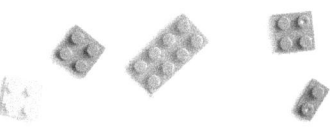

Bible Verse

"If we confess our sins, he is faithful and just and will forgive us our sins and purify us from all unrighteousness" (1 John 1:9 NIV).

Prayer

Lord, help us not to alienate or try to hide ourselves from You because of our sin. We wish to be close to You because we love You. We also need Your help in raising our children... Your children. Sin is darkness, and You are the Light. Help us break free from recurring sins, Lord, especially those that directly impact our kids. But also ones that indirectly impact our kids because motherhood is hard enough, and we need Your help, Lord. We need to feel close to You, without sin in between us. Lord, You know our hearts. Give us the courage to trust in You and break away from (recurring) sins by way of our repentance and Your forgiveness. Purify our hearts, Lord, so we feel like there is nothing in our way as we reach out and benefit from Your forgiveness, blessings, guidance, wisdom, and Your peace in motherhood. We love You. Amen.

Reflective Questions

1. Is there something in your heart that you've chalked up to mom guilt, but is perhaps Holy Spirit conviction instead? Said another way, ask God if there are any sinful behaviors in you that *directly* impact your children.

2. Next, ask God what sin in you *indirectly* impacts your children because it separates you from God, the giver of patience, strength, wisdom, guidance, peace, and all things we mamas need every day!

3. Take a heartfelt inventory of your sinful nature. Ask for God's forgiveness. Then ask Him to help you ask your kids for forgiveness as a part of modeling faith and restoring mistakes and sinful actions with them, prayerfully. Lastly, get in the habit of regularly considering whether your kids know that you're a sinner and that you personally need our Savior God's forgiveness, too.

Caring for Yourself when You Become a Mother

How are you feeling after last week, mama? That was a heavy one. It's good, though, to be honest with ourselves, with our kids, and with God. Hopefully, you asked Him for forgiveness and feel replenished by His loving forgiveness, grace, and peace. This week will hopefully replenish you as well but in a different way. When we became mothers, we changed (or we *shed layers*, like our one mama shared). We became someone new. Not entirely different, but a new, truer version of ourselves. Our transformation into motherhood is marked by God! Since I am a wellness professional, I'm passionate about encouragingly sharing ways mamas can take care of themselves. This is especially important for us; since in every way we care for ourselves, we also care for our kids. Before I continue, I want to be clear that the number one way to take care of ourselves is to submit our lives to Jesus Christ. He is our number one caregiver, always and forever. Here's what some of our contributing mamas shared about the care of Jesus.

Dianne is in her 40s, with three school-age children. She shares: *God will take care of me; He loves me more than the birds of the air, and He takes care of them* (Matthew 6:26-27). *He's our best caregiver.*

Kary is in her 30s, with two young to school-age children. She shares: *God continued to care for me by placing supportive people in my life.*

Heather is in her 40s, with two school-age children. She shares: *Jesus has guided and taken such beautiful care of me over the years on my journey through motherhood.*

My own share: *He loves me, cares for me, and wants to bring me joy!*

Gina is in her 30s, with four young to school-age children. She shares: *I know that to Him; I am not a mom. I am His daughter. He cares deeply for all of me: my health, dreams, anxieties, and my mother's heart.*

Jesus is our number one caregiver! Your physical and emotional health are important to Him.

Now, I'll share a few practical ways we can take care of ourselves as mamas. Because let's be honest, when we went from being our own sole responsibility to being responsible (in partnership with God) for another human being, our focus likely shifted. But it is possible to take good care of ourselves *and* our kids! It doesn't matter if you're a new mom or a grandmother to teenagers. It's never too late to take better care of ourselves. God's mission for us on earth is to serve others while expanding His kingdom for as long as He has us here. So, let's be and feel well while we're at it, mamas! I'll offer a few suggestions below, but please consider this list prayerfully. God knows you and your family best. Trust Him to guide you in what will make the most meaningful difference for you and, subsequently, for your family.

First, I suggest carving out some time to get to know your (new) self since you became a mother. Identify what's important to you and energizing for you. There's a lot of talk about self-care out there. This is a mix between self-care and soul-care (Abbie Halberstadt talks about this distinction in her book, *M Is for Mama*,[31] as well). What activities and types of people bring you joyful energy and joyful rest? Consider what you're doing when you find yourself having fun. What rejuvenates you, physically and emotionally? Then, mama, schedule it in! We are often the keepers of the family calendar, but kid activities can very easily take over if we let them! This may take intention, and it will most likely also take prayer. It is so important to fill ourselves and our time with things that make us feel good as a child of God (not necessarily as a mother)! God wants us to feel good, whole (in Him), and also healthy! It shouldn't be our number one priority—God should be—but focusing on our health is an important use of our time that yields significant results for us, our families, and also for God. Have fun with this, and remember, God is our number one source of wellness and care. Trust Him to guide you in this.

Secondly, I'll share five things we can do that don't take a lot of time or cost a lot of money but can greatly impact our overall well-being. These include, but are not limited to: 1) being in nature; 2) moving our amazing, God-given bodies; 3) serving others; 4) generating a gratitude practice; and 5) intentionally laughing every single day. Pretty simple and obvious things, right? But if we're not intentional, we can easily miss out on the amazing benefits of these God-given activities.

Nature: Science is catching up with creation! There's scientific research indicating, for instance, that being in the presence of colorful flowers can improve anxiety, help with sleep, improve our memory, make us more productive, and generally improve our mental health.[32] *God, You had fun creating all the flowers on earth, didn't You? Thank You!*

Movement: There's a lot I could say here, but just consider all the ways our bodies were designed to move. God created us with over 600 muscles to use! What movements feel good in your body? What activities do you enjoy doing? Seek clarity, schedule it in, have an earthly accountability partner, and ask God to help you consistently help yourself (and your family) by moving your amazing, blessing of a body on a regular basis!

Service: Yes, motherhood in and of itself is a HUGE act of service. But I know I don't always see it that way. Please join me in praying about this. And if your kids are a little older, or if you feel the Lord calling you to serve outside your home, I encourage you to serve those in need, especially "the least of these," according to (Matthew 25:40). Not only are we called

> WHEN WE SERVE OTHERS, WE *benefit* EMOTIONALLY AS WELL!

to do this as part of God's mission for His people, but I believe this was part of His intention, too: When we serve others, we benefit emotionally as well! (Tip: Serve others with your kids!)

Gratitude. How many times a day do you thank God for something or someone in your life? We can't do this too much! I highly recommend the book *The Magic* by Rhonda Byrne.[33] I'd consider it a secular book, although she mentions several times how gratitude is the foundation of every religion, Christianity included. The 28 gratitude practices in this book have helped me thank God more regularly and more automatically throughout my day. Additionally, our hearts cannot experience negative emotions at the same time as they experience gratitude! *Thank You, Lord!* If you're prone to complaining or feeling sorry for yourself, consider praying about a daily gratitude practice. And, who's going to be your earthly accountability partner?

Laughter. Talk about a gift from God! Similar to nature and gratitude, there's a lot of science surrounding laughter and what it does for our physical and emotional well-being. *You are so creative, God!* On social media, I love to post funny content (you can search the hashtag I use, #laughingisgoodforyou) because I know most people just don't laugh enough! There are a lot of serious things to focus on in life, especially in motherhood, but God gave us the gift of laughter, so let's commit to laughing more!

Another hashtag from which you may find value in terms of your physical and emotional health is my wellness business hashtag, #wellnessbymonicabstaley. Since 2015, from protein and sleep to energy and stress, I've been supporting (especially) women in feeling their best in the incredible bodies God gave us. (Tip: "Hanger" is a real thing. Do your best to always be well-fed, especially when you're with your kids!)

This is not an exhaustive list, but hopefully God has sparked something in you to commit to at least one of these ways you can care for yourself as a mother. Note: The value of an accountability partner cannot be underestimated! Maybe call on one of your Christian mom friends so you can hold each other accountable, logistically and also in prayer. Lastly, with whom we surround ourselves makes a difference in our overall well-being. Be supportive of yourself by surrounding yourself with other kind and supportive people. **(This week, you may also find value in reviewing weeks ONE, NINE, SEVENTEEN, and THIRTY-SIX.)**

Bible Verse

"Do you not know that you are God's temple and that God's Spirit dwells in you? If anyone destroys God's temple, God will destroy him. For God's temple is holy, and you are that temple" (1 Corinthians 3:16-17 ESV).

Prayer

Lord, thank You for our lives and the amazing bodies and minds with which You've blessed us. Please help us honor our bodies by not doing them harm and by making choices that support our overall well-being. Thank You for filling our spiritual cups, Lord. Help us to experience this life with as much vitality and energy as You intended, by prioritizing our well-being. You are our number one priority, Lord. Help us do Your will in motherhood and in our lives with minds, hearts, and bodies that feel as well as possible. We love You. Amen.

Reflective Questions

1. Prayerfully ask God how you can better care for yourself and your temple. Ask Him to help you do this regularly and joyfully for your own benefit and for the benefit of your children.

2. Prayerfully consider your accountability partner in wellness. Connect with at least one person about this before the end of the week.

3. How are you feeling about this week's topic? Take inventory of your feelings as part of your quiet time with the Lord. If shame, guilt, fear, overwhelm, or any other unproductive/unholy emotions surface, ask God to take them from you right now. Instead, pray and review questions one and two until you feel Christ's peace in your heart.

Reflection; Miracles in Motherhood (Vol. V)

M ama, I am so proud of you! *Thank You, God, for giving this mama the fortitude she needed to (nearly!) finish this devotional!* We've covered 49 different, often related topics now. My hope continues to be that you've been in prayer, in action, and in rest with the Lord. God continues to be on the move in our family, mama! He is our best friend. He helps us to discipline our kids with the love of Jesus. He helps us accept Christ's peace in our mama hearts.

Take some time to reflect on the last nine weeks:
1. How has God's love and peace for you changed you and impacted your family since you started this devotional, specifically in the last nine weeks (weeks 41-49)?
2. What have been your three to five biggest takeaways in the last nine weeks (week 41-49)?
3. Is there a week you'd like to re-read this week?

4. Is there a mama you thought of in weeks 42, 45, or 49, but you forgot to pray for her or reach out to her? Now is your opportunity! Don't let this week go by without praying for her or connecting with her.
5. Do you find yourself seeking, trusting, and relying on God for peace, wisdom, and guidance in motherhood, even 5-10% more than you did nine weeks ago?

Let's pray. *Lord, we thank You for being a God Who cares for us and our children. We're also grateful for other Christian mamas who've shared things with us that help us draw closer to You. Help us continue to see and experience the correlation between relying on You more and motherhood being "easier" and also more fun! Help us continue to find things to be grateful for in our motherhood, even (especially!) as we struggle. Lord, please deepen our prayer life and our relationship with You. You are our best friend, Lord! Thank You for loving us so perfectly. Help us to discipline our children with that same love. Thank You for blessing us with our children and for giving us peace in our mama hearts, Lord. We love You. Amen.*

One final time, I'll share a miracle of God – from Julie, a mama in her 60s, with four adult children. She shares: *Our three older children were very healthy, but our youngest child had several health issues. He had RSV when he was only about four months old. That was scary. The most unusual thing started when he woke up on Halloween from his afternoon nap, and his neck was stiff. He couldn't turn it from its position, looking over his shoulder. I couldn't get into the doctor at that time on a Friday, so I took him to the emergency room. The hospital sent us by ambulance to Children's Hospital.*

They released us that night and said he was fine in every way... But that he still couldn't turn his head. My doctor referred us to a pediatric neurologist, but we couldn't get in for six weeks. I just could not wait six weeks, and I actually called my friend, who was our PA. She invited me to come over and talk about it that evening. I didn't even know what they were thinking it might be! Was it a muscular disease? What were we facing? She said they suspected a brain tumor. I was like, "If it is a brain tumor, he could be dead in six weeks." I said, "I would imagine that they would do an MRI, CT scan, or the like when we went to the specialist. Could they just do it now, locally, so we could know and not delay?" That's what we did. We had to wait days for the results. Nothing showed up, no tumor! I just burst into tears! My son's neck problem lasted between two and three weeks total, and then it was gone. Our MD said it must have just been muscular. It was just very strange, and when I think of the grace of God, I often think of that.

As Christians, at times like these, we praise God for His care and for His grace. We praise Him for the health and safety of our kids. And we're reminded just how precious their health really is. Our God is a loving God! This mama is faithful! In a time of waiting, a time of unknowns, it can be easy to spiral away from God and toward trying to control and fix a situation ourselves. But I believe God provided a way for this mama to advocate for her child's health (and for her own peace of mind!). I can't imagine getting my baby up from his nap and him not being able to move his head. I can't imagine the words "brain tumor" and my child's name in the same sentence. *God, thank You for the resources You gave this mama!*

Our God extends His grace with open arms to protect us and our kids according to His perfect will. Sometimes, His perfect will brings our children to Heaven sooner than we want. Sometimes not. Every day, we must thank God for the blessing of our children! Mama, may we hold our kids tightly and have gratitude and praise toward God for every moment with them. Truthfully, when mamas of older kids tell me that, I wonder how I can do that during the hardest, most trying times of motherhood. But the thing is, we may not always be able to do so on our own. We need the help of God! A God in Whose will we trust!

> BUT THE THING IS, WE MAY NOT ALWAYS BE ABLE TO DO SO ON OUR OWN. WE NEED THE HELP OF *God*!

I hope this reflection week has blessed you. Some of the topics in this devotional are hard. Some we can relate to more than others. A week where we pause to review and reflect can be really helpful. And hearing a story about the gift of God's incredible grace reminds us how great our God truly is! It's also a reminder to ask God to protect our families, to be weak and vulnerable, pleading for God to keep our children healthy and safe. In place of fear for our children's safety, we can ask the Lord to give us His peace. If tragedy happens, we can still pray to the God Who loves us.

This week's Bible verse sums this up well, along with many of the topics we've read about so far:

"Rejoice always, pray continually, give thanks in all circumstances; for this is God's will for you in Christ Jesus" (1 Thessalonians 5:16-18 NIV).

Week Fifty-One

Worry, Worry, and More Worry in Motherhood

Can you believe we've been studying God's love and peace for mamas for almost an entire year now? Your commitment to God, to yourself, and to your family inspires me, mama! During our last two weeks, we'll revisit two very common buzzwords when it comes to both motherhood and Christianity: *worry* and *trust*. Worry, anxiety, and fear do not come from God. But with God's help, we can practice and learn to trust God more and to worry less. Let's review what our amazing contributing mamas shared about God and their worries in motherhood.

Dianne is in her 40s, with three school-age children. She shares: *In the midst of worry is right where Jesus meets me. Worry is spoken of really clearly in the Bible… God will take care of me; He loves me more than the birds of the air, and He takes care of them (Matthew 6:26-27). It was the test of giving back to Jesus, things that aren't mine; that was my worry. When worry arrives and overwhelms me, that's the Holy Spirit's reminder to pray. Pray for those who are in the midst of what I worry about, pray for other mamas, pray for the truth that God's got me and these sweet children. When I pray, that is when the calmness and peace of Christ falls over me, and I feel it, I know it, and then I feel good I had prayed for other mamas. It takes the focus off me and onto Jesus, the one who overcomes the worry. Anytime I begin to worry, I pray for wisdom and other mamas as we move forward in peace and confidence in the truth Jesus shared with us, that He's our best caregiver.*

Jonnie is in her 40s, with two young adult children. She shares: *Don't confuse fear and worry with guiding your children. As parents, we often parent from fear and not faith. We are to shepherd them and encourage them toward the Lord. Fear has the power to control you and your decisions or drive you straight to the person who has conquered fear and death itself. Fear and anxiety have been commonplace for me in parenthood, and I have to say, that experience has kept me super close to Jesus.*

We need Jesus, mama! This mama has stayed close to Jesus *because of* her worry, fear, and anxiety in motherhood. Rather than fear, this faith is how we best shepherd our children closer to our trusting, fear-and-death-conquering Savior! May we not allow worry and fear to control us; may we instead turn to Jesus Christ. And may our kids see us model this, too.

Cassandra is in her 50s, with six school-age to adult children. She shares: *I thought things would be easier as my oldest child grew and that once he became an adult, I would have fewer worries and responsibilities. However, as he grew and began to interact with the world, I realized that I had less and less control over his environment and who had access to him. Daily, I have to let go and let God have His way, and trust God to send angels to be a hedge of protection around my oldest child, even now that he's an adult.*

Brianna is in her 30s, with one young child (and one on the way). She shares: *My son had a stroke and now has cerebral palsy because of it. My faith was tested by constant worry. Worry about not doing enough and worry about what path to take for him to get the best care. I had to spend time in the Word and finally, just release all my worries on God and realize He cares more for my son than I ever could. In the end, everything did work out. I know He will continue to help us through this journey. We just have to "be still." The other night, I was flipping through the Word and crying, desperately seeking answers on what to do for my son's next level of care. I constantly landed on verses about trusting the Lord, and as I sat there, I literally felt God saying to me,*

"I've got this." All worry left me, and I felt a supernatural peace that only God could provide.

Worry followed by prayer, allows us to trust in Him as He replaces our worry with His perfect peace.

Kari is in her 60s, with three young adult children. She shares: *When my triplet daughters were born early at 28 weeks gestation, I was so scared and worried. I spent as much time as possible in the NICU, sitting by their incubators, worrying about and praying for my babies. I knew that there were many people praying for them, which gave me hope, strength, and peace.*

> **WORRY FOLLOWED BY PRAYER, ALLOWS US TO *trust* IN HIM AS HE REPLACES OUR WORRY WITH HIS PERFECT PEACE.**

Teresa in her 40s, with two school-age children. She shares: *During the last three years, while working full-time, I committed to my personal growth by advancing my education. This required me to sacrifice time with my family and ask for help in different ways. During this time, I worried my children would feel my absence, and that I was not showing up as a parent in full capacity. Daily prayer included asking the Lord for guidance and strength to trust that they would continue to grow and thrive under our new normal.*

I can relate to this; maybe you can, too. When I heard from the Lord to write this devotional, I was not looking for extra things to do in my life! But instead of worrying, over and over again, I trusted Him with my wellness business and with my children, as He helped me find the time to write. *Lord, I am so proud of what You and I have created. I praise You! Your peace has calmed my worries as I put my trust in You.*

My own share: *I was filled with worry and fear for the first 18 months of motherhood. I knew fear came from the enemy and not from God, but I struggled to overcome all the stresses and unknowns. I'm so grateful for The MomCo. I remember crying to my small group one night, just confessing how overwhelmed with worry and fear I was. I asked them to please pray for me. Prayer works. And while I'm in the thick of parenting young kids, and it's still hard every single day, between my community and taking time to be with Him, the worry and fear have nearly disappeared.*

Giving the Lord my worry about motherhood saved my mama heart and grew my faith in Jesus Christ! If I hadn't had that moment of clarity (*thank You, Jesus*) to have my Christian mom friends pray for me, you may not be reading these words right now. Our lives open up to God's goodness and peace when we step out of worry into trust in the Lord.

Gina is in her 30s, with four young to school-age children. She shares: *When I hear moms worry that they are losing themselves, I encourage them to lean in because shedding the old is how He makes way for the new (Ephesians 4:22-24). He makes all things new. Motherhood is our journey to Him.*

I just love the wisdom the Lord has given this encouraging mama! (I also have a whole new perspective when I see dog hair on the floor from our supposedly non-shedding dog, Leroy. I'm shedding, too, pup!) We mamas are shedding in the name of our trustworthy God, Who has blessed us with motherhood. Just as our babies were formed in our wombs, when we replace worry with trust, the Lord can form us into the person we need to be for Him and for our children. Just like worry in motherhood doesn't completely disappear overnight, this "shedding" process continues throughout motherhood. It's all for and done by the hands of our trustworthy God! So, let us not worry about losing ourselves in motherhood, mama. *Rather, Lord, help us trust You as we journey closer and closer to You through trusting in You and growing in You through Your gift of motherhood.* **(See: WEEK ONE: Losing Yourself in Motherhood.)**

Lastly, may we remember to seek the prayers of other Christians when worry brings us to our knees. Praying for others and asking others to pray for us is a true gift from the Lord!

Worry, Worry, and More Worry in Motherhood

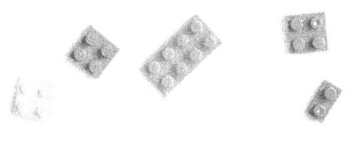

Bible Verse

"'Come to me, all you who are weary and burdened, and I will give you rest. Take my yoke upon you and learn from me, for I am gentle and humble in heart, and you will find rest for your souls. For my yoke is easy and my burden is light'" (Matthew 11:28-30 NIV).

Prayer

Lord, worrying for our children makes us weary. The burden of motherhood is worrisome itself. Help us trust in You more; we want to rest in You, Lord. Whether it's everyday struggles or life-threatening worries about our kids, help us to always feel Your trustworthy and peaceful presence in our hearts, Lord. May we fall on our knees as we give our worries to You over and over again throughout our journey of motherhood. Remind us always that You love our children more than we ever possibly could. Remind us that You have a wonderful plan for their lives. Remind us that worrying isn't actually helpful, Lord! I pray we transfer the energy we spend worrying into energy spent trusting in You and Who You are for our kids. Thank You for Your trustworthy peace, Lord. We love You. Amen.

Reflective Questions

1. Prayerfully consider a worry you have for your family/children. Vulnerably, ask the Lord to take this worry from you right now. Keep praying until you hear His voice and feel His peace in your heart.

2. Recall something in the past, regarding your children, about which you previously worried. Consider how the Lord replaced your worry with trust and peace. And then, thank the Lord!

3. Connect with and/or pray for another mama you know who's currently overwhelmed with worry for her children.

Week Fifty-Two

Trust, Trust, and Even More Trust in the Lord

After 51 weeks, it's hard to believe I have anything left to share with you about trusting God in motherhood. The word "trust" was (unsurprisingly), the number one buzzword used among the 33 Christian mamas who contributed to this devotional! It has been woven into nearly every other week, but this week, we'll focus on it. At the end of the day, while trusting the Lord can be challenging at times, I believe it is the most important and also the most rewarding aspect of faithful motherhood. We receive Christ's wisdom, guidance, and peace when we trust in Him. I hope this week encourages you and gives you the strength to fully trust in the Lord, mama.

Gina is in her 30s, with four young to school-age children. She shares: *He replaces control with trust. Motherhood is done in prayer because I trust Him to lead me forward.*

Jill J. is in her 50s, with two adult children. She shares: *I would say the challenge came when they entered high school when I was no longer able to take them from "here" to "there," when they were independent, and I had to trust and pray they were making the right decisions. It was at this time I truly dug deeper into my faith and my relationship with Jesus. I started attending daily Mass occasionally to have my time with the Lord, my time to pray for my family and my friends, and my time to trust and see that Jesus cared for me. Trust, trust, and trust. Sometimes, it's hard to trust and keep the faith when life is so busy and there is barely time for yourself. Step back and allow yourself just 10-15 minutes to be thankful and grateful for everything that is going on around you, as crazy as it may be at times. Trust me, before you know it, the "crazy" is gone, and your time to parent, teach, and mold your children is gone… And that is when you really do have to TRUST and have FAITH that you did your job as a mom!*

Julie is in her 60s, with four adult children. She shares: *Jesus proved so very worthy of our trust over and over again. Trust, trust, trust, trust. In your prayers, tell God that you trust in Him.*

Jan is in her 70s, with three adult children. She shares: *What a big job and a big blessing when you let Jesus in, trusting Him to guide you!*

Carmie is in her 70s, with three adult children. She shares: *I just keep praying, praying, praying. That's the only thing you can do; put it all in Jesus' hands because He will take care of everything. You just have to trust in Him.*

Alyssa is in her 30s, with four young to school-age children. She shares: *Trust that God can do more in six days than we can do in seven. Pray, Jesus, I trust in You.*

Her first sentence here has really stuck with me since I initially read it. *Help me trust You with my time, Lord!*

Pam is in her 50s, with five school-age to adult children. She shares: *And turn to trust in God and faith for the things you are grateful for as well as the things you struggle with.*

Cassandra is in her 50s, with six school-age to adult children. She shares: *God has already predestined everything in your life, so ease some of your stress and trust God! Daily, I have to let go and let God have His way, and trust God to send angels to be a hedge of protection around my oldest child, even now that he's an adult.*

Debi is in her 60s, with three adult children. She shares: *I had a peace I knew from learning to trust God in a previous crisis that even if the tornado* hit, if it wasn't her time, God would protect her somehow. And He did. The tornado made a drastic turn two blocks before it hit her dorm.

We must remember when we have trusted God in the past; His promises are true.

Beth is in her 60s, with three adult children. She shares: *It was a crossroads I was standing at that required me to lay down my personal life and choose to pick up the cross of Jesus and boldly claim His name, His grace, His mercy, His love, and trust in His provision.*

And:

As parents, we all felt the Lord leading us daily and lifting us up as we stepped one foot in front of the other, trusting in Him to guide us. We felt full of His peace and watched our son grow in his wisdom and his trust in the Lord. Although I would not wish this experience on any parent, it was a season of such growth, trust, faith, and grace from which we learned so much.

Brianna is in her 30s, with one young child (and one on the way). She shares: *I constantly landed on verses about trusting the Lord, and as I sat there, I literally felt God saying to me, "I got this." All worry left me, and I felt a supernatural peace that only God could provide.*

Kari is in her 60s, with three adult children. She shares: *There were many parenting decisions over the years where I needed to trust God to show me the right way. When my girls would spend time at their dad's, I was allowed no contact, so I learned to trust that God would take care of them. I knew that He loved them even more than I ever could. Trust that God loves your child even more than you do, and He is watching over them. You may be limited in what you can do, but God is omnipotent and omnipresent.*

My own share: *My mama heart was so full of worry and fear for the health and well-being of my son for the first 18 months of his life. That is, until I laid it all down at the Lord's feet, trusting that He would take care of my son, according to His perfect plans for his life. Once I did that, while also sharing with my MomCo group, who prayed for me, I felt the peace of Christ in my mama heart for the first time in motherhood. And, I've come to learn that that's from where all peace comes, from trusting the Prince of Peace Himself.*

As in any best friendship, God also trusts in us:

Her Prayer for Peace

Dianne is in her 40s, with three school-age children. She shares: *He's entrusted you to care for and raise them earthside and then give back to Jesus.*

Jan is in her 70s, with three adult children. She shares: *It was during these times that brought me the revelation that this child was not "mine," but a gift from God. God entrusted me to be her advocate while she grew.*

Jill J. is in her 50s, with two adult children. She shares: *As parents, we need to be reminded that our children are not ours; they are God's, and He trusted us to love, teach, and care for them while they are young so that when they do go off on their own, they do so with the faith, knowledge, and confidence we instilled in them.*

It has been a true honor to study God's Word and His love and peace for us with you, mama. I am beyond grateful for our contributing mamas, who took time away from their families to share how trusting in God has provided them and their families with so many blessings, including His peace. Mama, please don't keep what you've learned to yourself. Please don't keep what God's placed on your heart to yourself. Share it! We are called to discipleship. I am a different mother and a different child of God, thanks to the testimonies shared by these Christian mamas. Please pass God's goodness along. His love, truth, grace, and peace are meant to be shared!

> HIS LOVE, TRUTH, GRACE, AND *peace* ARE MEANT TO BE SHARED!

Bible Verse

"'But blessed is the one who trusts in the LORD, whose confidence is in him. They will be like a tree planted by the water that sends out its roots by the stream. It does not fear when heat comes; its leaves are always green. It has no worries in a year of drought and never fails to bear fruit'" (Jeremiah 17:7-8 NIV).

Prayer

Lord, You are our stream of goodness. Remind us to ground our roots in Your trustworthy waters every single day. Our confidence is in You, Lord. Remind us that we do not need to worry. When we trust in You, we and our families will never fail. You are so very trustworthy, Lord. Your perfect will and promises are always fulfilled. Surround our hearts with confidence from You, to trust in You, and to guide and protect our families within Your perfect will. We thank You for hearing our prayers for peace when we trust in You, Lord Heavenly Father. We love You. Amen.

Reflective Questions

1. Prayerfully reflect on this week's Bible verse. Speak, think, and pray it until you can say it by heart. What does belief in this verse do for your trust in God, your life, and your motherhood? Share this verse with at least one other Christian mama before the end of the week.

2. Consider a hardship in motherhood with which you have entrusted to the Lord. How did His peace show up for you and your family? How did this feel?

3. Reflect on one area of motherhood in which you have difficulty relinquishing control and trusting God. He knows your heart. Pray to Him now. Ask Him to help you trust in Him. Hold your clenched fists out in front of you, mama. As you pray, notice God working in your heart, opening your heart, opening your fists, releasing your desire to control, as you offer this hardship up to Him. Give Him your trust, mama; He is trustworthy. His love, His peace, never fail.

Next Steps

1. Share this devotional with at least three other mamas today.

2. Prayerfully create a list of at least ten mamas to pray for over the course of the next week.

3. Prayerfully review at least four weeks of this devotional over the course of the next month.

Things to Say or Not to Say when it Comes to Infertility

By Monica Staley

Things to say:
1. Simply say, I love you.
2. We pray for/think of you every day, night, week, etc. (I loved getting messages saying, "We just prayed for you" or, "We're praying for you right now.")
3. A genuine compliment about her spirit and strength. (These are even more profound if they are received out of the blue and are not necessarily in conversation about infertility. It's a constant reality, so it will always be appreciated.)
4. If you really want to "do" something, sometimes offering silent, physical support can be so meaningful. Offer to quietly (no words necessary) hug her. (She may weep in your arms.)
5. This is not for everyone! However, I found it extremely helpful to connect with other Christian women who were experiencing infertility. If you know this person well, use your best judgment and lovingly ask if she has or wants to connect with other Christian women on this journey. (See: The "Christian Infertility Support Group" on Facebook, at Footnote 12 in the Notes section.)

Things NOT to say:
1. Have a couple of drinks/just relax, and have sex.
2. Stop trying so hard.
3. My sister did/have you tried... (No unsolicited advice, please!)
4. Why don't you just adopt?
5. Even as a believer, I didn't always find it helpful to hear about God's perfect timing.

Acknowledgments

First and foremost, *Lord, thank You for the opportunity to draw other mothers closer to You. I sure do hope this is what You had in mind! I know this content will bless other Christian mamas! Thank You for my children and for Your peace in my mama heart, Lord.*

Secondly, thank you to my family, the source of so much of my joy and so many of my prayers for peace! A special shout-out to my dad for his simple yet powerful encouragement and belief in me. And a special thank you to my children's generous grandmas and four supportive aunties, too! Lastly, thank you for all the prayers, Matt!

Thank you to my husband for being my sounding board, for watching our toddlers, and for ensuring I was well-fed while I worked on this book! This book would not be what it is without your support and prayers, Ryan. I love you.

Third, thank you to my incredible friends in Christian motherhood, my contributors, who paused their lives as busy mamas to pour into the hearts and households of other Christian mamas. Your courage and willingness to share about your trust in and reliance on the Lord made this devotional possible.

To all my friends, church mom-group members, and (yep!) social media friends. Your prayers and support blessed me and greatly impacted this book.

To my publisher, Lisa Fahey of Farmhouse Publishings, LLC — the Lord is in you! Your quiet, clear guidance and prayers allowed me to learn and grow within the book-writing process, but most importantly, you always reminded me to simply trust in the Lord. Thank you for steering this ship!

To my editor, Kendra Paulton, thank you for catching grammatical errors, fixing sentence structure snafus, and for adding Biblical insights. (Your sweet personal comments within my Google Docs manuscript truly fed my soul!)

To my cover and book designer, Heidi Caperton, you are incredibly talented and extremely patient. Thank you for capturing all my visions, especially the final one!

Last but not least, while most of the dedication section is dedicated to you, thank you, Hope and John. My sweet kids, it's because the Lord has blessed me to be your mama that this devotional book exists. I love you.

Notes

Resources for Mamas

Introduction
1. Nilsen, Megan. *A Beautiful Exchange: Responding to God's Invitation for More.* Xulon Press, 2015.

Week Two
2. Thurling, Stephanie and Holmstrom, Sarah. *Raising Prayerful Kids: Fun & Easy Activities for Building Lifelong Habits of Prayer.* Tyndale House Publishers, Inc., 2022. https://www.raisingprayerfulkids.com/

Week Five
3. Mom's Life: https://grace.church/women/#csec-get-involved-women-moms-life
4. The MomCo: https://www.growthechurch.co/

Week Six
5. Vennard, Jane E. "The Breath Prayer." *The Upper Room*, n.d. https://www.upperroom.org/resources/the-breath-prayer
6. Lyda, Hope and Lind, Michelle. *One-Minute Prayers to Pray for Your Kids.* Harvest House Publishers, 2022.

Week Eight
7. "Trauma Noun - Definition, Pictures, Pronunciation and Usage Notes | Oxford Advanced American Dictionary at OxfordLearnersDictionaries.com," n.d.

8. Mental Health Sermon Series: "Longing for Better Days." Westwood Community Church. October-November 2023. https://www.westwoodcc.org/betterdays/

Week Fourteen
9. Halberstadt, Abbie. *M Is for Mama: A Rebellion Against Mediocre Motherhood*. Harvest House Publishers, 2022.

Week Fifteen
10. Rosevelt, Theodore quote: "Comparison is the thief of joy." n.d. https://www.goodreads.com/quotes/6471614-comparison-is-the-thief-of-joy

Week Sixteen
11. "Grace Noun - Definition, Pictures, Pronunciation and Usage Notes | Oxford Advanced American Dictionary at OxfordLearnersDictionaries.com," n.d.

Week Nineteen
12. "Christian Infertility Support Group" on Facebook: https://www.facebook.com/groups/1773912026169828/
13. Bethel Music, Kristene DiMarco. "It Is Well" (Radio Mix). Bethel Music Publishing (ASCAP), 2013. https://bethelmusic.com/resources/it-is-well-radio-mix/it-is-well
14. Rūmì, *The Essential Rumi*. HarperSanFrancisco NKA HarperOne, 1995. https://openlibrary.org/works/OL18987W/The_essential_Rumi

Week Twenty-Four
15. Dawson, Rachel. "What Is Agape Love? (And What Does it Mean for Me?)" Crosswalk, March, 2021. https://www.crosswalk.com/faith/spiritual-life/what-is-agape-love-and-what-does-it-mean-for-me.html

Week Twenty-Five
16. "Provision Noun - Definition, Pictures, Pronunciation and Usage Notes | Oxford Advanced American Dictionary at OxfordLearnersDictionaries.com," n.d.

Week Twenty-Six
17. Pastor Swindoll, Chuck. "How Do I Know God's Will?" *Insight for Living*, December 26, 2017. https://insight.org/resources/daily-devotional/individual/how-do-i-know-god-s-will

Week Twenty-Seven
18. Father Mattingly, Andrew. "Sunday Homily on Obstacles to Saving Souls." *Padre's Points Podcast*, July 6, 2022. https://creators.spotify.com/pod/show/padres-points/episodes/Sunday-homily-on-obstacles-to-saving-souls-e1ksl8e

Week Thirty-One
19. Murphy, Ian. *The Road to Self-Awareness: A Therapy Book for Christians*. Sophia Institute Press, 2023.

Week Thirty-Two
20. Mental Health Sermon Series: "Longing for Better Days." Westwood Community Church. October-November 2023. https://www.westwoodcc.org/betterdays/

Week Thirty-Seven
21. "Idol Noun - Definition, Pictures, Pronunciation and Usage Notes | Oxford Advanced Dictionary at OxfordLearnersDictionary.com" n.d.

Week Thirty-Nine
22. Halberstadt, Abbie. *M Is for Mama: A Rebellion Against Mediocre Motherhood*. Harvest House Publishers, 2022.

Week Forty-Three

23. Castor, Ken. *Make a Difference: 365 World-Changing Devotions.* BroadStreet Publishing, 2016.
24. TerKeurst, Lysa. "The First 5 Mobile app." *Proverbs 31 Ministries,* 2015. https://first5.org/

Week Forty-Five

25. Thurling, Stephanie and Holmstrom, Sarah. *Raising Prayerful Kids: Fun & Easy Activities for Building Lifelong Habits of Prayer.* Tyndale House Publishers, Inc., 2022. https://www.raisingprayerfulkids.com/
26. National GAL/CASA: https://nationalcasagal.org/
27. Nilsen, Megan. *A Beautiful Exchange: Responding to God's Invitation for More.* Xulon Press, 2015.
28. Ibid.
29. Halberstadt, Abbie. *M Is for Mama: A Rebellion Against Mediocre Motherhood.* Harvest House Publishers, 2022.

Week Forty-Eight

30. Ibid.

Week Forty-Nine

31. Ibid.
32. Department of Landscape Architecture, College of Architecture and Urban Planning, Tongji University, Shanghai 200092, China; Department of Horticulture, Faculty of Agriculture, Suez Canal University, Ismailia 41522, Egypt. "How Can Flowers and Their Colors Promote Individuals' Physiological and Psychological States during the COVID-19 Lockdown?" *PubMed Central,* September 29, 2021. PMCID: PMC8507779; PMID: 34639557. https://pmc.ncbi.nlm.nih.gov/articles/PMC8507779/
33. Byrne, Rhonda. *The Magic.* Atria Books, 2012.

About the Author

While this is Monica Staley's first published book, pre-motherhood, she enjoyed blogging on her personal wellness website. She's also very active (in a good way!) on social media. After being a paralegal for ten years, in 2015, Monica prayerfully pivoted into the health sector as a certified health coach, a health and beauty product sales and leadership executive, and a yoga instructor.

Monica grew up in the Minneapolis, MN area, went to college at Marquette University in Milwaukee, WI, and now she and her loving and supportive, "Iowa-boy" husband, Ryan, are prayerfully raising their twins, Hope and John, and their pup, Leroy, in the Minneapolis area.

In her spare time (ha!), Monica likes to practice yoga, paint, and blare Lauren Daigle! She has supported mamas within her wellness business for years, and is excited about the Lord's work through this devotional.

If you have been blessed by this book, please share the message with others by posting on social media using #herprayerforpeace

wellnessbymonicabstaley@gmail.com
www.wellnessbymonicabstaley.com/
linktr.ee/wellnessbymonicabstaley

www.ingramcontent.com/pod-product-compliance
Lightning Source LLC
Chambersburg PA
CBHW070635160426
43194CB00009B/1470

Praise for *Her Prayer for Peace*

Her Prayer for Peace, by Monica B. Staley, is a beautifully written, honest, yet very encouraging compilation of reflections of mothers, young and old. I found myself remembering, in tears, the realities of motherhood, passionate and sometimes painful. I look forward to sharing *Her Prayer for Peace* with new moms and young friends "in the thick of" parenthood.

— **Julie,** elementary school counselor

This book relates right to my life! It's by real-life moms who get it and point me to Jesus. I want to be that mom who has my eyes locked on Jesus while helping my kids see Him in and through me, too.

— **Dianne,** Westwood Church and The Hope House

This book will help you feel like you are not alone in motherhood. The ladies sharing part of their motherhood journey are so relatable and inspiring. This book will give you hope in your journey through motherhood.

— **Amara,** an amazing stay-at-home mom

I love Monica's heart for moms! I appreciate that this devotional fits any mom at any age or stage in motherhood. Well-written, easily understood, and beautifully applied Scriptures accompany every week. The reflective questions at the end of make this such a valuable resource as each week is read. Recording personal answers within each week will allow each mom to draw near to Jesus in the moment and SEE His answers to their prayers as they look back in the future.

— **Beth,** works with natural health solutions from home

Strong relatability within! This devotional resource offers a relatable twist of Scripture and skillfully written compilations of stories, viewpoints, and week-to-week hurdles of fellow moms with Christ. How they overcome obstacles, and how the support of Jesus comes in so many ways.

— **Angela**, an amazing stay-at-home mom

"It takes a village"… this book will bring the village right to you! Starting my day with other moms who understand the chaos and joys of my everyday life as a mom makes me feel seen and gives me the perspective I need for one more day.

— **Gina**, director in marriage and family ministry

One of my favorite games as a kid was Follow the Leader. Some leaders made the game more fun and interesting. Monica pulled together a variety of Christian mothers who wisely looked to Jesus as the Leader. His support and guidance are shown in personal ways, making this devotional very inspiring.

— **Jan**, retired

I love it! I love the format of hearing others' stories and then embed with Scripture, finishing with prayer and reflective questions. As a mother whose children are all grown, and I am now in my grandma stage, this made me reflect that being a mom is so much more than that. It really is serving just as Jesus has asked us to do. With this mindset, I think it's easier not to lose yourself. I also loved how they bring God into the every day, especially with those hard-to-do tasks. God always makes things easier when we rely on Him. Love, love this. Thank you, Monica, and these amazing mamas for sharing with all of us.

— **Billie**, owner of Shades of Divine, Christian & faith-inspired clothing and accessories

Monica is a woman of God. And best yet, she is a mom who deeply loves her children — and God. She is real and open about the ups and downs we face in motherhood. This book makes you feel less alone in this journey and reminds you to turn your eyes and heart to God for support and guidance. The weekly reflective questions are thought-provoking and hit home with my mama's heart at just the right time in my stage of motherhood. I cannot wait to spend an entire year filling up my cup with Him, Monica, and the other contributing moms.

— **Susan**, an amazing stay-at-home mom

Encouraging words, even for my sometimes devotional-jaded heart. Great nuggets of truth to think through and reflect on. I wanted to keep reading! This book caused me to stop and reflect at a deeper level than I daily do about motherhood, encouraging me to walk closer with Jesus as I parent!

— **Janette**, an amazing homeschool mama

Our Creator gave us motherhood for salvation. Come within these pages to find a community of women ordering their lives toward Christ, spouse, family, and beyond. May you be filled with the Holy Spirit and find peace that surpasses understanding!

— **Alyssa**, attorney

This devotional provides an insightful journey of faith in motherhood in a package that any reader can relate to. As I enter the vocation of marriage, I appreciate how Monica Staley shares the authentic experiences of women at all stages of motherhood. From daily chores to life's biggest moments, no topic is too big or too small. We see God's faithfulness everywhere through stories accompanied by narration, Scripture, and reflection questions.

— **Katie**, CPA